THE INVENTION OF EUCLIDE

DAVID ZIERLER

THE INVENTION OF ECOCIDE

AGENT ORANGE, VIETNAM, AND THE SCIENTISTS WHO CHANGED THE WAY WE THINK ABOUT THE ENVIRONMENT

THE UNIVERSITY OF GEORGIA PRESS • ATHENS AND LONDON

the
Friends Fund   Publication of this work was made possible, in part, by a generous
gift from the University of Georgia Press Friends Fund.

Parts of chapter 8, "Against Protocol," originally appeared in substantially different form as "Against
Protocol: Ecocide, Détente, and the Question of Chemical Warfare in Vietnam, 1969–1975," by
David Zierler, in *Environmental Histories of the Cold War*, edited by J. R. McNeill and Corinna
R. Unger, Copyright © 2010 the German Historical Institute. Reprinted with the permission of
Cambridge University Press.

© 2011 by the University of Georgia Press
Athens, Georgia 30602
www.ugapress.org
All rights reserved
Designed by Walton Harris
Set in 10.5/14 Minion Pro

Printed digitally in the United States of America

Library of Congress Cataloging-in-Publication Data

Zierler, David, 1979–
The invention of ecocide : agent orange, Vietnam, and the scientists who
changed the way we think about the environment / David Zierler.
    p.   cm.
Includes bibliographical references.
ISBN-13: 978-0-8203-3826-2 (hardcover : alk. paper)
ISBN-10: 0-8203-3826-5 (hardcover : alk. paper)
ISBN-13: 978-0-8203-3827-9 (pbk. : alk. paper)
ISBN-10: 0-8203-3827-3 (pbk. : alk. paper)
1. Nature — Effect of human beings on. 2. Extinction (Biology)
3. Agent Orange — Health aspects. 4. Agent Orange — Toxicology.
5. Vietnam War, 1961–1975 — Chemical warfare.
GF75.Z54 2011
576.8'4 — dc22   2010044005

British Library Cataloging-in-Publication Data available

To Sadie Vella

CONTENTS

ACKNOWLEDGMENTS

FOR THE PAST SEVERAL YEARS I have been surrounded by a wonderful mix of family, friends, and colleagues whose advice and support helped me to create this book. Without them, I would not have been able to bridge my ideas with a topic that has proved sometimes unwieldy and always emotionally charged.

All good things start at home. My family has lovingly sustained my scholarly endeavors in too many ways to count. The storage space and home office have been a great help, but the intellectual vitality and good humor of my wife's family and my own gave me the confidence and energy to see this project to its conclusion. To the Zierlers: Mom and Dad, Jeremy, Samantha, Jemma, Jonathan, and Zachary; and to the Akselrads: Mom and Dad, Rebecca, Benjamin, and Gila, and to my grandmothers, aunts, uncles, and cousins — thank you so much and I love you all.

From dissertation proposal to book binding, *The Invention of Ecocide* took shape alongside my association with two of the great historical institutions in this country. The Department of History at Temple University provided a more fulfilling and exciting academic environment than any I could have dreamed up on my own. The Office of the Historian at the U.S. Department of State, in existence since 1861, is both an engine of annotation and declassification of the most important U.S. national security documents, and a center for policy-oriented historical analysis. I have relied heavily on the office's output for my own work, and it is a great honor to be a part of it now. From 2004 to the present, one person has devoted superhuman levels of attention to my work. I came to Temple to study with Richard Immerman, that rare professor who is both a giant in his field and unbelievably attentive to his students. I would not be a historian without him. Richard is a gift to the historical profession, and it has been my good fortune to work with him at Temple and in his capacity as an advisor to the Office of the Historian.

I want to thank a number of people who generously shared their time and experience to help me gather and interpret my source material: Amy Crumpton of the American Academy for the Advancement of Science; George Clark of the Environmental Science and Public Policy Archives, Harvard University; Stephen Plotkin of the John F. Kennedy Presidential Library; John Wilson of the Lyndon B. Johnson Presidential Library; Samuel Rushay of the Nixon Presidential Materials Project; Joshua Cochran of the Gerald R. Ford Presidential Library; and Justin Hill of the Interlibrary Loan Staff, Temple University. I also want to express my deep gratitude to the individuals who graciously granted my requests for interviews. Their experiences as scientists and political actors form the core of this project's narrative, and my time with them enriched my understanding of their motivations against the backdrop of the Vietnam War and the rise of environmental consciousness. Thank you to the late Arthur Galston, Matthew Meselson, Phung Tuu Boi, Arthur Westing, William Haseltine, John Constable, Mrs. Jean Pfeiffer (wife of the late Bert Pfeiffer), Robert Cook, and Tuan Vo. Finally, Derek Krissoff and John Joerschke of the University of Georgia Press have ensured that the massive amount of documentation I have generated from my years of research actually became a book. Their professionalism and expert advice smoothed the painstaking work of assembling this manuscript.

My wife Aviva has been the light of my life for over ten years. We have studied together from our time as undergraduates through our terminal degrees, and we have traveled the country and world — much of it in the pursuit of my historical interests. She is my muse, my best friend, and of course, my last editor. The shortcomings of this book are mine alone, but its strengths I share with Aviva. In an instance of joyously good timing, we learned we would be expecting our first child just as I was wrapping up the manuscript. Our apartment was not big enough to house my filing cabinet and a bassinet when our daughter Sadie was born. It was the greatest trade I ever made.

ABBREVIATIONS

AAAS	American Association for the Advancement of Science
ABA	American Bar Association
ACDA	Arms Control and Disarmament Agency
AFB	air force base
AFSC	American Friends Service Committee
ARPA	Advanced Research Projects Agency
ARVN	Army of the Republic of Vietnam
AWG	Arthur W. Galston
BPI	Bureau of Plant Industry
BTI	Boyce Thompson Institute
CBW	chemical and biological weapons
CCA	Contemporary Culture Archives
CDTC	Combat and Development Test Center
CIA	Central Intelligence Agency
CINCPAC	commander in chief of the U.S. Pacific Command
CNI	Committee for Nuclear Information
DDT	dichlorodiphenyltrichloroethane
DMZ	demilitarized zone
DNSA	Digital National Security Archive
EWP	Egbert W. Pfeiffer
FAS	Federation of American Scientists
FRUS	*Foreign Relations of the United States*
GFK	George F. Kennan
GPO	Government Printing Office
GRFL	Gerald R. Ford Presidential Library
GVN	government of Vietnam
HAC	Herbicide Assessment Commission
IAA	indole-3-acetic acid
ICC	International Control Commission

ICI	Imperial Chemical Industries
ICJ	International Court of Justice
IWC	international war crimes
JCS	Joint Chiefs of Staff
JFKL	John F. Kennedy Presidential Library
LBJL	Lyndon Baines Johnson Presidential Library
MAAG	Military Assistance and Advisory Group
MACV	Military Assistance Command, Vietnam
MRI	Midwest Research Institute
MSM	Matthew S. Meselson
NARA	National Archives and Records Administration
NARMIC	National Association on Research of the Military-Industrial Complex
NAS	National Academy of Sciences
NCI	National Cancer Institute
NGO	nongovernmental organization
NLF	National Liberation Front
NSC	National Security Council
PPPUS	*Public Papers of the Presidents of the United States*
RG	record group
ROTC	Reserve Officers' Training Corps
RVN	Republic of Vietnam
SALT	Strategic Arms Limitation Talks
SCFR	Senate Committee on Foreign Relations
SCPC	Swarthmore College Peace Research Collection
SDS	Students for a Democratic Society
SR	Senate Resolution
SSRS	Society for Social Responsibility in Science
TCDD	2,3,7,8-tetrachlorodibenzo-para-dioxin
TIBA	2,3,5-triiodobenzoic acid
UN	United Nations
UNEP	United Nations Environment Programme
USAF	United States Air Force
USAID	United States Agency for International Development
USDA	United States Department of Agriculture
VC	Viet Cong
VNAF	(Republic of) Vietnam Air Force
WBC	War Bureau of Consultants

THE INVENTION OF ECOCIDE

CHAPTER ONE

INTRODUCTION

FOR THE PAST FOUR YEARS, I have followed 2,4-D (2,4-dichlorophenoxya-cetic acid) and 2,4,5-T (2,4,5-trichlorophenoxyacetic acid) through history. Plant physiologists classify these synthetic chemical compounds as selective auxins of the phenoxyacetic herbicide family. They were the first plant kill-ers developed by scientists to target specific "weeds"—any plants useless or counterproductive to human needs.

The discoveries that led to modern herbicides began in Charles Darwin's laboratory. Late in his life, Darwin discovered that some internal mechanism directs plants to grow toward sunlight and sources of water. American and European scientists later called this mechanism the plant's hormone system. On the eve of World War II, scientists discovered that certain chemical syn-theses could enhance the growth of a plant—and in higher concentrations, kill it. Via absorption through the leaf, 2,4-D and 2,4,5-T wreak havoc on the plant's hormones.[1] Several days after exposure, the treated plant experiences uncontrolled and rapid growth, until its leaves shrivel back to a brown mass and fall off.

The biochemical specificity of these herbicides has no cultural analog: no universally accepted characteristics distinguish weeds from other plants. The designation depends on what people want from land they seek to con-trol. On farms, sprayed applications of 2,4-D and 2,4,5-T can keep weeds out of cropland and animal pasture. After World War II, herbicides, along with pesticides, dramatically increased agricultural yields worldwide in what became known as the Green Revolution.[2] The massive application of herbicides for farming, forest management, and lawn care continues today at global annual rates exceeding a billion gallons.

This book focuses on one aspect of herbicide use that is now a relic of history. During the Vietnam War, the U.S. military combined 2,4-D and 2,4,5-T, named the 50:50 mixture Agent Orange, and defoliated approximately five million acres of forests in an attempt to expose communist guerrilla fighters loyal to the National Liberation Front (NLF, or Viet Cong) of South Vietnam. Known as Operation Ranch Hand, from 1961 to 1971 the herbicidal warfare program targeted not specific weeds but entire ecosystems. In Vietnam the forest was the weed.

The goals of agricultural use and military use of herbicides differ: one aims to increase crop yields, the other to win wars. But the logic of unburdening human labor through chemistry applies to both. For a wheat farmer determined to rid his crop of invasive weeds, an herbicide application may seem more economical in the short run than removing the plants by hand.[3] For President John F. Kennedy, determined to defend the government of South Vietnam from communist takeover, herbicidal warfare battled the NLF by chemical proxy. As part of the broader counterinsurgency mission, Kennedy sought innovative means to neutralize the NLF's ambush tactics. The president's strategy was simple: deny guerrillas their only tactical advantage with chemicals, not infantry.

Under President Lyndon B. Johnson, herbicidal warfare expanded dramatically: during a ten-year program, Ranch Hand crew members sprayed fifteen of the twenty million total gallons, or 75 percent, between 1966 and 1969. This escalation occurred generally because the "Americanization" of the war after 1965 amplified all the myriad U.S. military operations in Vietnam, but specifically because Johnson never considered his predecessor's use of herbicides to prevent—rather than to abet—an expansion of the war. The massively destructive effects of herbicidal warfare became known as "ecocide," so called by several academic scientists who protested herbicidal warfare beginning in 1964 and who ultimately won the right to inspect its effects in Vietnam six years later. What they found was not simply the elimination of "weeds" but the destruction of whole environments upon which humans depended—and the looming prospect that the chemicals themselves might harm humans and animals.

The ensuing herbicide controversy turned upside down a key component of President Richard M. Nixon's policy of détente, or relaxation of cold war tensions, with the communist world. One of Nixon's early détente initiatives attempted to establish American leadership in the global nonproliferation of chemical and biological weapons (CBW). To that end, the president unilaterally abolished the U.S. military's biological weapons program. In late

1969, he announced his plan to resubmit the Geneva Protocol of 1925 to the Senate for ratification. This international treaty binds its signatories to refrain from first use of chemical and biological weapons in war. It states that the use of "asphyxiating, poisonous or other gases, and of all analogous liquids, materials or devices, has been justly condemned by the general opinion of the civilized world."[4]

Nixon's initiative provided the critics of Operation Ranch Hand the ideal platform to end herbicidal warfare in Vietnam and in future wars. They convinced the Senate Committee on Foreign Relations (SCFR) to link renunciation of herbicidal warfare with ratification of the Geneva Protocol. Nixon rejected the deal, citing a legal rationale first advanced by the Kennedy administration: the Geneva Protocol prohibits only weapons that harm or kill people, not plants. The crux of the scientists' position was that wartime chemical destruction of plant life—the foundation of all ecosystems—could not be cordoned off as a convention of treaty interpretation. Ecologically, they argued, the rationale made little sense: herbicides sprayed in massive quantities undoubtedly harm more than plants. Further, the scientists argued that the ease of producing inexpensive herbicides made them a perfect "weapon of mass destruction," to use a current term, because virtually any state or revolutionary movement could employ herbicidal warfare wherever ecological and tactical conditions made defoliating the enemy's territory advantageous.

The scientists prevailed, thanks to support from powerful members of Congress, such as J. William Fulbright, Edward Kennedy, and others who were dismayed by the ecological destruction U.S. forces had wrought in Vietnam—and the war itself. In the run-up to the War Powers Act of 1973, the herbicide controversy served as an ideal opportunity to make a stand. At that juncture, many legislators were committed to extricating the United States from Vietnam generally and constraining the war powers of the executive branch specifically.[5] After a protracted deadlock, in 1975 President Gerald R. Ford renounced first use of herbicides in war, against the advice of military officials who remained committed to the strategic necessity of herbicides in future conflicts. By couching the antiwar protest slogan "No more Vietnams!" in ecological terms, the scientists therefore effectively codified an ethic of transnational environmental concerns into international law. The scientific movement against Agent Orange thus transcended—and helped to discredit—the bipolar cold war divisions that engendered herbicidal warfare in the first place.

The major thesis of this book explains why the scientists were able to end herbicidal warfare. Theirs was a unique achievement in the broad and diverse antiwar movement, whose members demanded change in the U.S. government's policy in Vietnam. I argue that the scientific campaign against Agent Orange succeeded because it fell squarely at the intersection of two major political transformations in the United States during the late 1960s and early 1970s: (1) the demise of interventionist anticommunism as the dominant expression of U.S. foreign policy; and (2) rising concerns that humankind's environmental impact was global in scope and a threat to international peace and even human survival. Both transformations, of course, extended beyond the herbicide controversy. The political, moral, and strategic calamity of the Vietnam War by the end of the 1960s likely would have eroded the salience of cold war containment if Operation Ranch Hand had never existed. And environmental activists and scientists likely would have raised the specter of global ecological apocalypse, as they did with the first Earth Day in 1970, had herbicides remained strictly a domestic tool of farmers and foresters.

The scientists' campaign was important not because it heralded these transformations but because it connected them in a way that expanded and reframed the meaning of international security beyond the previously dominant and singular U.S. imperative to rid the world of the communist menace. This accomplishment was an act of political prescience and fortuitous timing in which the scientists, led by Arthur Galston of Yale University, presented the ecocide of Vietnam as a product of a destructive and immoral war *and* an omen of a future techno-industrial ecological dystopia.[6] The following narrative connects trends in the cold war in the wake of Vietnam and postwar environmental consciousness that heretofore have remained almost entirely separate in the extant literature on environmental and diplomatic history.[7]

I became interested in Agent Orange and herbicidal warfare as a case study of a much broader historical question: What is the relationship between ecological issues and international relations? From a historiographical perspective, the question is largely unexamined: few environmental historians write about great power politics, and diplomatic historians have given little thought to the relationship between culture and environmental change. This project attempts to answer exhortations from within both the diplomatic and the environmental history subdisciplines to push scholarly work beyond its traditional parameters.[8] In recent years historians have done innovative work to bridge this divide, particularly in the area of war, diplomacy, and environmental impacts.[9]

This work examines the herbicide controversy as a struggle to control the meaning of global security in the wake of the Vietnam War. The protesting scientists were central to creating a new vision of environmental security that was at once a product of cold war destruction and a rejection of the bipolar ideology that created it. The imperative today to sustain global ecological health or risk worldwide catastrophe in the form of resource wars, global warming, drought, and massive species extinction has become an inescapable fact of modern international discourse. By suggesting that Operation Ranch Hand and its hypothetical, future incarnations could one day imperil the planet's ecological balance, the scientists helped to codify global environmental issues as a mainstay of both U.S. national policy and international diplomacy, demonstrated particularly by the launch of the United Nations Environment Programme (UNEP) of 1972.

Still, the scientists' achievement was tempered by their inability to halt the herbicide program in its heyday, which remained the staple of their agenda after 1964. If government and military officials had terminated the program at that juncture, Operation Ranch Hand would have remained a minor, mostly experimental program. Its impacts would have been limited to a relatively small land area. Instead herbicide operations expanded in lockstep with the overall war.

The logic of herbicidal warfare, repeated consistently in U.S. military evaluations throughout the war, was straightforward: the use of herbicides improved vertical and lateral vision in forested terrain, which thereby limited the guerrilla enemy's capacity to resupply its forces and to attack soldiers, convoys, and bases. Correspondingly, Operation Ranch Hand dramatically increased its geographical scope and frequency of spray missions during the war's zenith between 1966 and 1970. In the military rationale, herbicidal warfare would hasten both the end of the war and the reconstruction of a victorious South Vietnam.[10] Together with the dominant strategy of U.S. policy makers, the American military's conviction of herbicidal warfare's importance to the war effort ensured that Agent Orange and its complex legacy would remain a burning issue decades beyond the conclusion of the Vietnam War.

The ecological and human health legacy of Agent Orange remains today a topic of intense study.[11] Health specialists continue to debate the various illnesses—including cancers, diabetes, and birth defects in Vietnamese civilians, U.S. and Vietnamese war veterans, and their progeny—that can be traced definitively to Agent Orange exposure. Such concerns are not limited to persons who experienced the war firsthand. Vietnamese government ecologists and Western nongovernmental organizations (NGOs) also continue to locate and repair ecological damage wrought by herbicidal warfare. Efforts to "re-green" rural areas that sustained repeated herbicide attacks began under the reunified Vietnamese government in 1976. The program has achieved some spectacular results. Swampy coastal forests called mangroves sustained the greatest herbicidal damage of any of the region's environmental systems, yet mangrove preserves have experienced ecological restoration nearly to their prewar state. One Vietnamese government scientist, Phung Tuu Boi, has created an ingenious method to rid inland rainforests of invasive species that first took root when dominant trees died following a spray attack. Boi has planted high value and nonnative commercial trees to shade native saplings until they can absorb the sun's full force. Nearby residents can then harvest the shade trees and sell them for profit.[12]

Operation Ranch Hand also created dioxin "hot spots" in heavily sprayed areas and depots that once stocked and shipped herbicide drum containers by the thousands. Dioxin, short for 2,3,7,8-tetrachlorodibenzo-para-dioxin, or TCDD, is a highly toxic by-product of military-grade 2,4,5-T, which persists in these areas.[13] This nasty and curious chemical compound has made Agent Orange notorious, while few have heard of the herbicide code names Agent Blue (an arsenic-based rice killer) and Agent White (composed mostly of 2,4-D, which is still widely used for lawn and agricultural weed control). Vietnamese scientists are generally convinced that dioxin hot spots are responsible for thousands of congenital malformations (birth defects) among Vietnamese.[14] "Peace Villages" in Vietnam, which house children and adults with such deformities, as well as public history exhibits, purport that such people, who were not alive during the war, are victims of herbicidal warfare (figure 1). Leading Western scientists are skeptical of such a link but cite the need for more research, particularly because some studies have found elevated levels of TCDD among residents near Agent Orange "hot spots."[15]

Similar uncertainties exist over the health legacy of herbicidal warfare and American soldiers who served in Vietnam. Those who associate a given cancer or genetic disorder with exposure to Agent Orange can trace the problem to the supply demands of the U.S. military machine in the midst of

Figure 1 Agent Orange exhibit, War Remnants Museum, Ho Chi Minh City. Author's photo.

an escalating war. By the mid- to late 1960s, the Pentagon's enormous herbi-cide orders strained the production capacity of Dow, Monsanto, and other chemical companies. In order to meet its quotas, the companies produced herbicide chemicals as quickly as possible and in the process sometimes eschewed standard production procedures. Most important, the military supply orders compelled the manufacturers to "cook" 2,4-D and 2,4,5-T at higher than normal temperatures. As one toxicological study noted, the amount of dioxin created in the production of 2,4,5-T "can be minimized by regulation of temperature, pressure, and solvent conditions, but when the production process goes out of control, large amounts of TCDD can be pro-duced."[16] According to one U.S. official, the existence of dioxin was known to military officers at the height of the war. James Clary, a U.S. Air Force (USAF) scientist stationed in Vietnam, noted in 1988 in a letter to former senator Tom Daschle, "When we initiated the herbicide program in the 1960s, we were aware of the potential for damage due to dioxin contamina-tion in herbicides. We were even aware that the 'military' formulation had a higher dioxin concentration due to the lower cost and speed of manufac-ture. However, because the material was to be used on the enemy, none of us were overly concerned."[17] Statistically, this revelation—the only one of its kind—has not realized the potential problems to which Clary admitted. Epidemiological studies on U.S. veterans dating back twenty years have so far been unable to establish a conclusive link between Agent Orange and a variety of cancers and other health maladies that some servicemen have attributed to the herbicide.[18]

But this logic can be easily turned around: no one can categorically tell a sick veteran that his illness was *not* caused by Agent Orange; consequently, the failure to establish causation, in the author's view, makes neither the U.S. government nor the corporate producers of dioxin-laden Agent Orange any less negligent in the massive procurement and dispersal of a chemical compound whose dangers were not fully understood during the war or now. This is the basic rationale behind the Agent Orange Act of 1991, in which the U.S. government determined that it would treat U.S. soldiers whose ill-nesses carried a "presumptive" association with Agent Orange exposure.[19] Alvin L. Young, a former project scientist for the U.S. Air Force who has been deeply involved in studying Agent Orange and its legacy, goes further. He offers what is perhaps the wisest policy prescription to avoid playing the losing game of causation: "Vietnam and Agent Orange are now public policy issues as well as medical and scientific issues. There are strong public policies favoring our veterans, and rightly so. The [U.S.] government should have acknowledged that many Vietnam veterans do appear to be at risk for a range of diseases and health problems due to the 'Vietnam experience' as a whole. Why focus on Agent Orange instead of on providing treatment and benefit for all these veterans?"[20]

Notably, this prescription mirrors identically the policy view of one diplomat in the U.S. embassy in Hanoi, who agreed to talk with the author on the basis of anonymity. The official, a specialist in public health and development issues, noted, "Due to the widespread poverty in Vietnam and ongoing difficulties in defining who exactly counts as an Agent Orange victim, why expend energy and resources isolating these people from a broader aid package from Washington to Vietnam?"[21] This framework offers the best path to full normalization of relations between the two countries, a process that continues apace to this day.[22]

As a historical topic, Agent Orange has received surprisingly little attention by historians. But there is a robust historiography on chemicals and American national policy. Two exemplars are Thomas Dunlap's *DDT: Scientists, Citizens, and Public Policy* and Edmund Russell's *War and Nature: Fighting Humans and Insects with Chemicals from World War I to Silent Spring*. Dunlap's *DDT* examines the complex interplay of scientific knowledge and public anxiety over widespread exposure to pesticide chemicals. Like *DDT* this project crescendos in the early 1970s with an environmentally based victory over the government and corporate champions of dominating weeds and pests through chemicals. Unlike Dunlap's discussion on citizen participation, this project does not include a sustained examination of the public's reaction to the Agent Orange controversy. There are several reasons for this distinction.

The Environmental Defense Fund comprised scientists and lay citizens who led the crusade to ban DDT. There was no such complementing institution during the herbicide controversy and no blockbuster literary equivalent of *Silent Spring* to engender widespread concern. The scientists devoted to ending herbicidal warfare did not work alongside lay citizens who shared their concerns, nor did they devote much energy to influencing public perception during the course of their campaign. Instead the scientists focused first on gaining the support of scientific organizations, including the American Association for the Advancement of Science (AAAS). Then they cultivated relations in government and military bureaucracies to secure safe passage to war zones in Vietnam to examine the effects of herbicidal warfare. Finally the scientists focused on the arcane matter of international treaty law surrounding the Geneva Protocol of 1925, which they correctly identified as the most promising avenue to banning a wartime practice that was international by definition. In this schema, the scientists saw little reason to join forces with broader environmental movements of the day.

Unlike DDT, "Agent Orange" in the early 1970s was not a household term but a wartime code name for a liquid chemical compound that the military was using on the other side of the planet. As late as 1970, well before Agent Orange became both shorthand for all the herbicides used by Ranch Hand crews and for dioxin-tainted 2,4,5-T, journalists commonly referred to the herbicides as "agents orange, white, and blue" if they used those terms at all.[23] At that juncture, Agent Orange had not achieved its status as a proper noun. Few Americans knew the extent of herbicide usage on American, let alone Vietnamese, land, and what they did know about the spray program in Vietnam came from newspaper reports based on the scientists' findings and subsequent lobbying in Washington as the war was winding down. Although Rachel Carson noted the potential dangers of herbicides in *Silent Spring*, her major focus was on DDT, the anti-mosquito chemical (which she alleged was killing birds, hence making the spring silent). That chemical compound left the greatest impression on millions of Americans, including President Kennedy, who took an active interest in the subject.[24]

Operation Ranch Hand lacked the publicity that Carson had bestowed on DDT. Agent Orange achieved widespread attention only later in the decade when Vietnam veterans began to complain of various illnesses possibly related to their exposure to the herbicide. The protesting scientists, who had been skeptical of these claims, remained aloof from the litigation. At that point, defense lawyers, dramatic by trade, embarked on one of the most complex and sensational class-action lawsuits in U.S. history. Before Agent Orange had "hit home" in America, in the form of sick and frustrated veterans, there is little reason to believe that the herbicide scientists would have enhanced their agenda had they embarked on a public relations mission to gather popular support. It is not that they saw no value in such a project. But the urgency of the scientists' agenda required them to focus their efforts on policy makers whose antipathy to the Vietnam War was well established and who were receptive to their linkage of ecological issues and international security. Public campaigning was a project the scientists left to others, most notably the organizers of the first Earth Day, who cited the herbicidal destruction wrought in Vietnam at the beginning of their inaugural address in 1970.[25]

Although this book maintains a chronological focus that proceeds in tandem with Dunlap's *DDT*, it also picks up where Edmund Russell leaves off in *War and Nature*. Russell shows in fascinating detail how scientists and military researchers developed chemicals that killed humans and pests side by side, to the point that the pesticides and antipersonnel chemical weapons blurred the distinction between war abroad and peace at home. Russell's narrative ends on the eve of the Vietnam War with a brief reference to Agent Orange. The herbicides 2,4-D and 2,4,5-T, as this project will show, followed a nearly identical conceptual trajectory as the one Russell traces with DDT. Researchers first understood the properties and potential of herbicides and pesticides as a direct result of the exigencies of World War II and the demands of total wartime mobilization in Europe and the United States. Both pesticides and herbicides became commercially available after the war, and chemical corporations heralded their products as miracles that defended and expanded American power in the postwar era. Russell stretches his study back to World War I, when modern science and the Industrial Revolution combined to create the horrors of chemical warfare on Europe's battlefields. The present work pushes the story to the end of the Vietnam War, when the protesting scientists ensured that the Geneva Protocol of 1925—designed by its framers to prevent chemical and biological warfare in the future—extended to protect not only humans but the environments in which they live.

Three significant works focus explicitly on Agent Orange. I also situate my work within this literature. Paul Fredrick Cecil's *Herbicidal Warfare* is based in part on the author's personal experiences—Cecil was a pilot for Operation Ranch Hand. In addition to providing valuable nuts-and-bolts information on specific missions and the command structure of the program, Cecil's account offers insight into a group of soldiers who served in one of the most unique and dangerous military programs in modern history.[26] The first U.S. Air Force deaths in Vietnam were members of Ranch Hand, and herbicide spray planes sustained the most enemy ground fire of any U.S. air operation. Cecil offers an exciting narrative concentrating on the dangers and adventures of defoliation missions. His work is an important reminder that the herbicide program, while controversial, was staffed by a dedicated and tight-knit group of soldiers who believed their operation was in the best interest of their country.

Ranch Handers, Cecil points out, were uninvolved in the high policy that launched herbicidal warfare; they were tasked with a mission to provide optimal fighting conditions for the American soldier in Vietnam, and they accomplished that mission. Critics who opposed herbicidal warfare, for whom Cecil has expressed little patience and who figure centrally in the following narrative, made their case under entirely different parameters, so different, in fact, that the ideas supporting "ecocide" and "tactical necessity" need not be seen as mutually exclusive arguments battling for sole possession of the truth. The question of herbicidal warfare's value in Vietnam simply had little to do with critics' concern regarding its ecological and human health impacts and the possibility that this cheap and widely available weapon would proliferate in wars all over the globe.

Fred Wilcox's *Waiting for an Army to Die* is an account of Vietnam veterans who fell ill after the war and who blame their illness on Agent Orange. Wilcox poignantly captures their grievous circumstances of wasting away from cancers and other horrific illnesses amid the vast and uncaring bureaucracy of the U.S. Department of Veterans Affairs and other federal agencies, which did not seriously begin to study the health effects of Agent Orange until 1984.[27] But Wilcox devotes insufficient attention to the uncertainty among health researchers regarding Agent Orange exposure and statistical correlation to specific health maladies once the federal research began. If a Vietnam veteran is dying of lung cancer, did he fall ill because of a tour of duty in Vietnam, an unlucky genetic inheritance, or a twenty-year smoking habit? Defining what makes an Agent Orange victim is trickier than Wilcox's work suggests. Still, *Waiting for an Army to Die* elevates Agent Orange as a powerful symbol of the forgotten and traumatized U.S. soldier in the post-Vietnam era. Both its title and the powerful anecdotal evidence Wilcox brings to bear serve as important reminders that the absence of "conclusive" data linking Agent Orange to almost all the health maladies that veterans and their families have claimed may say more about the limits of epidemiology than the true health legacy of herbicidal warfare in Vietnam.

Finally, Peter H. Schuck's *Agent Orange on Trial* examines the landmark litigation pitting American Vietnam veterans against the corporate producers of Agent Orange in the early 1980s. A legal scholar, Schuck elucidates many of the correlative nuances missing from Wilcox's narrative. Schuck's riveting account of the largest (and arguably most complex) civil-action lawsuit in U.S. history explains why sick Vietnam veterans could not sue for and win court-ordered damages. First, the U.S. government exercised sovereign immunity, which made it impossible for veterans to sue any federal agency.[28] Second, the chemical companies asserted that their product conformed to government specifications, and their lawyers effectively denied any link between fatal illnesses and Agent Orange exposure.[29] Before the trial began, veteran plaintiffs settled out of court for $180 million, although lawyers for Dow and Monsanto maintained that the settlement was not an admission of guilt but a gesture of goodwill. In a partial repeat of history, down to the decision of Judge Jack Weinstein, who also presided over the court case brought by American veterans, Vietnamese nationals recently attempted to sue the chemical manufacturers of Agent Orange for a range of health illnesses and for lasting ecological damage wrought by herbicidal warfare. In 2005 Weinstein dismissed the lawsuit. He found that Operation Ranch Hand did not violate any international law (such as the Geneva Protocol) to which the United States was bound, and therefore foreign nationals had no basis to sue. In March 2009, the U.S. Supreme Court denied the Vietnamese plaintiffs' application to hear an appeal, thereby ending the lawsuit.[30] It is perhaps the only aspect of the complex legacy of Agent Orange that has ended with some degree of decisiveness.

Each of these works has greatly informed my understanding of the vast complexities and drama surrounding Agent Orange. But there is more to this story, one that should make Agent Orange resonate equally with scientists, intellectuals, cold warriors, and evolving notions of international security. This project offers a historical explanation for the rise and fall of herbicidal warfare. The narrative follows 2,4-D and 2,4,5-T along the path of scientific discovery, national-security strategy, and environmental and antiwar protest in the Vietnam era. All the actors in this narrative in some way contributed to the invention of ecocide.

CHAPTER TWO

AN ETYMOLOGY
OF ECOCIDE

FROM THE PELOPONNESIAN WAR to the present-day Palestinian-Israeli conflict, combatants have accused the other side of committing atrocities. It is a
unique form of propaganda — a condemnation that the enemy has crossed
a normative boundary whose authority supersedes the objectives of both
combatants. The Latin term for this is *jus in bello*, or justice in war.[1] To
violate this principle of justice is to commit, or stand accused of committing, a war crime. *Jus in bello* is a building block of the modern international system dating back to eighteenth-century Europe, and its principles
were at the core of the Nuremburg trials immediately after World War II.
During the Vietnam War, a group of scientists coined and propagated the
term "ecocide" to denounce the environmental destruction and potential
human health catastrophe arising from the herbicidal warfare program
known as Operation Ranch Hand. In the long history of war crimes allegations, the scientists' accusation was doubly unique: they leveled the charge
against their *own* government and then effectively forced national policy to
renounce first use of herbicides in future wars.

The movement against ecocide sparked a flurry of interest across disparate groups including legal theorists, radical demonstrators, and environmental activists. Ecocide was one of many variants of the idea that some aspect of the Vietnam War violated international law. This form of dissent was
unique to whoever employed it; for example, in 1967 Martin Luther King
Jr. posited his "Declaration of Independence from the War in Vietnam" as
a philosophical proposition that racism at home and the war in Indochina
were each illegal enterprises that could not be challenged as discrete entities.

That same year, John H. Messing, a law student at Stanford University, was among the first Americans to dissect U.S. foreign policy by the stringent criteria of international treaty law. Taking a cue from the strenuous televised debate in the SCFR in 1966 over the legality of the war, Messing found no grounds to justify a lawful source of American involvement in Vietnam.[2] But the question that truly vexed most dissenters in the Vietnam era was not *if* but rather *how* the war was illegal. That is, to challenge the entire basis of the American intervention in Vietnam required a certain intellectual detachment from the war as it was being waged day to day. Thus broad condemnations that confronted the war as a prima facie criminal enterprise generally served as a step to censure particular tactics that struck dissenters as uniquely illegal.

The connections that might have been drawn between specific atrocities and the legitimacy of the war as a whole usually remained tacit or were altogether unacknowledged. Put another way, a belief in the basic illegality of the war may have been deeply held among opponents of the war, but it was not the primary factor that compelled them to act. To denounce the actions of one's government required a more visceral aversion to any number of wartime tactics employed by U.S. forces in Indochina. Finally, as a utilitarian strategy of protest, in the later years of the war dissenters denounced particular American actions in Vietnam as specific crimes of war.

In February 1970, a conference titled "War Crimes and the American Conscience" was attended by dozens of American scholars who had gathered to survey the full gamut of war crimes committed by the United States in Vietnam.[3] Among the participants was Arthur W. Galston, a plant biologist and chair of the Department of Botany at Yale University (figure 2). It was here that Galston coined the word "ecocide," culminating four years of herbicide research and his attempts to end Operation Ranch Hand. In 1966 Galston became one of the first scientists to voice concern over the ecological and human health effects of the herbicidal warfare program in Vietnam.[4] The strategy of defoliation and crop destruction had been in effect since 1961 as an integral component of American counterinsurgency operations throughout South Vietnam and its borderlands with Laos and Cambodia. The herbicidal component of counterinsurgent doctrine sought to deny the guerrilla forces of the NLF food and forest cover, protect American soldiers from ambush, and destroy any agricultural areas thought to be under NLF control.[5]

By 1966 Operation Ranch Hand had expanded to a scale of chemical war-

Figure 2 Arthur W. Galston in his office at Yale in the early 1990s. Galston Family photo.

fare unseen since World War I. By the end of the decade, Ranch Hand crewmen had sprayed approximately twenty million gallons of Agent Orange and other chemical herbicides over an area of South Vietnam equal in size to the state of Massachusetts.[6] Although by early 1970 there were signs that the herbicide program was drawing to a close, the ecological damage sustained in the coastal mangrove swamps, in rice paddies and croplands, and in the dense rainforests in South Vietnam's interior was only beginning to be surveyed by scientists. At the same time, reports surfaced that the chemical 2,4,5-T, which comprised one-half of the chemical compound Agent Orange, was proved mutagenic and possibly carcinogenic in lab rats.[7]

But Galston and the scientific colleagues who shared his views were not merely alarmed at the massive and deliberate environmental destruction in Vietnam and the possibility that the United States had exposed millions of people — including its own soldiers — to potentially cancer-causing chemicals. These scientists also imagined *more* ecological dystopias and human health epidemics created by future wars fought with more sophisticated chemical weapons and advanced methods of environmental warfare.

As Galston understood, soldiers at every rank and with direct knowledge of the tactical and political value of herbicidal warfare had produced assessment reports from the field that extolled its virtues since the beginning of the operation.[8] The reports convinced officials at the Pentagon to include herbicidal warfare in contingency planning for future conflicts in which the United States might face insurgents.[9] Throughout the presidential administrations of John F. Kennedy, Lyndon B. Johnson, and Richard M. Nixon, civilian government leaders assured the military advocates of defoliation that the United States would never relinquish its herbicidal capacity despite charges that it constituted chemical warfare and as such was prohibited by international treaties such as the Geneva Protocol of 1925.[10] In the words of one newspaper editorial, against these odds how might one stop the U.S. military from "defoliating the world?"[11]

Arthur Galston was determined to ensure both the ecological reconstruction of Vietnam and the prohibition of herbicidal destruction in future wars: the Agent Orange controversy remained Galston's cause célèbre until his death in 2008.[12] Galston's colleagues have characterized his concern with herbicidal warfare as something of a mania; Galston himself surmised that his interest stemmed from a guilt complex arising from his inadvertent contribution to the development of herbicides during research on his doctoral dissertation in 1942–43.[13]

The scientists who campaigned to end herbicidal warfare, wholly committed as they were to limiting the ecological destruction of Vietnam and in future war zones, never considered themselves part of the environmental movement as they understood it. Indeed, the scientists' discomfort with the label "environmentalist" was one ideological platform uniting a group that is otherwise difficult to narrate with a single voice. E. W. "Bert" Pfeiffer of the University of Montana — among the first scientists to demand action against Operation Ranch Hand — readily identified himself as a socialist. Matthew Meselson of Harvard University, who led the major scientific herbicide investigation in Vietnam in 1970, counted among his friends and allies the elite among Washington's foreign-policy establishment. What linked these disparate scientific actors beyond their efforts to terminate herbicidal warfare was their insistence that the antiherbicide campaign was not an expression of contemporary environmentalism.[14]

Arthur Galston summarized the sentiment best during an interview with the author:

> I wasn't a big part of Earth Day or the Sierra Club, [and] I did not consider environmental agitation as "where it was at"; we have finite energy, finite time . . . you want to apply the pressure where it's likely to do the most good. To my way of thinking it wasn't environmentalism but a bioethical approach. In other words, every time you make a scientific advance, you have a potential to create problems for society. You discover a new antibiotic; it has the potential for good to prevent disease, or it has the potential for being misused so it's going to favor the evolution of resistant varieties. Environmentalists to me . . . there are some kooks in that movement . . . dilettantes . . . people who want to pick up Coke bottles from a stream. That's fine . . . these people call themselves environmentalists, but that's not where I'm at. I want to pursue things that are of greater biological impact.[15]

Galston went on to offer a critique of the environmental movement, using the public uproar over DDT to illustrate what he saw as a Manichean anti-intellectualism that pervaded environmental "agitation," as he called it: "To say something is natural does not mean that it's good. Those two [terms] are not equitable. If I could get rid of mosquitoes, I would. Well, that's anti-natural, and yet it's pro-human."[16]

In other words, Galston was not motivated to preserve some indigenous ecological Eden from Western technological predations. If Ranch Hand was an operation of resource extraction, it would not be ecocide. Galston's framework illustrates one of the founding distinctions (and tensions) between environmentalists and environmental historians. The former tend to advance a duality between active and destructive humans and passive and fragile nature. Further, modern environmentalists generally equate nature with leisure — something to be enjoyed, not exploited. Environmental historians complicate this separatism by emphasizing the interconnectedness of human culture and natural change throughout history.[17] In shunning the environmental movement, the scientists made a self-conscious decision to avoid what they saw as the simplistic entrapments of "agitation."

Yet the fact that the scientists did not actively identify with environmentalism does not automatically exclude them from such a broad and ideologically diverse club — one that Galston caricatured somewhat crudely. Still, the scientists' actions matched their ideologies: they did not seek an alliance with the major environmental organizations of the day, nor did they couch the travesty of herbicidal warfare in fashionable phrases such as the "rape" of the land in order to whip up popular indignation. Moreover, the scientists correctly predicted that by emphasizing the "cide" over the "eco" in their lobbying effort, policy makers and jurists would be more likely to recognize Operation Ranch Hand as a preventable ecological war crime. Under the mantle of international law, the scientists determined that ecocide could become categorically banned by treaties governing the rules of warfare. This plan thus served two closely related goals: preserving global security in a world facing grave environmental threats and protecting human populations living in areas suitable for unleashing herbicides in future wars.

Finally, we cannot underestimate the scientists' sense of intellectual vanity when assessing their motivations. Galston made no effort to mask his disdain for "kooky" and parochial environmentalists; for him and his colleagues, the company of Hannah Arendt and Jean-Paul Sartre at European war crimes symposia, and J. William Fulbright in the U.S. Senate, was far more preferable.

During a panel at the "War Crimes and the American Conscience" conference, titled "Technology and American Power," Galston defined ecocide:

> After the end of World War II, and as a result of the Nuremburg trials, we justly condemned the willful destruction of an entire people and its culture, calling this crime against humanity *genocide*. It seems to me that the willful and permanent destruction of environment in which a people can live in a manner of their own choosing ought similarly to be considered as a crime against humanity, to be designated by the term *ecocide*. I believe that the most highly developed nations have already committed autoecocide over large parts of their own countries. At the present time, the United States stands alone as possibly having committed ecocide against another country, Vietnam, through its massive use of chemical defoliants and herbicides. The United Nations would appear to be an appropriate body for the formulation of a proposal against ecocide.[18]

At the relatively late juncture of 1970, Galston's indictment fit tightly within a strong antiwar activist movement in Europe that emphasized war crimes, but in the United States the specter of Nuremberg had only begun to loom large. Only a few months earlier, the investigative reporter Seymour Hersh had broken the story of the My Lai massacre, which the army had covered up since the occurrence of the incident in March 1968.[19] Hersh's reporting received headline coverage around the country, earned him a

Pulitzer Prize, and provided chilling testimony to millions of Americans that U.S. forces would kill defenseless civilians if their village was suspected of harboring "Viet Cong."[20] In a letter to the editor of *Life*, one reader lamented, "If the principles of the Nuremberg War trials mean anything at all, then these men who killed women, children and old men should never be allowed to hide behind the excuse that 'I was just following orders.'"[21]

In Western Europe, and particularly in Sweden, France, and Britain, intellectuals opposed to the war had generally grappled with the notion of American war crimes earlier than their counterparts in the United States; for them My Lai was not a starting point that helped spur war crimes symposia such as that attended by Galston but the logical culmination of an industrialized power intent on the destruction of an agrarian peasant country.[22]

The British moral philosopher Bertrand Russell — who had built his reputation as a staunch anticommunist with the 1920 screed *Practice and Theory of Bolshevism* — founded the International War Crimes (IWC) Tribunal for the Vietnam War in November 1966. The title of the published book resulting from the tribunal was *Prevent the Crime of Silence*, reflecting its premise that unpunished war crimes are bound to be repeated. Jean-Paul Sartre, IWC Tribunal executive director, explained the group's mission: "A tribunal such as that of Nuremberg has become a permanent necessity . . . before the Nazi trials, war was lawless." Sartre went on: "The judgment of Nuremberg had necessitated the existence of an institution to inquire into war crimes, and if necessary, to sit in judgment." The decisions were intellectual only; the group, of course, had no enforcement capacity. But the group did claim ownership of the legal relevance of the judgment at Nuremburg: the Nazi defendants in 1945 stood accused of perpetuating war crimes, not "just following orders." For the IWC Tribunal, protesting to end an ongoing criminal war was Nuremburg's mandate.[23]

Edgar Lederer, a Parisian biology professor, first raised the issue of chemical warfare at an IWC Tribunal meeting. Lederer provided a broad overview of the environmental destruction and human suffering wrought by herbicidal warfare in Vietnam and made a strong case that Operation Ranch Hand encapsulated nearly every criminal dimension of the American war in South Vietnam, namely, the lavish use of advanced technology to subdue an unidentifiable enemy, thereby negating any practicable distinction between obliterating civilians and enemies.[24] Lederer went on to contribute to the resolution of the "International Meeting of Scientists on Chemical Warfare in Viet Nam" in Orsay, France, in December 1970. The resolution commended American scientists for "their courageous stand" taken against their government in protest of herbicidal warfare: "In the face of the terrible and widespread destruction of the ecology of Viet Nam whose extent passes [*sic*] the human imagination, we launch this appeal . . . to offer appropriate and helpful assistance to the Vietnamese people and to extend the study of the poisonous effects of the chemical substances used in this war, and to find means of fighting those effects."[25]

The Orsay resolution associated ecocide with genocide more explicitly: "The volume of human loss and the widespread destruction of nature lead us to the conclusion that we are not only faced with genocide but *biocide*."[26] Neither Galston nor any of the American scientists involved in the herbicide controversy were comfortable with this conflation. Agent Orange, in their view, was ecocidal to humans insofar as humans were ecologically connected to their surroundings. There was no moral or legal equivalence between the deliberate destruction of plants and humans.

Galston invented ecocide within a broader transatlantic dialogue on American war crimes and in an intellectual atmosphere that valued scientific authority on moral and political matters. But it was the NLF — the *target* of herbicidal warfare — and its allies in the Democratic Republic of Vietnam (North Vietnam) that most vigorously brought the resulting calamities to the world's attention. Although the propagandistic value in making public the horrors of herbicidal warfare was obvious enough, the word "propaganda" is not an adequate description. The tone and purpose of NLF documents, leaflets, and speeches denouncing herbicidal warfare were remarkably similar to those of Americans and Europeans writing on the same subject. If one allows for a degree of hyperbole and anti-American rhetoric in the NLF materials, those generated by protesting Americans and their European counterparts shared the same objective: to spread the word on how the United States was fighting its war in Vietnam.

One of the earliest such examples of a Vietnamese denunciation of herbicidal warfare came in April 1963 in a radio message broadcast by the Liberation Press Agency of the NLF. Broadcast out of Hanoi, the message challenged official American assertions of the safety of herbicides for human exposure and its limited use in counterinsurgency operations: "The fact is that the United States and the Ngo Dinh Diem administration have used these chemicals to carry out reprisals against the people, destroy the crops and vegetation, and plunge the inhabitants into misery and compel them to join 'strategic hamlets.'"[27] In a September 1965 speech titled "We Are

Determined to Defeat the U.S. War of Destruction," Colonel-General Van Tiên Dung of the NLF described herbicides as a "test ground," or a kind of military laboratory to prepare for future wars, against the people of Vietnam and a "policy of terror" that was destined to fail.[28]

In the early years of the war, Vietnamese communists were keenly aware of the value in establishing a common purpose between their own political objectives and the concerns voiced by dissenters in the United States and elsewhere.[29] In 1966 researchers in Hanoi compiled an impressive collection of international reactions to the American use of chemicals in Vietnam. With denunciations pouring in from Japan to Italy and from Lebanon to Tanzania, the Hanoi government portrayed the isolation that the United States was creating for itself by its actions in Vietnam. Notably, it was clear that the international condemnations directed against the United States did not conform to the ideological divide of the cold war. Insofar as reactions to the U.S. military's use of chemicals in Vietnam was a reliable gauge of general sentiment in the international arena, the United States early on had alienated allies and enemies alike.[30] By 1967 the NLF had organized its own war crimes committees, apparently modeled after the Russell tribunal, and the following year the North Vietnam Social Sciences Institute issued a wide-ranging survey on American war crimes. The section on chemical warfare cited a 1966 petition created by Arthur Galston and sent to Lyndon Johnson urging the president to halt the use of herbicides as evidence that Americans understood the catastrophe in Vietnam and protested that it was being carried out in their name.[31]

Throughout the war, the literature and broadcasts coming out of communist Vietnam strove to establish the existence of solidarity with the majority of the world's peoples on the issue of herbicides. But coverage in newspaper articles on Operation Ranch Hand brought the issue to public attention in the West only in 1965, and it took another year before the defoliation issue began to rouse the consciences of antiwar activists, of which there were few in 1965–66.[32] Hanoi and the NLF counted on wide-ranging solidarity against herbicidal warfare largely as a presupposition that the severity and inhumane character of Ranch Hand would forge a dissenters' bond across the first, second, and nonaligned worlds. The Vietnamese communists' persistence indicates that it was not only the American military that set out to "win hearts and minds"; when herbicidal operations reached their peak in 1967 and 1968, the NLF could also boast a veritable alliance with the war crimes movement as it positioned itself against the U.S. government. By that time, the herbicide controversy figured prominently — even centrally — in the litany of cited reasons for why and how the American war amounted to a criminal enterprise.

As a case of deliberate ecological destruction in which civilians had clearly suffered enormously, Operation Ranch Hand united activists in the West and communists in Vietnam in opposition without reference to the ideological battle that had precipitated the Vietnam War in the first place. If the first notable similarity in the war crimes literature and Vietnamese communist propaganda is the indignation expressed at the inhumanity of leveling high-technology destruction against a rural peasantry, the second is the shared absence of almost all reference to the cold war. To those who saw undeniable evidence of war crimes in Vietnam, the question of American containment versus communist expansion in Southeast Asia remained almost irrelevant throughout the herbicide controversy. In the West, it was possible to denounce Operation Ranch Hand without calling into question the fundamental tenets that had guided American foreign policy since 1947 or even the "logical culmination" of those tenets in the form of American intervention in Vietnam.[33] For herbicidal warfare protestors, debating the merits of containment detracted from their cause — there were more pressing issues. This was powerfully expressed by Paul Ehrlich, a biologist who achieved fame in 1968 with his neo-Malthusian book *The Population Bomb*. Ehrlich estimated that natural resource extraction and food production would soon fail to keep pace with human needs. In 1971 he determined that the crop-destruction variant of the herbicide program was a grave but preventable omen of a future global catastrophe.[34]

The week after the "War Crimes and the American Conscience" conference, where Galston had introduced ecocide, the American Bar Association (ABA) reasserted its decades-long opposition to the United Nations (UN) Genocide Convention of 1948.[35] Although the United States played an instrumental role in bringing the convention before the UN General Assembly, interest groups had repeatedly blocked Senate ratification.[36] In February 1970, ABA officials surmised that the time was appropriate to display the organization's lobbying clout again. According to a *New York Times* editorial, an ABA resolution held that Senate ratification of the Genocide Convention would "enable Communist countries to haul American citizens before an alien court on charges arising out of racial practices at home and military actions in Vietnam."[37] The *Times* took sharp issue with this position; the editorial avowed that the United States had not violated the Genocide

Convention, and the ABA's stance reinforced the perception that the United States was vulnerable to the charge of genocide. Meanwhile, the second part of the editorial strongly endorsed Galston's proposal on ecocide: "A world that is increasingly mindful of the threat to all life inherent in heedless tampering with the environment cannot be indifferent to the consequences of deliberate interference with the ecological balance."[38]

It was a curious line of reasoning. First, the *Times* editorial board apparently did not recognize the logical connection between the mounting war crimes movement in the United States and subsequent efforts such as that by the ABA to ensure that the United States did not legislate itself into a war crimes charge issued by the International Court of Justice (ICJ) or some other official body. As the ABA perceived the situation, nongovernmental groups like the Russell tribunal might have been an embarrassment to the United States, but an ICJ case would have been serious indeed. Second, the editorial operated on a cognitive dissonance: the *Times* asserted that the United States had not violated the Genocide Convention but simultaneously supported Galston's solution to ban ecocide. Galston had not meant to be as quaint as perhaps the *New York Times* had thought — ecocide was not merely a crime against trees such as that caused by overdevelopment.[39] To Galston, Operation Ranch Hand amounted to a crime against humanity.[40] As the ABA likely recognized, foreign communists were not the only activists who sought to haul the United States into an "alien court."

As a biologist and a humanitarian, Galston had staked a claim well beyond the reaches of his expertise; his major concern was that U.S. reconstruction efforts in Vietnam would not abandon the lives and land ruined by Agent Orange and, of course, that his government would renounce herbicidal warfare for all time.[41] But in the absence of any evidence that U.S. officials had such plans in the offing, implementing the legal mechanisms to enshrine ecocide as a crime required expertise in international law. It was Richard Falk, Milbank Professor of International Law at the Woodrow Wilson School at Princeton University, who laid out the case.

In 1968 Falk published an article titled "United States Policy and the Vietnam War: A Second American Dilemma." The title referred to the 1944 book *An American Dilemma: The Negro Problem and Modern Democracy*, by the Swedish economist Gunnar Myrdal. Taking an "objective" stance as a foreign observer, Myrdal had identified America's basic dilemma as the gap between "conduct and creed," that is, between America's guiding principles of liberty and equality with the racist realities of everyday life in a white-dominated society. Falk identified the Vietnam War as America's *second* dilemma because it replicated in foreign policy the gap Myrdal had identified in domestic affairs. In Vietnam, Falk charged, the United States departed radically from its creed in the realm of international relations; the war had proved so disastrous that the United States should "give up its pretensions about creating a world order."[42]

Falk's critique was devastating, yet compared to his writings following Arthur Galston's identification of ecocide, the notion of a second American dilemma seemed timid. By the early 1970s, Falk had come to believe that the United States stood guilty of war crimes in Vietnam that amounted to genocide. But why ecocide? For Falk, the strategy of environmental destruction for military purposes represented "the demonic logic of counterinsurgency warfare," a logic that proceeded on the "basic rationale of separating the people from their land." Paraphrasing Mao's famous likening of guerrillas to fish swimming in a sea of peasants, Falk characterized counterinsurgency doctrine as an "attempt to dry up the sea of civilians . . . This drying up process is translated militarily into making the countryside unfit for civilian habitation."[43]

The most pertinent questions had far transcended the intramural debates on U.S. foreign policy that had occupied Falk's attention in earlier years. With the knowledge of ecocide, the stakes of the war had become, in Falk's mind, elevated from a bankrupt adventure to an act of genocide. By contextualizing ecocide as a central component to the wider strategy of the destruction of South Vietnam, Falk identified "Agent Orange as an Auschwitz for environmental values . . . And just as the Genocide Convention came along to formalize part of what had already been condemned and punished at Nuremberg, so an Ecocide Convention could help carry forward into the future a legal condemnation of environmental warfare in Indochina."[44] Falk went on to argue that Operation Ranch Hand violated international treaty law and the U.S. Army's own laws of land warfare, contradicted overwhelming majority opinion as expressed in several UN General Assembly resolutions, and threatened to nullify the precedent of the Nuremberg trials.[45] On this last point, Falk was hardly the only legal scholar to grapple with the implications of Nuremberg for the Vietnam War.[46] Nor does it appear that lawyers were the first to consider Nuremberg as an avenue to protest American actions: beginning in 1965 college radicals and dissident U.S. servicemen routinely invoked Nuremberg to justify their resistance to American policy in Vietnam.[47]

Vietnamese communist pronouncements regularly characterized the American war generally and herbicidal warfare specifically as a genocidal act in the making.[48] At the Scientists' Conference on Chemical Warfare in Vietnam organized by Edgar Lederer, NLF Central Committee member Nguyen Van Hieu declared that scientific fears regarding the mutagenicity (or birth defect–causing) properties of Agent Orange had elevated the idea of genocide even beyond that seen during World War II. His prediction remains unsubstantiated: "Observations regarding chromosomic mutations and congenital malformations confirm the theoretic forecasts . . . The American Army is thus attacking not only the present generation but future generations as well, a crime never before committed in any war, not even that waged by the Nazis."[49] The theme of genocidal genetic warfare had become a staple by the late 1960s and early 1970s. In 1968 the Boston-based Committee of Concerned Asian Scholars titled an essay "Defoliation: The War against the Land and the Unborn." Citing Arthur Galston and other Western scientists, North Vietnam's English language *Vietnam Courier* ran numerous stories on the genetic destruction of Vietnam.[50]

No simple precedent existed for comparison with the ecological effects of herbicidal warfare. The denuded landscapes formed in the days and weeks after a Ranch Hand spray mission created a bizarre spectacle of destruction unlike anything that occurred in the course of peacetime activity. War, as recent studies have demonstrated, is always damaging to natural environments, yet few contemporary observers made reference to the "moonscape battlefields" of World War I or other potential analogs.[51] Accounts during and after the war were far more likely to draw parallels to the atomic attacks that laid waste to Hiroshima and Nagasaki, which leveled urban rather than rural environments.[52] Noam Chomsky was among the first Western observers to articulate why the Japanese precedent offered a more forceful analogy than other wars: "Three times in a generation American technology has laid waste a helpless Asian country. In 1945 this was done with a sense of moral rectitude that was, and remains, almost unchallenged. In Korea, there were a few qualms. The amazing resistance of the Vietnamese has finally forced us to ask, 'what have we done?'"[53]

The basis for the pattern drawn by Chomsky might be understood in racial terms, that is, that a racist presumption of white superiority had some basis in America's destructive wartime tactics against its Asian enemies, and more generally, that racism exerts an excessive and dangerous influence in international relations.[54] This is undoubtedly true. Yet in the case of herbicidal warfare, the explanatory power of race must be considered salient but not preeminent. Operation Ranch Hand worked in tandem with the Army of the Republic of Vietnam. ARVN officers proved to be energetic participants in the herbicide strategy who also believed that Ranch Hand would hasten the defeat of the NLF and hence the reconstruction of rural South Vietnam.[55] Accordingly, racial factors ranked low in characterizations of Operation Ranch Hand as an ecocidal or genocidal act. As Chomsky's analysis suggests, the basis for establishing a pattern of American tactics focused instead on the toxic and indiscriminate character of herbicidal warfare made possible by the fusion of science and air power.[56] For this reason, the case of Hiroshima figured prominently, even though the devastated coastal mangrove swamps and highland rainforests of Vietnam represented a calamity more visually and ecologically akin to the fields of the American South in the Civil War and France in World War I. For participants in the war crimes movement, it was never the ecological destruction *in itself* that mandated denunciations of Operation Ranch Hand as an act of genocide; it was the centrality of herbicides to a war strategy that portended the deliberate technological destruction of a nation.[57]

In the years since the end of the Vietnam War, the term "ecocide" has entered the popular lexicon, almost invariably without reference to its original context. It has proved a versatile term. Environmental activists soon adopted ecocide as their own. In 1971 one writer declared: "The message of our day is ecocide, the environment being murdered by mankind . . . Our dense, amber air is a noxious emphysema agent; farming — antihusbandry — turns fertile soil into a poisoned wasteland; rivers are sewers, lakes cesspools, and our oceans are dying."[58] More recent works have deployed the word to condemn the Euro-American destruction of American Indian cultures; the destruction of rainforests around the equatorial world; the corporate takeover and consequent destruction of a Pacific island; the neoliberal debt crisis in developing countries; the alarming trend of accelerated species extinction in recent decades; and the environmental ravages wrought across Eurasia in the pursuit of a totalitarian command economy.[59] Two works have described ecocidal military activities in the post-Vietnam era.[60] *Collapse*, a recent book by the evolutionary biologist Jared Diamond, frames ecocide as the organizing principle of his study. Diamond defines ecocide as "unintended ecological suicide," which has ended many great civilizations.[61] Finally, ecocide has found its way into what is probably the overriding environmental concern of the present day: global warming. Activists have more recently taken to the phrase "climate genocide" in denouncing carbon dioxide–emitting corporate operations and the governments that have hesitated to place strong curbs on emissions rates.[62]

These unique definitions should not obscure the original meaning and context of ecocide. The story of environmental destruction in Vietnam and the protests demanding and ultimately securing the termination of herbicidal warfare point to strong connections between America's counterinsurgency war in South Vietnam, antiwar protest, and environmental consciousness and activism in the 1960s and 1970s.

The work of the protesting scientists, as well as the political atmosphere that gave rise to ecocide, can be understood as a whole when one considers *how* the movement arose in the first place, and more crucially, *why* it succeeded in achieving its stated objectives. Although the concept of ecocide was always at the heart of the scientists' actions throughout the herbicide controversy — whether they concentrated on clarifying weapons disarmament policy, articulating the intersections of international law and science, or exposing government perfidy — ecocide alone did not and cannot provide an all-encompassing explanatory framework. The scientists most closely involved with the herbicide controversy were operating more broadly in a historical period that saw, as a result of the political, strategic, and moral calamity of the Vietnam War, a fundamental reorientation of the meaning of international security and human survival. By pointing at once to the criminality of American tactics in Vietnam and the rippling effects those tactics might have at a global level, the concept of ecocide fit squarely within a much broader political transformation over the course of the Vietnam era.

No one captured this change more powerfully than George Kennan, architect of the strategy of containment against the Soviet Union after World War II, who came to believe that his ideas on the cold war had been usurped by an excessively militant ideology that had led to the morass in Southeast Asia.[63] By 1966 Kennan was convinced that the Vietnam War threatened America's long-term viability. In a speech in support of Eugene McCarthy, senator from Minnesota and antiwar presidential aspirant in the 1968 election, Kennan devoted his talk to protesting President Lyndon B. Johnson's policies in Vietnam: "My friends . . . I do not see how we can view what our government has done with relations to Vietnam as anything other than a massive miscalculation and an error of policy, an error for which it is hard to find many parallels in our history, an error rendered doubly serious and inexcusable by the number and quality of the warning voices that have been raised against it."[64]

As a foreign-policy theorist, Kennan was less concerned with the counterinsurgency tactics in Vietnam that had exercised the conscience of so many antiwar activists; in his more global view such methods were symptomatic of the fundamental intellectual bankruptcy that had gotten the United States into this situation in the first place. If Vietnam had become the dominant symbol of American resolve to defeat the international expansion of communism, then the time had come to rethink America's purpose in world affairs. Kennan reached further: he incorporated the war within a broader matrix of issues that indicated, in his view, that the United States had lost its way. Kennan wrote and spoke repeatedly of the alienation of America's "Negro population" and "the steady process of destruction and pollution of [America's] natural resources," and finally, "the extremely disturbed and excited state of mind of a good portion of [the country's] student youth, floundering around . . . in its own terrifying wilderness of drugs, pornography and political hysteria."[65]

In a 1970 article appearing in the same journal that published "X," Kennan identified impending ecological doom as the preeminent security threat facing humankind. Environmental issues, Kennan observed, required an international oversight body such as the UN because the basis of global environmental protection required international cooperation. Kennan hoped that such an institution could avoid what the political scientist Robert Jervis has defined as a classic international-security dilemma, in which, given "the absence of a supranational authority that can enforce binding agreements, many of the steps pursued by states to bolster their security have the effect — often unintended and unforeseen — of making other states less secure."[66] The security threats that Kennan had in mind were immense: "Indeed, the entire ecology of the planet is not arranged in national compartments; and whoever interferes seriously with it anywhere is doing something that is almost invariably of serious concern to the international community at large."[67]

For Kennan the specter of some future "world wasteland" and the present reality of the American catastrophe in Vietnam were inseparable: both problems had arisen because of short-sighted and misplaced priorities. Militant anticommunism, as it was being applied in Vietnam, had damaged America's national security and at the same time threw into question the primacy of communist expansion as the dominant security threat facing the

United States. Even more worrisome in Kennan's view was that the decade-long fixation on Vietnam had obscured a threat that, if left unchecked, pointed to a struggle for human survival that would render irrelevant the ideological conflicts that had animated the cold war. Therefore, the scientific movement that invented ecocide — which simultaneously minimized the strategic relevance of the cold war and sought through legal mechanisms to prevent future environmental catastrophes — must be understood directly within the transformative context that Kennan had illustrated.

To demonstrate the magnitude of this transformation, we can examine popular conceptions of global destruction only ten years earlier. The newly elected John F. Kennedy vowed in his inaugural address that America should "pay any price, bear any burden, meet any hardship, support any friend, oppose any foe, in order to assure the survival and the success of liberty."[68] In the struggle against communism, what was the new president prepared to pay? Could the Kennedy administration maintain President Dwight Eisenhower's record of avoiding nuclear confrontation with the Soviet Union, while promising a fundamental shift from his predecessor's cold war strategy?[69] If a crisis situation erupted into intercontinental nuclear war, would human life on Earth continue? On this last point, at least, John Kennedy and his advisors had the semblance of a concrete answer to these untested questions. According to Herman Kahn, a researcher for the RAND Corporation, both the notion of survival in a postnuclear environment and the possibility of a U.S. victory in a nuclear war became entirely conceivable.

In 1960 Kahn published *On Thermonuclear War* to instant acclaim in the media and Washington's foreign-policy establishment. His ideas were given close attention in the Kennedy administration, which had hired many of Kahn's colleagues from RAND.[70] The title was an unsubtle reference to *On War*, a major treatise on military strategy written by the Prussian theorist Karl von Clausewitz in the early nineteenth century. In the book's famously chilling question, "Will the survivors envy the dead?" after a nuclear holocaust, Kahn offered an emphatic no.[71] What is significant is not how Kahn arrived at his conclusion — which relied on a mind-boggling sequence of genetic algorithms to calculate human survival rates — but in the author's noninterest in the ideological underpinnings that would precipitate a war of "mutually assured destruction." For Kahn, the point was to devise a strategy for the United States to "win" a nuclear war.[72] Stanley Kubrick based his macabre comedy and title character *Dr. Strangelove* (1964) on Kahn; the final scenes depicting mushroom clouds demonstrated in Kubrick's view what nuclear "victory" looked like.

Over the course of the decade, two major developments rendered Kahn's study irrelevant. First, in 1963 the Limited Nuclear Test Ban Treaty helped reduce nuclear tensions between the superpowers after the Cuban missile crisis pushed the United States and the Soviet Union to the brink of war.[73] That same year multilateral assurances of a nonnuclear West Germany virtually cemented the impossibility of strategic nuclear war between the United States and the Soviet Union.[74] Second, by the end of the decade the Vietnam War had essentially destroyed the idea that a policy of militant anticommunism was worth risking the physical survival of the United States or, for that matter, the world. At the same time, widespread ecological concerns reoriented the basic meaning of survival — both in the United States and globally. Taking a cue from the wider environmental movement that had steadily gained steam since Rachel Carson published *Silent Spring* in 1962, George Kennan was among the first to articulate the relationship between the decline of cold war fears and the rise of ecological fears.[75]

By 1970 visions of global environmental calamities thus bore scant resemblance to the postnuclear holocaust world imagined by Herman Kahn only a decade earlier. What had changed was not the extent of imagined destruction but its source. In place of nuclear devastation came a more gradual but no less apocalyptic vision of planetary environmental destruction that included desertified cropland, clear-cut forests, smog-filled air, and oil-slicked beaches.[76] The idea that humans were altering the planet's ecology for the worse and that something needed to be done about it had become a widely held belief — and for many it was an issue that had more salience and urgency than America's prosecution of the cold war. The historian John McNeill locates the realization that humans were creating "something new under the sun" as a process in the 1960s that depended, in large measure, on the fact that all over the world "received wisdom and constituted authority came under fierce attack" during that turbulent decade.[77]

But where was the evidence that the sum of the various environmental problems that had caused widespread concern by the late 1960s had justified the vision of a world wasteland? Was the very idea of humans slowly but surely destroying the world merely a reincarnation of unrealized anxieties born in the chaos of nineteenth-century industrialization? Furthermore, did this idea advance a false divide between rapacious humans and a passive nature that discounted the dynamism of the natural environment?[78] In

Vietnam many environmentalists saw strong evidence that such apocalyptic fears were not merely hypothetical. Channeling the introductory sentences of *Silent Spring*, the Sierra Club *Bulletin* published what amounted to an environmental obituary of a nation: "Once upon a time there was a small, beautiful, green and graceful country called Vietnam." The article went on to survey the mammoth environmental destructiveness of the "Orwellian" and "macabre" Operation Ranch Hand, concluding: "By the time deformed fetuses began appearing and signs of lasting ecological damage were becoming increasingly apparent success had been achieved. Vietnam had been saved. But the country was dead."[79] The theme of a "dead" country as an omen of things to come was struck repeatedly among environmentalists; one author suggested that the destruction of Vietnam offered a blueprint of planetary death.[80]

The scientists who identified ecocide fashioned themselves as neither specialists in security affairs nor environmental activists. But their agenda existed at the center of a complex transformation of priorities over the course of the Vietnam War. At a broad level, an examination of this transformation situates the herbicide controversy beyond the narrow parameters set by activist scientists and their supporters who protested ecocide, first as an ecological calamity in need of independent scientific investigation, and soon afterward as an ecological variant of genocide. The significance of the scientists' actions thus has wider ramifications for our understanding of the interplay between the counterinsurgency tactics of the Vietnam War and the protest it engendered.

CHAPTER THREE

AGENT ORANGE
BEFORE VIETNAM

AGENT ORANGE HAS A SPLIT LINEAGE. The history of its component chemicals, 2,4-D and 2,4,5-T, begins with one of Charles Darwin's lesser-known biological theories. The history of the military weapon Agent Orange begins on the eve of World War II, when the demands of total war sparked one scientist's insight that weed killers had military value. In the late 1870s, Darwin began to study the mechanisms that regulated plant growth; at the time there were no accepted answers to questions that would form the basis of plant physiology: Why do plant shoots grow upward in defiance of gravity? What causes stems to bend around objects that obstruct sunlight? Is there a particular part of the plant that controls growth, or is the process decentralized throughout the organism?

With the assistance of his son Francis, Darwin conducted experiments with 320 plant species, paying particular attention to the movement of seedlings when exposed to varying degrees of light. At nearly six hundred pages, the resulting publication, *The Power of Movement in Plants* (1880), reads like an endless scientific diary. Still, Darwin managed to fit his central hypothesis into a concluding paragraph:

> Circumnutation [bending] is of paramount importance in the life of every plant; for it is through its modification that many highly beneficial or necessary movements have been acquired. When light strikes one side of a plant, or light changes into darkness, or when gravitation acts on a displaced part, the plant is enabled in some unknown manner to increase the always varying turgescence [swollenness] of the cells on one side; so that the ordinary

circumnutating movement is modified, and the part bends either to or from the exciting cause; or it may occupy a new position, as in the so-called sleep of leaves.[1]

In other words, Darwin discovered that the stimulus of growth transferred from one part of a plant (the tip of a shoot) to another (the stem). When Darwin either shaded the tip with miniature cups or snipped it from the plant altogether, the stem would not bend toward light as it would under normal conditions, thus demonstrating the existence of "some unknown manner" of transmission that directed plant growth from top to bottom. These were the last of Darwin's major scientific discoveries; he died in 1882.[2]

Darwin's transmission hypothesis provided the foundation for all future discoveries involving plant growth regulation, on two levels. First, his experiments demonstrated the existence of a growth stimulus that could be isolated and studied. Second, researchers could concentrate their efforts on the tip of the plant. Over the next thirty years, scientists' understanding of plant growth expanded rapidly. E. H. Salkowski discovered indole-3-acetic acid (IAA) in 1885, which turned out to be the growth substance whose existence Darwin had postulated five years earlier. In 1911 Peter Boysen-Jensen replicated Darwin's earlier manipulation of plant tips, adding the step of placing pieces of gelatin between the tip and the stem. Boysen-Jensen observed that the gelatin separator did not affect the stem's growth response and hypothesized that the growth "messenger" was likely a chemical process.

Subsequent experiments by Arpad Paal (1918) and H. Soding (1925) involving observations following plant cuttings and light variations further confirmed the Boysen-Jensen chemical hypothesis. Then in 1926 a Dutch graduate student, F. W. Went, isolated the growth substance into a nonliving medium rather than allowing it to diffuse into the stem as his predecessors had done. Went chose agar, a seaweed-derived jelly that absorbed the growth substance from the isolated tips. When Went placed the agar back on the shoot, the young plant behaved as if it had never been severed in two. This proved the existence of a growth substance. Went named this substance auxin, from the Greek *auxein*, "to grow."[3]

The discovery and identification of unique plant hormones proved to be the methodological counterpart to Darwin's scientific process. Darwin had opened a Pandora's box for hormonal manipulation of a given plant's physiology with the knowledge that plant growth was controlled by biochemical reactions that could be isolated and quantified. Scientists in Germany, Britain, and the United States subsequently raced to create chemical solutions that could influence natural growth-regulating reactions. In 1933 the potential for hormone manipulation expanded greatly when Fritz Koegl, F. W. Went's laboratory partner at the Organic Chemistry Institute in Utrecht, successfully isolated IAA from several plant species, thus making possible the external application of synthesized hormones on plants. The following year, Kenneth Thimann and F. W. Went (who had recently joined Thimann at the California Institute of Technology) synthesized IAA and, more importantly, discovered that synthetic IAA was capable of manipulating plant growth in an identical manner to naturally produced hormones within the plant.[4] The promises of harnessing hormone regulation to promote growth seemed self-evident to researchers looking to create larger, faster-growing cash crops.[5]

A somewhat more counterintuitive approach to the potential benefits of hormone manipulation — using synthetic chemicals as plant killers — can be traced to Folke Skoog and Kenneth Thimann. Shortly following Thimann's own breakthrough in hormone synthesis, the team demonstrated that when IAA was distilled in higher concentrations it effectively inhibited plant growth.[6] The discovery was the first to push the conceptual boundaries in the field beyond attempts to make plants grow larger through hormonal regulation. This research helped usher in the era of phenoxy herbicides and their two most prominent formulations, 2,4-D and 2,4,5-T.

But the first chemical herbicide preceded the Skoog-Thimann discovery by thirty-five years. In 1900 scientists working for the burgeoning chemical industry introduced sodium arsenite as the first commercially available weed killer.[7] Although the compound proved an effective herbicide, from an agricultural standpoint sodium arsenite was problematic. It acted as a soil sterilant, whereas herbicidal chemicals that manipulated plant growth could prove at once harmless to soil and capable of selectively targeting certain plants.[8] As the botanist James R. Troyer observed, the discovery of growth-inhibiting herbicides "later made the control of weeds no longer a matter of hazardous corrosive chemicals, hit-or-miss results, or hard manual labor."[9]

The quest to displace the physical toil of agriculture with the labor-saving "magic" of biochemistry became a central mission of the Boyce Thompson Institute (BTI) for Plant Research, launched in 1924 in Yonkers, New York. Thompson, who had made his fortune in copper mining, created the institute in his name because of his concern over the widening gap between population growth and the feeding capacity of American agriculture. A close friend of Herbert Hoover, who directed the American Relief Administration during and after World War I, Thompson witnessed firsthand the mass starvation in Russia following the 1917 revolution. Thompson saw the catastrophe as an omen of what could happen in the United States. In 1919 at an exploratory meeting for the institute, Thompson declared: "There will be 200 million people in this country soon. It's going to be a question of bread, of primary food supply. That question is beyond politicians and sociologists. I think I will work out some institution to deal with plant physiology, to help protect the basic needs of 200 million. Not an uplift foundation, but a scientific institution dealing with definite things, like germination, parasites, plant diseases, and plant potentialities."[10]

Following the exciting developments in Europe, plant hormone regulation commenced at BTI under the direction of Percy Zimmerman. At that juncture, the future of biochemical applications in agriculture simultaneously promised greater crop yields at a dramatically lower cost of labor. In 1935 BTI scientists began to synthesize acids such as naphthalene acetic acid that proved to be far more powerful plant growth regulators than IAA in its original formation. Over the next four years, Zimmerman and his colleagues synthesized over fifty compounds that demonstrably manipulated the growth of roots, stems, and leaves via aerosol application.[11] This research yielded commercially significant results. By 1940 BTI-patented synthetic hormones designed to enhance root growth in young plants and to strengthen the stems of tree fruit (so that the fruit would ripen on the tree) hit the market in the United States.[12]

By the eve of World War II, researchers on both sides of the Atlantic had established conclusively the fantastic potential of chemical regulation of plant growth. Conceptually, all the groundwork was in place for a major breakthrough. At that stage, plant physiologists knew that various combinations of chemicals applied in various concentrations could affect plant growth in many ways. As one plant physiologist noted, "The ultimate objective of a considerable number of workers in the field of biology is *growth control*. The familiar phrase that 'once normal growth is better understood it should be possible to control abnormal growth' is in the minds of all."[13] The task ahead was to match the myriad chemical variables with the desired effects on plants, whether it was growth promotion, growth inhibition, or the outright killing of weeds. Most researchers continued to direct their efforts toward promoting plant growth until laboratory experiments confirmed that the brightest future in the field lay in weed control.

The path to discovering the first hormone herbicides was virtually preordained to occur simultaneously and independently. Disparate groups on both sides of the Atlantic claimed many "firsts" in the discovery of modern herbicides, although these distinctions are less important than the fact they were achieving similar goals. The first scientist to demonstrate conclusively the herbicidal effects of a specific chemical via hormonal manipulation was William Gladstone Templeman, a plant physiologist who worked for the Imperial Chemical Industries (ICI) in the United Kingdom. Like most of his peers, Templeman devoted his early work to plant growth promoting substances. After seven years of research, however, he abandoned this path in favor of studying the herbicidal effects of the same substances when applied to plants at higher concentrations. In 1940 Templeman's experiments showed that IAA killed broadleaf weeds that grew in cereal fields yet left the crops intact and caused no demonstrable harm to the soil.[14] Buoyed by this discovery but unsatisfied with the short persistence of IAA, Templeman collaborated with his fellow scientists at ICI in search of more persistent (and therefore cheaper) acids, one of which was 2,4-D.

The first published account of 2,4-D was produced by a chemist named R. Pokorny in June 1941.[15] The following year, another American chemist, John Lontz, applied for and received a patent for 2,4-D on behalf of E. I. du Pont de Nemours and Company.[16] That same year, Zimmerman and his colleagues at BTI, who had been testing numerous chemical combinations for the past six years, were the first to state explicitly the potential of 2,4-D as a synthetic plant growth regulator.[17] In 1943 Franklin D. Jones, of the American Chemical Paint Company, discovered the herbicidal properties of 2,4-D after a year of searching for a chemical to eradicate poison ivy. Jones was also the first scientist to conduct detailed experiments with 2,4,5-T, which Pokorny had also mentioned in his 1941 article.[18] Meanwhile, Arthur Galston, who became a leading critic of herbicidal warfare, inadvertently discovered in 1942 the herbicidal capacity of 2,3,5-triiodobenzoic acid (TIBA) on soy plants while conducting his dissertation research at the University of Illinois.[19] Galston's research helped to make soy beans commercially viable in the United States, while his herbicidal discovery added another synthetic compound to the nascent field of hormone weed control.

The concurrent and independent discoveries of hormone herbicides in the United States were not known to William Templeman and his ICI associates in Britain, who were both the first to synthesize 2,4-D and the first to recognize its plant-killing potential. In April 1941 Templeman filed with the British Patent Office, but officials froze the patent until 1945 due to the British government's wartime censorship of new scientific information to prevent sensitive materials from falling into enemy hands.[20] This fact helps to explain why Templeman was unaware of the work being done at Britain's other major center of plant research, Rothamsted Agricultural Experiment Station, where Philip S. Nutman, H. Gerard Thornton, and John H. Quastel discovered the herbicidal properties of 2,4-D at the same time.[21]

In the decades after Darwin's initial work, the field of plant growth research proceeded in bursts. The overlapping discovery of 2,4-D and its related synthetic compounds illustrates the effectiveness of government-imposed wartime restrictions that prevented the scientists from learning of one another's advances.[22]

Agent Orange offers a new perspective on the scientific origins of hormone herbicides. Ezra E. J. Kraus, chair of the University of Chicago's Department of Botany, first recognized the potential military value of herbicides at America's entry into World War II. Although the British scientists at ICI have a double claim on the innovation of hormone herbicides as agricultural tools and military weapons, the chronology favors Kraus's insight by two years. In contrast to the concomitant discoveries that led to the synthesis of 2,4-D and the consequent recognition of its herbicidal properties, the originality of Kraus's idea might be understood as a matter of political rather than scientific innovation. The significance of this innovation merits our attention before discussing the details of Kraus's work.

Whereas early research in plant growth manipulation required a cognitive leap to shift the field from growth promotion to weed destruction, the idea that herbicides could become a military weapon necessitated a similar reorientation of the social function of plant physiology in a time of total war. Just as the idea of favoring herbicides over growth promoters required new ways to unlock the potential of biochemistry, so too did the notion of herbicidal warfare require innovative thinking about national security and the environmental dimensions of battle.

Chemical weed killing initially developed as one dimension of humanity's age-old search for the most productive strategies of land use: even if a given herbicide's primary function was death in the form of targeting specific weed species, scientists' ultimate goal was to create optimal growing conditions for a particular forest or agricultural product that would otherwise have to compete with undesirable plant species for diminished amounts of sunlight, water, and soil nutrients.[23] The insecticide DDT, another chemical born in World War II that later achieved notoriety in the 1960s, followed a far more linear path between war and peace, for mosquitoes posed grave health dangers to soldiers and civilians alike.[24]

In stronger concentrations, military-grade herbicides would extend their weed-killing properties to all plant life to ensure the *minimization* of the productivity of land under the control of enemy forces. In the context of war, the term "herbicide" without the modifier "military" does not adequately convey its purpose, namely, to achieve widespread and unrestricted plant killing.[25] Therefore the "productivity" of the military use of herbicides (in contingency planning in World War II and in actuality during the Vietnam War) can only be measured in the unquantifiable concepts that citizens and national leaders use to employ and justify their war efforts.[26]

Ezra Kraus was well positioned to grasp the military potential of herbicidal warfare. Chicago's botany department boasted cutting-edge laboratory equipment, due in part to large grants from the Rockefeller Foundation. Kraus enjoyed inside access to the Bureau of Plant Industry (BPI) of the U.S. Department of Agriculture (USDA), located in Beltsville, Maryland, which he had helped to create in the late 1930s.[27] By 1940 Kraus had overseen several collaborative research efforts on plant growth manipulation involving his department and the USDA; he even secured jobs for several of his graduate students at BPI.[28] Kraus, like many of his colleagues in the United States and Britain, independently recognized the herbicidal potential of synthetic growth compounds. According to one of his graduate students, Kraus initially discussed his discovery in August 1941, although the nature of his research suggests the first inklings came to him in 1940.[29]

In the fall of 1941, Kraus and his student John Mitchell commenced research on the herbicidal potential of several synthetic growth compounds. Almost immediately after the Japanese attack on Pearl Harbor on December 7, Kraus offered his services to the government. Again Kraus found he was well situated to enlist plant physiology in the service of the public; he had been a founding member of a highly classified project on chemical and biological warfare under the auspices of the National Academy of Sciences convened by Secretary of War Henry L. Stimson and chaired by the pharmaceutical magnate George W. Merck.[30] In a top-secret meeting of the Biological and Chemical Weapons Committee of the War Bureau of Consultants (WBC) held on February 17, 1942, Kraus presented a position paper titled

"Plant Growth Regulators: Possible Uses." The paper was dated December 18, 1941; Japan's surprise attack had prompted Kraus to complete the paper as quickly as possible. What is less apparent is whether Pearl Harbor provided the "tipping point" that allowed Kraus to conceive of herbicides as military weapons or if the idea had occurred to him earlier. Regardless, the United States' abrupt entry into World War II gave Kraus an audience at the highest levels of the national defense establishment. Military and political officials, staring into the abyss of war, were receptive to new classes of weapons that promised tactical advantage on the battlefield.

Kraus outlined the strategic utility of herbicides, which he thought would make a greater contribution defoliating Japanese-held island forests in the Pacific than on the western front of Europe. He called for greater government support to advance the field of plant growth manipulation as a matter of national security:

> Projected Plans: Further investigations are proposed to determine the effects of compounds other than those now in use. There remains much to be done on those already partially investigated in relation to effects of various concentrations dependent upon character of soil or other medium in which plants are grown, stage of development of plant, effects of environmental factors such as humidity, light and temperature, and most effective method of application in each case.

> Significance of National Defense: These substances are especially important in the present war effort because of the relative speed with which practical results can be obtained in both offensive and defensive warfare.

> Offensive Significance: Release of growth destroying substances in the dry, solid state over rice fields would be a feasible and comparatively simple means of destruction of rice crops, the staple food supply of the Japanese. Distribution of sprays or mists over enemy forests would, through killing of trees, reveal concealed military depots. These are examples of many obvious uses of these compounds.[31]

The proposal is significant for three reasons. First, Kraus came up with his idea to make herbicides into a military weapon at a time when scientists were still making rudimentary discoveries about the characteristics of herbicides and their effects on plants. Second, from the perspective of Operation Ranch Hand and its awesome destructive power, Kraus's conceptualization of the military value of herbicides was more advanced than the state of herbicide research. Third, Kraus recognized the ease with which herbicides could join the American arsenal. This was precisely the concern of the scientists who sought to prohibit herbicidal warfare in the late 1960s — the accessibility of Agent Orange meant it could be readily available to any nation at war.

Kraus was one of dozens of scientists to offer expertise as a representative of his field; the WBC committee heard twelve papers on various methods to destroy cropland and forests alone. Discussions about unleashing potato blight microbes against Germany's staple crop served as the European analog to Kraus's plans to starve out the Japanese-occupied islands throughout the Pacific.[32] The WBC committee approved several of the position papers, Kraus's included. Shortly thereafter, Kraus wrote to Percy Zimmerman of the Boyce Thompson Institute to request samples of 2,4-D; Zimmerman's pioneering work on phenoxyacetic compounds had become known to Kraus the previous year. Kraus did not divulge his plans for 2,4-D to Zimmerman, although it is hard to imagine that in the intense anti-Japanese atmosphere in the weeks and months following Pearl Harbor Zimmerman would have had second thoughts about contributing to American retaliatory measures in the Pacific theater.[33] Arthur Galston, who worked on a federal emergency synthetic rubber project in 1943, recalled that few scientists engaged in biological or chemical warfare projects placed their moral qualms — if they had any — about the application of scientific knowledge toward destructive ends above their sense of national duty to win the "good war."[34] The exception came almost exclusively from several scientists involved in the atomic project who tried desperately to prevent a nuclear attack against Japan.[35]

By the beginning of 1943, Kraus and John W. Mitchell were running large-scale research projects on the crop-destruction potential of 2,4-D in the botanical labs at the University of Chicago and at the Beltsville research station. Kraus was impressed by the herbicidal capacity of 2,4-D against broadleaf plants, particularly in aerosol form, but he found that inorganic toxins such as arsenic proved most effective against rice. This discovery led to the military's creation of the arsenical rice-killer Agent Blue during the Vietnam War.[36]

The official nature of Kraus's research attracted the interest of military officials impressed by the potential tactical advantages offered by herbicides. The U.S. Army included herbicide research as a cornerstone of its fledgling chemical and biological research program at Camp Frederick, Maryland, following Kraus's acquisition of 2,4,5-T (which would eventually constitute, along with 2,4-D, one-half of the compound Agent Orange) from the Sherwin-Williams Chemical Company in the fall of 1943. By 1944 Kraus, Mitchell, and Charles Hamner, another of Kraus's students who had recently moved from BTI to Cornell University, had established the herbicidal properties of dozens of plants and in a variety of application methods. This research constituted the most comprehensive research on plant growth manipulation — for either war or peacetime applications — up to that point.[37]

With Kraus as a consultant, military scientists at Fort Detrick, Maryland, continued research on 2,4-D and 2,4,5-T in simulated wartime conditions, in other words, with military aircraft outfitted with crop-dusting equipment flying spray sorties over the Florida Everglades. Fort Detrick scientists chose the Everglades because its ecology most closely resembled the tropical Pacific island climates for which the herbicides were destined.[38] Kraus became the WBC's chief censor of scientific publications that contained potentially sensitive information pertaining to herbicides.[39] He proved a success in this position as well; the literature up to 1945 on hormone herbicides gives no indication that plant physiologists had joined the war effort. Hormone herbicides were the most viable component of America's incipient chemical and biological program — not to mention the one area of chemical and biological weapons research that showed tremendous commercial potential — and this secrecy attests to the seriousness with which military officials regarded the possibility of waging herbicidal warfare. Despite enormous advances in hormone herbicide research and a consensus among civilians and military officials involved in the program that herbicides would be an effective addition to the military's arsenal in the Pacific theater, the military would not use herbicides until the beginning of Operation Ranch Hand in 1961.

There are two major reasons why this crash-course program was unfinished when the war concluded in August 1945. First, obviously, the atomic blasts over Hiroshima and Nagasaki ended the war before George Merck and his military colleagues deemed herbicide operations at Fort Detrick battle ready. In 1946 Merck told a newspaper reporter, "Only the rapid ending of the war prevented field trials in an active theater of synthetic agents that would, without injury to human or animal life, affect the growing crops and make them useless."[40] In 1965 Charles Minarik, a biologist with the USDA who would soon devote his work to studying the ecological effects of Operation Ranch Hand in Vietnam, bluntly echoed Merck's sentiment: "The chemicals were never used abroad, and the war terminated before we could get the materials in the field."[41]

The second explanation for the absence of herbicide operations in World War II is less specific to the work of Kraus and his partners at the USDA and Fort Detrick, yet key for understanding strategic and moral attitudes toward chemical and biological weapons during the war. Although the unfinished state of herbicide planning reveals why that particular program never saw "action," it does not explain the Allied decision to refrain from *any* method of chemical and biological warfare throughout the war. With the horrors of gas warfare in World War I a fresh memory, mutual deterrence doubtless prevented the outbreak of unconventional warfare during the war's entirety. Even Franklin Roosevelt, who stood out among national leaders for his strong condemnation of chemical and biological weapons, intimated that the United States was prepared to retaliate in kind against such an attack.[42] On June 8, 1943, Roosevelt declared: "The use of such weapons has been outlawed by the general opinion of civilized mankind. This country has not used them, and I hope that we never will be compelled to use them. I state categorically that we shall under no circumstances resort to the use of such weapons unless they are first used by our enemies."[43]

In the midst of the controversy over herbicidal warfare in Vietnam, Roosevelt's statement became a major point of conflicting interpretations concerning the signatory status or prohibitory scope of the Geneva Protocol of 1925, which effectively banned first use of biological and chemical warfare among its signatories.[44] Although the United States did not sign the protocol, the statement prompted debate on whether Roosevelt's affirmation bound the United States to its provisions as a matter of customary (i.e., normative) international law.[45] This fact prompted further disputes about whether Operation Ranch Hand violated an international law; that is, do antiplant weapons fall under the scope of the Geneva Protocol?

There is no indication that American war planners during World War II considered these nuances.[46] Ezra Kraus lobbied and ultimately won U.S. Army support for herbicidal warfare planning as one part of what war planners saw as a broad strategic need for unconventional weapons. For a military preparing for total wartime mobilization, debate about the details of what the Geneva Protocol prohibited was of minor concern — even though the very purpose of the protocol was to place limits on the weapons that combatants were willing to deploy. At the same time, no obvious correlation exists between the military's appetite to acquire the largest variety of new and unconventional weapons and Roosevelt's (and later President Harry Truman's) reluctance to use them first in war.[47] The case of herbicides is further complicated by the fact that the United States was not racing its enemies to develop an herbicidal capability. Unlike a retaliatory gas attack — which is likely what Roosevelt had in mind in his June 1943 statement — the use of herbicides by definition would require first use in war. Had the herbicide plans reached maturity, such an action might have required a contravention of the Geneva Protocol and consequent reversal from Roosevelt's long record of supporting the protocol.[48] The explanations offered by Merck and Minarik, which consider the absence of herbicidal warfare from the Pacific theater solely in terms of timing, obscures this larger story. Although the incomplete state of herbicidal warfare planning freezes the question as a counterfactual, it cannot be assumed that if the missions envisioned by Kraus had been ready at an earlier stage in the war the civilian leadership ultimately responsible for such decisions would have approved the operation.

The academic-military research on plant growth manipulation during World War II proved tremendously valuable despite the absence of herbicides on the battlefield. Without government resources at the disposal of Kraus and his colleagues, the field would have been set back as many as ten years. As George Merck reasoned in a rather self-serving assessment, "Perhaps no other type of warfare can bring with it such a guaranty of good: economic advantages in agriculture, parallel gains in animal husbandry, and, above all, vital contributions to the fight against human ills and suffering."[49] If by early 1945 Americans had reason to believe that the war abroad was drawing to a close, another on the home front had yet to begin — a "war against weeds."[50]

One magazine story explicitly drew parallels between the two wars while improbably extending racist sentiment to the world of plants: The February 1945 issue of *Better Homes and Gardens* sang the praises of 2,4,5-T and its ability to combat Japanese honeysuckle, a longtime bane of American gardeners. The article characterized the honeysuckle as a "Jap invader [that] has taken over large areas in the eastern United States," which Americans could now annihilate thanks to the new miracle chemical.[51] Had the public known of the WBC's plans to use these "miracle chemicals" in the war against actual Japanese, the program would have garnered wide support. Such a perspective was not unique to the World War II era; the alliance of military needs abroad and the domestic benefits of the scientific and commercial utility of herbicides would continue through the Vietnam War.[52]

At the conclusion of World War II, Kraus successfully urged government censors to lift the ban on weed-control literature related to war research. Because such literature contained the most valuable available information about such chemicals, the policy soon ensured a booming market in chemical weed control. As the botanist Alden Crafts recalled, "Almost overnight the story of this miracle herbicide spread throughout the land; supplies were brought up, large scale applications were made, and commercial weed control became a going business."[53] Crafts continued his description of the postwar excitement in the agriculture and forestry sectors, explaining at once what botanists call the "mode of action" of the chlorophenoxy herbicides and the reason they became an instant success: "2,4-D not only killed plants by contact action; it translocated from the tops into the roots of perennial weeds; it was selective against many broad-leaved weeds in cereal and grass crops; it was absorbed from the soil by young seedlings with fatal results and hence could be used by the pre-emergence method; it was nontoxic to man and animals; and it was a cheap and potent chemical capable of controlling weeds at a cost as low as $1.00 per acre or less for the chemical."[54] At a November 1945 plant physiology conference, Kraus delivered a speech bordering on the giddy. Without making reference to his wartime work — probably because this was a sore subject among many of his colleagues who had not enjoyed access to the same cutting-edge research — Kraus talked of a revolution in humankind's capacity to control all plant life. Likening his colleagues' knowledge of hormone herbicides to children poking sticks in ant hills, Kraus declared an agricultural utopia was at hand:

> We are going to make plants grow taller, if you wish them taller, and shorter, if you wish them shorter. We are going to have them grow thicker, if you want them thicker, and thinner, if you want them thinner. When I start prophesying, the sky is the limit . . . If we have been able to bring about an increase in the yield of apples in two and three tons per acre, without loss of quality; if we are able to produce blueberries which are larger and seedless and if it is possible to get tomatoes that will be larger, and if we have a ripening process for fruits and can delay the sprouting of potatoes and fruit trees in the spring and if we can control weeds, we will have our results.[55]

The speech drew from the conceptual block that most scientists had come up against on the eve of World War II, when the burgeoning field generally approached synthetic hormones as promoters of plant growth. Kraus explained, "All one had to do was turn his spy glass the other way around," meaning that growth hormones had already proved far more valuable as selective herbicides. The cause of increased agricultural yields following the right mix of chemicals, concentrations, and delivery methods to destroy unwanted surrounding weeds was self-evident and well established. Yet Kraus saw this development as only the beginning of a grander process whose end point was total mastery of plant life at the cellular level. This point offered the sole hint of humility that Kraus offered in the speech; now that the war was over his objective was to enlist his colleagues to join this quest.

In the next few years, the market performance of the new hormone herbicides demonstrated that consumers were most interested in their properties as selective weed killers. Although more-exotic uses of synthetic plant hormones sounded appealing to many, Kraus's own research helped to ensure that the future of the field was in weed killing. Meanwhile, his vision that humans could one day precisely direct cellular processes by chemical means remained largely in the realm of scientific fiction. At the relatively late juncture of 1961, plant physiologists still dreamed of harnessing the true potential of plant cell manipulation. In terms vaguely expressing envy of the power of nature, one botanist predicted, "The person who can control the activities of the living cell without destroying its life can determine the ultimate fate of the individual plant."[56]

The combination of government secrecy, claims of intellectual property, and, above all, the economic boon that herbicides would bring to the lawn-care, agriculture, and forestry sectors set the stage for a competitive market in commercially available herbicides. The American Chemical Paint Company of Ambler, Pennsylvania, was the first to offer a 2,4-D-based hormone herbicide under the brand Weedone thanks to its employee Franklin Jones. Jones filed for the first 2,4-D patent in March 1944 and received it in December 1945. Almost immediately American Chemical Paint found itself in a maze of legal disputes with its competitors. Dow Chemical and Sherwin-Williams, for example, both claimed wartime collaboration with Charles Hamner at Cornell University, while attorneys for Du Pont claimed primacy for John Lontz's patent application — which preceded Jones's by two years but did not single out the weed-killing properties of 2,4-D. American Chemical settled against its adversaries with an elaborate licensing agreement, thereby creating an open market for the major agricultural corporations to market various herbicidal products by the winter of 1946–47.[57]

Production levels increased exponentially. According to the U.S. Tariff Commission, in 1945 the chemical corporations produced 917,000 pounds of 2,4-D; by 1950 the amount reached 14 million. By 1964 — the first year that the Department of Defense began to siphon off domestic stocks for its quickly escalating strategy of herbicidal warfare in Vietnam — the production level of 2,4-D was 58 million pounds, much of it bound for the millions of acres of lawns sprouting in new suburbs throughout the country.[58] In 1949 the U.S. Chamber of Commerce estimated that "weeds cause[d] an annual loss in [the] country of around *three billion dollars*" — a figure that surely delighted the chemical companies and their stockholders.[59] That figure increased over time; by 1961 the herbicide industry blamed weeds for losses totaling 5 billion dollars.[60] Considering especially the low inflation rate during that period, the numbers indicate a negative correlation between herbicide application and loss margins. Even if the herbicide industry had been able to boast that it had kept weed costs at a constant, this alone might have given critics sufficient cause to question the entire enterprise.

Over the course of the 1950s, chemical industry executives reinvested the enormous profits reaped by the booming herbicide market back into research and development. They lured scientists employed with the USDA and other government agencies during World War II to the private sector, which in turn created hundreds of variations of herbicide products marketed under dozens of brand names. Dow Chemical's in-house journal *Down to Earth* provides the best overview of the staggering influence of the chemical industry. Launched in 1945, *Down to Earth* featured articles on nearly every imaginable combination of chemicals, application methods, and their effects on testing grounds from Hawaii to Maine. In keeping with Ezra Kraus's injunction to his colleagues in November 1945, the theme of *Down to Earth* was control of an unruly natural world through chemicals.[61] As we will see in the following chapters, hormone herbicides had a pendulum-like quality regarding their utility in the United States during war and peace. Born in World War II as part of a monumental alliance of science and the defense establishment, the herbicide industry reached maturity in the postwar years in the hands of the private sector. The transition from peace to war, this time in South Vietnam in the early 1960s, proved to be as smooth in the short history of 2,4-D and 2,4,5-T as their introduction to the American domestic market in 1945.

CHAPTER FOUR

GADGETS AND
GUERRILLAS

THE DECISION TO LAUNCH military herbicide operations in Vietnam in November 1961 was a key component of President John F. Kennedy's grand strategy to contain the spread of communism and roll back the global influence of the Soviet Union. Three years before Lyndon B. Johnson "chose war" against North Vietnam through sustained bombing campaigns and the large-scale introduction of U.S. ground troops, Kennedy committed the United States to a wide array of counterinsurgency tactics in an attempt to defeat the NLF, known also as the Viet Cong.[1] The NLF was a communist revolutionary organization, allied with the Hanoi government, whose guerrilla soldiers controlled much of South Vietnam's countryside. By the fall of 1961, the NLF seemed poised to topple the pro-American government in Saigon led by President Ngo Dinh Diem. Following military and diplomatic setbacks elsewhere, particularly in Cuba and Berlin, Kennedy and his foreign-policy advisers committed technologically innovative military operations to the conflict in Vietnam as a symbol of the United States' resolve to confront communist expansionism.[2] The herbicides designed by Ezra Kraus during World War II would become the centerpiece weapon in a strategy of counterinsurgency to expose and starve out NLF guerrillas operating throughout rural South Vietnam.

At the outset of his term, Kennedy sought to change the means, if not the ends, of U.S. containment policy as it had been implemented by his predecessor, Dwight D. Eisenhower. Kennedy emphasized the need to develop novel methods to check Moscow's ability to foment and support communist revolutionary movements beyond Europe. Launched at the president's order on May 25, 1961, the umbrella strategy of "Flexible Response" called for a vast expansion and diversification of the U.S. military's offensive capacity to defeat the global communist menace: "I am directing the Secretary of Defense to undertake a reorganization and modernization of the Army's divisional structure, to increase its non-nuclear firepower, *to improve its tactical mobility in any environment*, to insure its flexibility to meet any direct or indirect threat, to facilitate its coordination with our major allies, and to provide more modern mechanized divisions in Europe and bring their equipment up to date, and [to provide] new airborne brigades in both the Pacific and Europe."[3]

Kennedy and his foreign-policy advisers formulated "Flexible Response" primarily as a critique of Eisenhower's "New Look" policy. As the historian John Lewis Gaddis observes, the New Look sought "the maximum possible deterrence of communism at the minimum possible cost" through heavy reliance on strategic nuclear deterrence as a substitute for a large standing army.[4] More recent scholarship by Richard H. Immerman and Robert R. Bowie indicates that Eisenhower's New Look encapsulated more than nuclear deterrence — it was the "basic national strategy" from which the president and his advisors assessed and acted upon all real and potential Soviet threats.[5] Yet for the sake of distinguishing his policies from Eisenhower's, Kennedy focused primarily on reforming Eisenhower's nuclear policies. The idea behind Flexible Response was that new times required new strategies of vigilance. In his inaugural address, for example, Kennedy declared, "The torch has been passed to a new generation of Americans," thus emphasizing that the United States had reached a crossroads in its cold war strategy.[6]

Notwithstanding the "missile gap" claim that helped secure Kennedy's bid for the White House in 1960, the newly elected president criticized Eisenhower's national-security policy largely in terms of its inability to mitigate future threats in a changing world.[7] During his campaign for the presidency, Kennedy focused less on the past effectiveness of the New Look, for good reason. Eisenhower's foreign policies had proved remarkably effective at meeting the same set of goals that Kennedy advanced regarding America's secure future. At the end of his term, Eisenhower and his secretary of state John Foster Dulles (who died in 1959) could boast of ending the war in Korea, ensuring long-term stability in Western Europe, slowing the tide of communist expansion in the third world, and most crucially, avoiding nuclear war despite — or perhaps because of — the threat of "massive retaliation."[8] Furthermore, Kennedy's platform downplayed the somewhat inconvenient fact that Eisenhower himself engaged in a variety of anticommunist tactics far removed from the nuclear brinkmanship upon which, according to his detractors, he had excessively relied.[9]

The military theorist who coined the term "Flexible Response," and who went on to play a role in its implementation in Vietnam, was Maxwell D. Taylor, chief of staff of the U.S. Army from 1955 to 1959. Taylor was not persuaded that the relative stability of the international system in the 1950s should be understood as the logical conclusion of Eisenhower's policies; he saw the United States circa 1960 as a nation on the verge of catastrophe precisely because those policies had ignored or even precipitated threats to the security of the United States. Less encumbered by the political considerations that tempered Kennedy's public pronouncements on such issues, Taylor attacked the New Look immediately following his retirement from military service. For his ideas, Taylor soon found a key role in the Kennedy White House as a special military adviser.

Taylor published *The Uncertain Trumpet* in 1959 to expose the "great fallacy" of Eisenhower's cold war strategy, which he paraphrased as a false rationale, that "henceforth the use or the threatened use of atomic weapons of mass destruction would be sufficient to assure the security of the United States and its friends."[10] For Taylor the matter boiled down to credibility: given the burden the Eisenhower administration placed on nuclear weapons to ensure the defense of the United States and its allies, when would its leaders resort to nuclear warfare?[11] The all-or-nothing terms demanded by nuclear diplomacy offered, in Taylor's view, "only two choices, the initiation of general nuclear war or compromise and retreat."[12] Two developments convinced Taylor that U.S. leaders would increasingly find themselves choosing the latter. First, nuclear deterrence had failed to prevent the outbreak of guerrilla or insurgency warfare in diverse areas such as Latin America and East Asia. Local conflicts, Taylor surmised, even those that threatened to tilt the balance of power toward the Communist Bloc, did not pose a major threat to the United States and therefore did not merit the risk of nuclear confrontation. Second, in Taylor's view, the Soviet Union not only recognized the strategic impotence of America's nuclear deterrent but also sought throughout the 1950s to match and even surpass the technological sophistication of America's nuclear and conventional military arsenal. Taylor articulated unequivocally the likely consequences of these developments:

For years it has been predicted that in a period of mutual deterrence the Soviets would indulge in a rising level of provocations. In 1959, we are in such a period and many episodes have verified the prediction. The Communist tactics in Taiwan, the Middle East, Berlin, and Laos provide examples of the growing use of military power to support an aggressive course of action under the conditions of cold or limited war. As the Soviets become more assured of their superiority in general-war weapons, particularly in intercontinental ballistic missiles, and if they sense American timidity, they may be expected to press harder than ever before, counting upon submissiveness arising from our consciousness of weakness. They will not believe, nor will our friends, that we will use our massive retaliatory forces for any purpose other than our own survival. How then are we to meet the anticipated Communist provocations of the future?[13]

As other theorists recognized, Flexible Response also fit well within a broader movement in the military to expand America's nuclear deterrent with a new generation of chemical and biological weapons. In the rationale of Maj. Gen. Marshall Stubbs, an officer of the Chemical Corps of the U.S. Army:

> The fear of nuclear war could conceivably inhibit the Soviets from using atomic weapons, if other means could achieve their purpose. Should this prove true, we are right now in a period of development of other weapons which would not carry with them the threat of total destruction — for we are subject to the same pressure as they, perhaps to greater pressures, in that we are more concerned with the welfare of our people and our allies. If the Communists succeed in attaining a superiority in these new chemical and biological weapons, which we cannot match or which we cannot defend against, our nuclear strength could be of academic value.[14]

The Kennedy administration interpreted Soviet statements and actions in a way that justified both components of Maxwell Taylor's analysis. On January 6, 1961, two weeks before Kennedy's inauguration, Soviet premier Nikita Khrushchev declared: "Liberation wars will continue to exist for as long as imperialism exists, as long as colonialism exists. These are revolutionary wars. Such wars are not only admissible but inevitable, since the colonialists do not grant independence voluntarily."[15]

Khrushchev's ostensible blank-check endorsement of wars of national liberation, along with Moscow's concurrent bluster over the brewing crisis in

Berlin, became Kennedy's chief foreign-policy concern. A national-security memorandum attests to the seriousness with which the new administration regarded Khrushchev's pronouncement: "The Communist Bloc has announced its intention to transform the Free World by a succession of acts of subversion or wars of 'liberation.' If successful they [will] reduce the physical power of the Free World and reduce its will to resist . . . [The United States] and its allies must therefore deter or, if necessary, be prepared to meet local aggression *wherever and however such aggression may take place.*"[16]

The key to Flexible Response was diversification. If the New Look relied too heavily on the ultimate form of warfare, and if America's enemies had become convinced that a range of "provocations" was unlikely to trigger a nuclear response, then the basic goal for the 1960s was to develop new war-fighting methods adaptable in nearly every imaginable battle scenario. By emphasizing the need to create low-intensity tactics tailored for protracted conflict against guerrillas, Flexible Response would allow the United States to maneuver effectively out of the nuclear trap that, theoretically, had constrained the power that nuclear weapons were supposed to guarantee. As the historian William Duiker observes, the new strategy sought "to permit the United States to strengthen friendly forces against internal or external adversaries without the threat of escalation into a nuclear confrontation between the Great Powers."[17]

The energy and resources the White House committed to a revamped defense establishment were significant: in the summer of 1961 Kennedy's congressional budget request sought to increase nonnuclear military expenditures by $5 billion and an additional 250,000 soldiers for active-duty troops on the grounds that a Soviet-American confrontation could erupt anywhere and at any time.[18] The crisis atmosphere, or what the historian George Herring has called a "siege mentality,"[19] among administration officials at the outset of Kennedy's term begged two questions for those who wondered how the new president's rhetoric and accompanying militarization would translate into action: What innovations would the U.S. military incorporate into its contingency operations? Against what enemy would U.S. forces test the various components of Flexible Response — and how would Moscow respond? The deteriorating situation in South Vietnam soon provided answers to both.

Kennedy's personal authorization to launch herbicidal warfare against the NLF was a preeminent manifestation of Flexible Response as its architects envisioned the strategy to contain Soviet influence on a truly global scale. Three dimensions comprise this assessment. First, without a battle-ground to test the concept, Flexible Response would remain theoretical. By mid-1961 South Vietnam had become the sole nation that could plausibly demonstrate the effectiveness of the new strategy. Second, administration officials saw the threat of South Vietnam falling into the communist orbit as sufficiently grave to justify the application of Flexible Response on a large and long-term basis. Third, political and geographical conditions in South Vietnam provided an attractive "laboratory" for testing counterinsurgent doctrine, fostered by the keen interest in the subject by the president and his brother, Attorney General Robert F. Kennedy.[20]

As the historian Lawrence Freedman observes, "Where Kennedy re-ally wanted flexible response was not at the nuclear or conventional lev-els, but with counterinsurgency."[21] By 1963 military theorists and advisors close to Kennedy had created a veritable library of articles and books that together might be called "counterinsurgency studies," a genre that arose largely in reaction to the writings of communist revolutionaries such as Mao Zedong and Che Guevara. Kennedy's top foreign-policy advisors closely read this literature on the assumption that effective counterinsurgency methods required a strong understanding of the communist revolutionary mind.[22]

Although the entire basis of Flexible Response centered on the strate-gic assumption that the United States had to confront communist revolu-tionary movements wherever they might arise, the international situation proved more constraining than Kennedy's early rhetoric suggested. In Cuba, where the administration first demonstrated its penchant for elaborate and clandestine plans to overthrow the communist regime led by Fidel Castro, Flexible Response proved to be a disaster: the botched Bay of Pigs invasion of April 1961 eliminated any chance for pro-American dissidents to assume control of Havana; the Central Intelligence Agency's (CIA's) outlandish at-tempts on Castro's life proved ineffective; and U.S. interventionism in Cuba and Khrushchev's consequent decision to place nuclear warheads there helped to force the Cuban Missile Crisis of October 1962. The crisis was, ironically, just the kind of showdown that Kennedy aimed to avoid with his emphasis on nonnuclear weapons and strategies.[23]

Meanwhile, the showdown over Berlin — where the antirevolutionary imperatives of Flexible Response were basically inapplicable — took a turn for the worse when Khrushchev ordered construction of the Berlin Wall soon after his confrontational summit meeting in Vienna with Kennedy in June 1961. Between the summit and the building of the Berlin Wall, a National Security Council (NSC) staff member ably summarized the beleaguered administration's default rationale: "After Laos, and with Berlin on the horizon, we cannot afford to go less than all-out in cleaning up South Vietnam."[24]

The second reason is more unique to the political situation in Vietnam and its relation to the evident spike in communist expansionism. Khrushchev's speech in early January 1961 was widely interpreted in the new administration as a vow of full support to the NLF. As Assistant Secretary of State William Bundy characterized the sentiment among the new occupants of the White House, "What was going on in Vietnam seemed the clearest possible case of what Khrushchev in January had called a 'war of national liberation.'"[25] The new president had built his reputation as one of Washington's staunchest supporters of an independent South Vietnam; whatever Khrushchev's real intentions, his speech and its apparent relation to the situation in Vietnam ensured it would be that country where the United States would "draw the line" against Moscow.

As a senator from Massachusetts, Kennedy made his strongest foreign-policy pronouncements on the paramount importance of securing the long-term stability of South Vietnam: in 1954, Kennedy supported the ascension of Ngo Dinh Diem to the presidency of South Vietnam; two years later Kennedy became an outspoken critic of the 1954 Geneva Accords, which split Vietnam at the seventeenth parallel and formally ended France's failed bid to reassert its traditional colonial control over Vietnam. The agreement provided for a reunification of North and South Vietnam under a democratically elected (and likely communist) government. In recognition of the fact that South Vietnam was little more than a political creation of the United States—and one constantly in danger of falling into the communist orbit—Kennedy's memorably paternalistic declaration in June 1956 foreshadowed his determination as president to ensure the viability of the government in Saigon: "If we are not the parents of little Vietnam, then surely we are the godparents . . . This is our offspring."[26]

By the summer of 1961, Kennedy had decided on the need to increase significantly U.S. military operations in South Vietnam. The combination of pressure from the Joint Chiefs of Staff (JCS) and increasingly grave reports issued by the U.S. embassy in Saigon convinced the president of the need for direct action. Whereas compared to Laos the situation in Vietnam remained a low priority in the first few months of the administration, Kennedy had come to fear the effect of "falling dominoes" throughout Southeast Asia should the NLF succeed in its stated goal to "overthrow the camouflaged colonial regime of the American imperialists and the dictatorial power of Ngo Dinh Diem."[27] An NSC meeting in May 1961 outlined the administration's South Vietnam policy, calling for the United States to "prevent communist domination of South Vietnam; to create in that country a viable and increasingly democratic society, and to initiate, on an accelerated basis, a series of mutually supporting actions of a military, political, economic, psychological, and covert character designed to achieve this objective."[28]

The plan was universal both as applied "on the ground" in South Vietnam and for the political reverberations its architects hoped to generate around the world as a sign of America's anticommunist resolve. Deputy National Security Advisor Walt W. Rostow, the former MIT economist and one of the Kennedy administration's most enthusiastic proponents of an American commitment in Vietnam, had advised the president two months earlier that communists everywhere would see Vietnam as a deterrent to revolution: "We shall have demonstrated that the Communist technique of guerilla warfare can be dealt with."[29]

The decisions that informed Kennedy's May 1961 pronouncement can be traced to the weeks preceding his inauguration. The U.S. embassy in Saigon completed a detailed counterinsurgency report on January 4, 1961, which awaited Kennedy's attention later that month. The report comprised the views of military and diplomatic officers stationed in Saigon, and the committee that authored it was chaired by Joseph Mendenhall, a State Department official. It characterized the situation in grave terms: the Saigon government would likely collapse in a matter of months if President Diem did not take immediate and concerted steps to challenge the NLF insurgency. The tone of the embassy's plan suggested that the survival of the Saigon government was Diem's duty alone: with sufficient U.S. support his government had sole responsibility to keep the communist insurgency at bay. The basic message was that the United States should either launch counterinsurgency operations or prepare for the toppling of the pro-American government in Saigon.[30]

At this early juncture, the U.S. embassy commanded relatively little influence over Kennedy's Vietnam policies. The president was far more impressed with the assessments of Brig. Gen. Edward G. Lansdale based on Lansdale's visit to Vietnam in early January 1961 and subsequent meeting with Kennedy during an NSC meeting later in the month. At that meeting,

Lansdale underscored the seriousness of the situation in South Vietnam. Lansdale's reputation preceded him. Over the past several years, he had earned a reputation as a "maverick" in the military establishment and was widely admired by Kennedy officials, including Rostow, who commented that Lansdale "knew more about guerilla warfare on the Asia scene than any other American."[31]

Lansdale was a tireless self-promoter involved with several covert operations dating back to his work fighting insurgents in the Philippines following World War II, and by the late 1950s he was spending much of his time in South Vietnam, where he cultivated a close rapport with Diem and advocated on his behalf in Washington. Lansdale's major contribution to U.S. strategy in South Vietnam was threefold: (1) he believed that embassy officials had failed to appreciate that Diem was the only leader capable of maintaining South Vietnam as a noncommunist state; (2) he criticized the prevailing military sentiment that the overriding threat to the Saigon government came from North Vietnam; that is, the NLF should be confronted on its own terms with novel counterinsurgency techniques rather than contingency plans premised on the threat of a North Vietnamese invasion; and (3) he argued that offensive military tactics could be successful only if applied in conjunction with numerous development and aid programs designed to win support of South Vietnam's peasantry.[32] Lansdale's emphasis on counterinsurgent operations as a holistic enterprise appealed to Kennedy's dual interests in "nation building," and at the same time it provided a realistic framework for the application of Flexible Response. Following his report to the president at the NSC meeting, Lansdale secured his role as a link between the administration and the United States Military Assistance and Advisory Group (MAAG), Vietnam, under the command of Gen. Paul D. Harkins.[33]

At the outset of formulating a political-military policy for South Vietnam, the basic bone of contention between those confident of a quick victory and the pessimists who predicted a "quagmire" lay at the tactical rather than the strategic level. Among NSC members and military officers, few disputed the strategic value of Southeast Asia as a key battlefront in the global cold war. The problem centered on how to accomplish the mission. Was Diem — widely perceived among U.S officials as corrupt and ruthless — the only leader on whom the United States would stake its reputation, as Lansdale insisted? Furthermore, how might the United States wage a war of counterinsurgency on a foreboding terrain and against an enemy difficult to detect? Vice President Lyndon B. Johnson, returning in May 1961 from a trip to South Vietnam, where he had met with Diem, was less sanguine about the prospects of victory than many of his colleagues, particularly those who extolled the value of counterinsurgency operations. "Before we take any such plunge," Johnson warned, "we had better be sure we are prepared to become bogged down chasing irregulars and guerillas over the rice fields and jungles of Southeast Asia while our principal enemies China and the Soviet Union stand outside the fray and husband their strength."[34] The assessment indicated the chasm between Johnson's private concerns and public grandiosity; his famous declaration in Saigon during the May 1961 trip that Diem was the "Winston Churchill of Asia" was obviously political theater.

The notion of becoming "bogged down" in South Vietnam's jungle terrain, along with the prospect of fighting an undetectable enemy, had been a prevailing concern and object of counterinsurgent theorists, as well as a source of resistance to intervention in Vietnam among military leaders.[35] Maxwell Taylor characterized the NLF guerrilla strategy: "They strike at isolated government forces — then disappear into the jungle."[36] As the political scientist Samuel P. Huntington noted at the time, the value of concealment offered by the jungle allows insurgents to turn their weakness to advantage: "Guerrilla warfare is a form of warfare by which the strategically weaker side assumes the tactical offensive in selected forms, times, and places."[37]

Taking the jungle theme to its logical conclusion, one army colonel characterized the guerrilla as a fighter "secretive and ruthless in his actions [who] moves like a tiger in the night with the cunning of a fox to make his attacks . . . A guerilla, with his hit-and-run tactics, terror and assassination techniques does not pretend to have or follow the traditions of the military profession."[38] Gen. Curtis LeMay, advocating a counterinsurgent role for the U.S. Air Force to commence aerial detection operations to defeat the NLF, argued, "The very characteristic of the guerilla is his ability to disappear from regular intelligence surveillance."[39] MAAG Chief Lionel McGarr cited the jungle as the major obstacle to security in South Vietnam: "The Communists have chosen the physical battlefield well. The vast and rugged jungle area and border [are] perfectly 'preconditioned' for infiltration."[40] Perhaps the dominant metaphor in counterinsurgent literature was the shadow, suggesting at once the asymmetrical tactics of the guerrilla and the consequent inability of forces trained in conventional warfare to detect him (figure 3).[41]

The nation-building aspects of counterinsurgency alluded to in Kennedy's

Figure 3 The August 4, 1961, cover of *Time* magazine conveyed the idea of the "hidden enemy" above a portrait of Ngo Dinh Diem. Courtesy of *Time* Magazine.

TWENTY-FIVE CENTS

AUGUST 4, 1961

SOUTHEAST ASIA "Where the Borders Are Less Guarded, the Enemy Harder to Find"

TIME

THE WEEKLY NEWS

SOUTH VIET NAM'S NGO DINH DIEM

$7.00 A YEAR

VOL. LXXVIII NO. 5

May 11 proclamation — what President Lyndon B. Johnson termed in 1965 America's goal of winning "hearts and minds" in Vietnam — could not proceed without a concerted effort to confront and destroy NLF dominance in the hinterlands of South Vietnam.[42] As David G. Marr, an intelligence officer for the U.S. Marine Corps who later became a prominent historian of twentieth-century Vietnam, recalled: "From the very beginning, counterinsurgency in Vietnam emphasized military considerations over political ones, enforcement of 'physical security' over more subtle questions of social change or psychological loyalties. In short, it was blatant counterrevolution over revolution, although few Americans involved at the time seemed prepared to acknowledge this."[43]

The emphasis on physical security over the more productive, aid-oriented aspects of counterinsurgency explains why the decision to launch aerial herbicide operations occurred at the earliest stages of the administration's contingency planning for Vietnam. On April 12, 1961, Walt Rostow handed Kennedy a memo that listed nine courses of action that the United States should pursue in South Vietnam. The fifth recommendation called for the president to send a military research team to Vietnam to work with Lionel McGarr to explore various "techniques and gadgets" to be used against the NLF.[44] Rostow did not elaborate on the specific "techniques and gadgets" he had in mind. On April 26 the deputy secretary of defense, Roswell L. Gilpatric, gave President Kennedy a "program of action" on South Vietnam that reiterated Rostow's call for new counterinsurgent techniques to be developed by a new research and development center in South Vietnam. The memo cited the lack of aerial surveillance techniques to locate guerrilla movement.[45] Two weeks later, Vice President Johnson secured Diem's approval to launch the research center. With Diem's acceptance of the proposal the Pentagon's Advanced Research Projects Agency (ARPA) created the United States/Government of South Vietnam Combat and Development Test Center (CDTC), which was soon headed by MAAG Lt. Gen. McGarr.

Edward Lansdale, who issued the Pentagon directive, defined the objective of the CDTC "to acquire directly, develop and/or test novel and improved weapons and military hardware for employment in the Indo-Chinese environment."[46] Among the first of the CDTC's tasks was to identify herbicidal chemical compounds best suited to destroy forest cover and crops known to be used by NLF guerrillas. The testing phase, codenamed Project Agile, was directed by James W. Brown, the deputy chief of the Crops Division at Fort Detrick, where he had been involved in military herbicide experiments. The CDTC received its first shipment of herbicides and spray equipment on July 10, 1961. Brown experimented with Dinoxol, an herbicide compound that contained 2,4-D and 2,4,5-T (the chemicals that would later comprise Agent Orange), on manioc, sweet potatoes, rice, as well as forest cover. Impressed with the results of early tests, Brown noted that herbicidal chemicals would likely become a central component of the strategy to defeat the NLF. "No one appreciates food or visibility," he noted, "more than those deprived of it."[47]

As a component of MAAG, Vietnam, defoliant operations were initially designated an "advisory" project, meaning that the United States sought only to equip and train the South Vietnamese Air Force (VNAF) in herbicidal warfare. On August 10, only a month after the center's first herbicide shipment, the VNAF conducted its first spray missions on roadside foliage in U.S.-issued H-34 military helicopters. On August 24 the VNAF conducted its first fixed-wing spray mission with C-47 planes against forest targets selected personally by President Diem, who immediately appreciated the tactical and strategic value of herbicidal warfare.[48] Both aircraft had been in wide use for several years in the U.S. Navy and Air Force, primarily for aerial insecticide missions in and around military bases.[49] At a September 29 meeting with U.S. ambassador Fredrick Nolting and General McGarr, Diem requested a massive herbicide operation throughout the central highlands to deny the fall harvest to NLF guerrillas. The meeting ended without a formal U.S. commitment to aid a crop-destruction mission of that magnitude—likely because administration and military officials feared the negative publicity and communist propaganda value that such a program would attract.[50]

To the consternation of the Kennedy administration, the chances of a collapse of the Diem government seemed to increase in step with U.S. involvement in South Vietnam. In September 1961, NLF forces seized the provincial capital Phuoc Thanh, only fifty-five miles from Saigon. Although the number of VNAF sorties for Project Agile had increased daily since the first test runs in early August, the areas sprayed were hardly sufficient to make a significant impact on surveillance capacities to track guerrilla movements. The White House aide Arthur Schlesinger Jr. relayed to Kennedy a letter from the journalist Theodore H. White, who was stationed in Vietnam. White summarized the situation in stark terms: "The guerrillas now control almost all the southern delta—so much so that I could find no American who would drive me outside Saigon in his car even by day without military convoy."[51]

Displaying restraint, President Kennedy rebuffed calls from both the JCS and members of the NSC to introduce combat forces in South Vietnam, opting instead to send Maxwell Taylor and Walt Rostow to gather more information on local conditions.[52] They commenced their trip on October 17; their many duties included assessing the progress of the herbicide operations, during which they were informed by James Brown that aircraft at Langley Air Force Base (AFB) could be outfitted with spray mechanisms to augment the VNAF force.[53] The resulting Rostow-Taylor report confirmed the negative assessments that precipitated their mission and advocated an across-the-board increase in the U.S. presence in South Vietnam, including troops that could become engaged in combat operations.

Kennedy did not follow every recommendation put forth in the report (particularly the promotion of troop deployments), partly because several administration officials, including Undersecretary of State Chester Bowles and Assistant Secretary of State W. Averell Harriman, argued strongly against any move toward direct war involving U.S. forces. Still, the president, ever cognizant of the nightmare scenario of "falling dominoes" in Southeast Asia, accepted and acted on the main thrust of the Rostow-Taylor report's call for "vigorous action," namely, to prevent the loss of South Vietnam, which was "not merely a crucial piece of real estate, but [emblematic of] the faith that the U.S. ha[d] the will and the capacity to deal with the Communist offensive in that area."[54] Kennedy's decision to intensify U.S. efforts in lieu of a large ground-troop presence ensured the expansion of counterinsurgency operations, including herbicidal warfare.

Events in Washington anticipated the Rostow-Taylor report. Although the prospect of sending ground troops to South Vietnam remained an open question throughout September and October, all signs pointed to a massive expansion of Project Agile. On September 23 a jointly written State Department and Defense Department memorandum outlined several emergency measures to support the Diem government. The plan covered a wide range of counterinsurgency military operations that, if successful, would obviate the need for regular ground troops. Based on test results from the CDTC, the memo listed four basic objectives of herbicidal warfare:

- Stripping the Cambodian-Laotian-North Vietnam border of foliage to remove the protective cover from Viet Cong reinforcements
- Defoliating a portion of the Mekong Delta area known as "Zone D" in which the Viet Cong have numerous bases
- Destroying numerous abandoned manioc groves which the Viet Cong use as food sources
- Destroying mangrove swamps within which the Viet Cong take refuge[55]

The plan called for these operations to be completed in 120 days. The speed of the proposed operation was magnified by its projected breadth and cost: the total forest and cropland area to be targeted for spray missions was in excess of thirty thousand square miles, or one-half the size of South Vietnam, and at a cost of $55.9 million.[56] Although the recommendations proffered by the CDTC were soon replaced by a similar but far more limited spray program (scaled down to a tenth of the original cost) developed by officials at the U.S. embassy in Saigon, the report represented a turning point in herbicide operations in South Vietnam.[57]

First, the CDTC successfully lobbied for an "Americanization" of herbicidal warfare, which would be called Operation Farm Gate (and soon Operation Ranch Hand) to be conducted under the leadership of the Air Force Special Air Warfare Center based at Eglin AFB, Florida. In October 1961 there existed no set protocol on where and how herbicidal chemicals would help to defeat the NLF guerrilla insurgency; the direct involvement of the USAF aimed to correct this gap. Second, the September 23 report advanced the idea that herbicidal warfare should be conducted for the broadest possible purposes: for safeguarding international borders against furtive deployment of men and matériel; for defoliating in any forested area thought to conceal guerrilla operations; and for destroying cropland thought to be under NLF control. On the last point, the JCS and its chairman, Gen. Lyman L. Lemnitzer, expressed serious misgivings. On November 3 the JCS issued a memorandum to Secretary of Defense Robert S. McNamara that concurred with plans to commence with Operation Farm Gate but urged a considered approach to crop destruction:

> The Joint Chiefs of Staff are of the opinion that in conducting aerial defoliant operations against abandoned manioc (tapioca) groves or other food growing areas, care must be taken to assure that the United States does not become the target for charges of employing chemical or biological warfare. International repercussions against the United States could be most serious. In this connection, it is recommended that the operations be covered concurrently with a publicity campaign as outlined by Task Force Vietnam in Saigon.[58]

The JCS memorandum singled out crop destruction as a potential source of international condemnation for biological and chemical warfare. It was a political rather than a legal concern; the United States was neither a formal party to nor a professed follower of any international law — including the Geneva Protocol of 1925 — that forbade the destruction of crops in war.[59] Still, in a battle for "hearts and minds" in which propaganda would prove as potent a tool as any military weapon, crop destruction struck the JCS as a particularly sensitive activity. Beginning in 1962, denunciations of the program from the communist media organs of Moscow, Peking, and Hanoi would justify the concerns of Lemnitzer and his colleagues.[60] The decision to commence with the program, despite these justified concerns, is suggestive of the hopes that Kennedy's advisors invested in the herbicide program. The president never would have allowed the communist orbit an easy propaganda "score" if he were not convinced of the potential of herbicide to maintain stability in South Vietnam.

The issue was resolved when William P. Bundy, acting assistant secretary of defense for international security affairs, sent a memorandum to Robert McNamara, informing his boss that Diem had agreed that crop-destruction missions would remain a U.S.-assisted South Vietnamese program.[61] Given Diem's avowed keenness for crop-destruction operations, U.S. officials in Washington and Saigon concluded that this allocation of operational control was the wisest course — no matter how hollow the distinction. Meanwhile, on November 14, Secretary McNamara ordered the commander in chief of the U.S. Pacific Command (CINCPAC), Adm. Harry Felt, to lead U.S. herbicide operations. At the same time, mechanic crews at Pope AFB in North Carolina outfitted C-123 transport aircraft with spray equipment in anticipation of their departure for South Vietnam.

The remaining piece of the puzzle before large-scale U.S. herbicide operations could commence was the direct authorization of President Kennedy. The decision-making process over the last several months had leaned toward an increased U.S. presence in South Vietnam in general, and herbicidal warfare in particular was poised to become an enduring manifestation of Flexible Response. But the president's decision was not a foregone conclusion. Kennedy had received written recommendations to commence herbicide operations from his key advisors on foreign policy, including Secretary of State Dean Rusk and Secretary of Defense McNamara, but both recognized the controversial nature of herbicidal warfare. Rusk assured the president that such an operation was lawful; in a memo dated November 24, 1961, he advised Kennedy that "the use of defoliant does not violate any rule of international law concerning the conduct of chemical warfare and is an accepted tactic of war." Rusk cited as sufficient legal precedent Great Britain's limited use of herbicides during the 1950s against insurgents in Malaya, where Sir Robert Thompson conducted successful counterinsurgency operations. Nevertheless, Rusk believed that legal precedent alone was not likely to stanch international criticism. He made no mention of the Geneva Protocol of 1925, suggesting that antiplant chemicals remained outside the scope of the laws governing the U.S. military as well as international law. On this count, Rusk's analysis was consistent with prevailing legal views of the time.[62]

Secretary McNamara also expressed concern about the international repercussions of herbicidal warfare in all its forms — not only in terms of crop destruction, as the JCS had noted. As insurance against this possibility, McNamara requested that President Diem make a public pronouncement that herbicides posed no danger to humans or animals.[63] This request is the only available record before the president's authorization in which a Kennedy administration official acknowledged (by dismissing it) that the

United States would stand accused of using chemicals whose health effects on humans remained uncertain.

President Kennedy relied on Deputy Defense Secretary Roswell Gilpatric to present the liabilities and advantages of herbicidal warfare. Gilpatric's assessment was that clearing convoy paths was absolutely necessary to prevent NLF ambushes; if the president decided to restrict herbicide use in Vietnam to one task, the most sensible was to ensure the safe passage of U.S. and ARVN men and matériel. He informed Kennedy that Radio Hanoi had already denounced crop-destruction missions as poison gas attacks mounted by South Vietnam. He also emphasized that the president's authorization to commence with herbicidal warfare could become a fruitless gesture if South Vietnamese forces did not receive the necessary support to monitor and pursue NLF guerrillas in defoliated areas.

The president incorporated this advice into a memorandum drafted by McGeorge Bundy, special assistant for national security affairs, which accepted the joint recommendations of the Departments of State and Defense, thereby committing the United States to a strategy of herbicidal warfare in South Vietnam that lasted under a flurry of international and domestic controversy until its end in 1971 (figure 4). Kennedy's decision to launch U.S.-led herbicide operations was part of a broader move by the administration to "Americanize" the war in South Vietnam. A week earlier, Kennedy had announced a "sharply increased joint effort" of U.S. and South Vietnamese forces to combat the NLF, which included the deployment of uniformed American soldiers operating under U.S. command.[64] Under the circumstances, it would have made little sense for Kennedy to have commenced with herbicide operations without a greater U.S. presence in South Vietnam, or alternatively, with a greater U.S. presence without herbicides.

Like so many "what-if" questions that propel debates on the long-term legacy of President Kennedy's Vietnam policies, it is worth assessing the extent to which the tremendous damage wrought by Operation Ranch Hand over the following ten years can be traced back to the decision-making history in the fall of 1961.[65] The language of Kennedy's authorization of November 30 indicates that the president did not sign on to a program of unlimited proportions, as the CDTC had originally advocated. The terms of the authorization fully squared the character of the herbicide program with Kennedy's broader efforts to avoid escalating the war into an open-ended conflict. The parallels remained when the war did escalate: herbicide operations reached their zenith in step with the broader contours of the overall

DECLASSIFIED
E. O. 11652, SEC. 3(E), 5(D), 5(E) AND 11
Committee Print of Pentagon Papers
BY H22 NARS, DATE 7/15/77

November 30, 1961

TOP SECRET

NATIONAL SECURITY ACTION MEMORANDUM NO. 115

TO: The Secretary of State
            The Secretary of Defense

SUBJECT: Defoliant Operations in Viet Nam

        The President has approved the recommendation of the Secretary
of State and the Deputy Secretary of Defense to participate in a selective and carefully controlled joint program of defoliant operations in
Viet Nam starting with the clearance of key routes and proceeding
thereafter to food denial only if the most careful basis of resettlement
and alternative food supply has been created. Operations in Zone D
and the border areas shall not be undertaken until there are realistic
possibilities of immediate military exploitation.

        The President further agreed that there should be careful
prior consideration and authorization by Washington of any plans
developed by CINCPAC and the country team under this authority before such plans are executed.

                                        McGeorge Bundy

Information Copies to:

        The Director of Central Intelligence
        The Director, U. S. Information Agency
        The Director, Bureau of the Budget
        The Administrator, Agency for
          International Development
        The Military Representative of the President   cc: Mrs. Lincoln
                                                             Mr. McG. Bundy
                                                             B. Smith/C. Johnson
                          TOP SECRET   Robert Johnson
                                                             NSC Files

additional cy to Defense 6/21. Rept # 459

Figure 4 Memorandum authorizing herbicidal warfare in Vietnam. "National
Security Action Memorandum 115," November 30, 1961, Meetings and Memoranda
series, National Security file, John F. Kennedy Library, Boston, Mass.

conflict; the total volume of herbicides sprayed in South Vietnam shot up from approximately one million liters in 1964 to over twenty million liters in 1966.[66] For this reason, Kennedy cannot be blamed directly for the subsequent destruction caused by Operation Ranch Hand — he explicitly sought to prevent the program from running amok.

Still, herbicidal warfare remained throughout the Vietnam War solely a counterinsurgency operation in South Vietnam as it had been designed under Kennedy's direction; no matter the extent to which herbicide missions expanded under Lyndon B. Johnson, the complicated infrastructure that procured and transferred herbicides from chemical plants in the United States to South Vietnam was firmly in place by the time Johnson assumed the presidency. To the extent that it is possible to isolate particular military operations from the war as a whole, the answer must be considered in terms of what Kennedy's successors inherited versus what they innovated.

As with all aspects of Flexible Response, as it became implemented by the U.S. military in South Vietnam, one cannot ignore Kennedy's ultimate responsibility for committing American technology and soldiers to a war against the communist NLF insurgents. Even if Kennedy neither wanted nor envisioned the massive devastation created by Operation Ranch Hand by the late 1960s, the decision to authorize the mission or to abandon it altogether was his alone. The promise of tactical control and stability offered by 2,4-D and 2,4,5-T in the rural terrain of South Vietnam — like the control already demonstrated by these herbicides in the fight against weeds at home — proved too enticing to the president. Kennedy's choice was informed by his understanding of the future direction of the cold war and the available tools necessary to win it. In the absence of Kennedy's considerations and unique views on counterinsurgency, it is possible, even likely, to imagine the Vietnam War without Agent Orange.

CHAPTER FIVE

HERBICIDAL WARFARE

IN EARLY DECEMBER 1961, immediately after President John F. Kennedy authorized herbicide operations, C-123 transport aircraft retrofitted with fixed-wing spray mechanisms took off from several U.S. Air Force bases. Although the merits of the term "chemical warfare" became a contentious issue in the latter part of the decade, when antiwar and environmental protestors merged to denounce the "ecocide" of Vietnam and the dubious legality of Operation Ranch Hand vis-à-vis the Geneva Protocol of 1925, administration officials used the term from the beginning. The U.S. Army referred to the defoliation program as chemical warfare well after U.S. disengagement from the conflict.[1] In preparation for Kennedy's authorization of November 30, 1961, his aide Walt Rostow explained the necessity of presidential sanction because the deployment of "weed killers" by the U.S. military constituted a "kind of chemical warfare."[2] Rostow's note suggests his ambivalence toward the implications of Operation Ranch Hand on a legal and political level, and a desire to sacrifice long-term liabilities to immediate tactical advantage. Although herbicide assessment reports written by various military agencies from 1962 to 1970 consistently extolled the tactical and strategic virtues of Operation Ranch Hand for the United States' broader counterinsurgency mission in South Vietnam (and thereby vindicated the program's early boosters), no justification for the program had ever fit within the parameters of *jus in bello*, or acceptable wartime practice.[3]

If the beginning of Operation Ranch Hand in the winter of 1961–62 marked the beginning of large-scale chemical warfare — unseen in major battles since the western front of World War I — why did the warnings of administration skeptics go unheeded? Roger Hilsman, director of intelligence and research at the State Department and later assistant secretary of state for Far Eastern affairs, recalled his opposition to herbicide operations in March 1962, when herbicidal warfare remained in its testing phase:

> Defoliation is just too reminiscent of gas warfare . . . It [could] cost us international support, and the Viet Cong [could] use it to good propaganda advantage as an example of Americans making war on the peasants.[4]

The immediate answer is that most of Kennedy's advisors felt that herbicidal warfare was *not* on a par or even in the same league as the gas attacks of World War I. Secretary of State Dean Rusk emphasized to the president that the term "weed-killer" was preferable to "chemical warfare," thus anticipating future denunciations of the program.[5] At the same time, a growing chorus in the military establishment was calling for the enlistment of those weapons in military operations against guerrilla soldiers. In a region of battle unsuitable to the conventions of American tactics and weaponry, only chemicals promised victory. As one military official advocated:

> The best way for the U.S. to achieve its military aims in Southeast Asia would be to rely on chemical warfare. The United States will never have enough counterinsurgency troops to comb every rice paddy in the battle zones of South Vietnam. We cannot send armored personnel carriers down every irrigation canal. Not enough helicopters can be produced and manned to track down every band of guerillas hiding in wooded areas. But it *is* possible to "sanitize" an area with chemical weapons, with gases and sprays that destroy animal life and crops. We can create a no-man's land across which the guerrillas cannot move. We can clean up an area so that the enemy won't dare attempt to operate in it.[6]

The distinction between antipersonnel and antiplant weapons ultimately explains why Kennedy authorized herbicide operations. Yet at the same time, the distinction obscures the fact that the president knew from the beginning that Operation Ranch Hand would mark the first time a major power introduced chemicals in war since World War I. The president never bought into the widely espoused idea that chemical warfare represented a more "humane" way to wage war. Hence the president drew the line at herbicides among the weapons he deemed suitable for use in South Vietnam.[7] In step with the rest of his Vietnam policies, Kennedy recognized the order of magnitude of his decision to "Americanize" the war in South Vietnam where his predecessors had not. Such a decision required novel techniques and tools to subdue the NLF insurgency, but in the president's view the United States would not be the first country to reintroduce chemical weapons lethal to humans in combat.

The C-123 aircraft and the air force personnel who first volunteered for the herbicide operations began their trip from Pope AFB, North Carolina, on November 28, 1961. Making their way west en route to South Vietnam, the crews made stopovers at Travis AFB in California, Hickam AFB in Hawaii, and Wake Island and Guam, in the North Pacific Ocean. On December 6 the C-123s landed in formation at Clark AFB, Philippines, thus completing their last stop in the Pacific island empire that the United States had built since the 1890s. The crews received instructions to wait in the Philippines for several weeks until logistics with MAAG-Vietnam could be worked out. Capt. Carl W. Marshall, commander of the mission, newly christened Operation Ranch Hand, made good use of the hiatus; given the dearth of experience among the crew, Marshall spent the month practicing dummy, chemical-free flight patterns near the air base on the Philippine coast.[8]

Although Operation Ranch Hand was about to enter South Vietnam on a combat mission directed and operated by U.S. forces, the question of civilian versus military identification for the crews and aircraft remained open through December 1961. While the White House had already decided that the crop destruction would remain masked as a Republic of Vietnam (RVN) program, Secretary of Defense Robert McNamara recommended that herbicide missions be flown in unmarked planes by personnel dressed in civilian clothing.[9] The U.S. ambassador in Saigon, Frederick Nolting, agreed, fearing that incoming shipments of herbicidal chemicals, clearly marked for an American military program, would be protested by the International Control Commission (ICC). The ICC was mandated by the Geneva Accords of 1954 to inspect incoming military shipments to South Vietnam.[10] Deputy Secretary of Defense Roswell Gilpatric prepared a "tit for tat" strategy should ICC inspectors consider blocking herbicide shipments: North Vietnamese aggression against South Vietnam had already violated the Geneva Accords; herbicidal warfare constituted a justifiable response by the United States to aid its ally. Gilpatric instructed the JCS and the air force, army, and navy secretaries to repeat the following statement should they encounter any questions about the Ranch Hand program: "The United States has acceded to GVN's [Government of Vietnam's] request for expanded aid in men and matériel and is determined to help preserve its independence. This is the sole objective of the United States. The United States will terminate these measures as soon as North Vietnam ends its acts of aggression."[11]

Operation Ranch Hand thus served a curious dual purpose: it became one of the first "carrots" or diplomatic inducements by the United States intended to end North Vietnamese aggression. But to the extent that the NLF and its guerrilla forces operated independently of Hanoi, herbicidal warfare had nothing to do with the Geneva Accords and the threat that President Diem faced from the north.

Such justifications failed to satisfy all U.S. officials involved in the matter. Nolting believed that the justification for Operation Ranch Hand, based on President Diem's request for herbicide operations, was an insufficient "cover" for the program. Almost immediately thereafter, the air force halted any movement to conceal the national identity of the Ranch Hand crews. A memo sent to Assistant Secretary of Defense William Bundy from Philip F. Hilbert of the Office of the Undersecretary of the Air Force emphasized the absurdity of any attempt to conceal the real source of Operation Ranch Hand and the herbicide shipments. Although no government official involved in the herbicide program discounted the adverse propaganda that the United States and South Vietnam would sustain, the position of the air force prevailed: if Operation Ranch Hand was to proceed, it would do so overtly. On December 14, 1961, the Departments of State and Defense jointly declared, "The identity of United States crews and aircraft participating in the spraying operations of the defoliation program will not be disguised."[12] Adverse political repercussions aside, the goal of Operation Ranch Hand was to expose hidden NLF guerrillas without being disguised itself.

Meanwhile, James Brown returned to South Vietnam in mid-December 1961, after a month conferring with colleagues at Fort Detrick about the promising results of the herbicide test runs. Before his departure, Brown met with William Godel, the deputy director of the Pentagon's Advanced Research Projects Agency, where Brown learned of President Kennedy's authorization to commence herbicide operations and the decision of the Defense Department to bestow on Brown near-total authority over the spray missions.[13] As a scientist, Brown was an unusual choice to command a military operation. The directive for a scientist to outrank military personnel was evidence of the anxiety in Washington to "rein in" herbicide operations at the outset. Otherwise the military's enthusiasm for spray missions could have led to an expansion of Operation Ranch Hand well beyond the president's mandate "for a selectively and carefully controlled" spray program.[14]

PLEASE!

SMOKEY

Only you can prevent a forest

Brown's first order of business upon his return to Vietnam was to carry out the three-phased program that would kick off U.S. herbicide operations. As detailed by Lt. Gen. Lionel McGarr, of MAAG, Vietnam in October 1961, the plan called for spray missions concentrated in an area known as Zone D, south of Saigon and known to be an NLF base camp. Herbicide targets included destruction of cropland, forest defoliation along supply and ambush paths, and roadside defoliation along routes frequented by South Vietnamese troops and U.S. advisors.[15]

The coding system for herbicides, which identified particular chemical compounds by the colored band around their drum-barrel containers, began during Brown's earlier testing under the auspices of the CDTC. Awaiting Brown's return to South Vietnam were twenty thousand gallons of Agents Pink and Green, which contained formulations of 2,4,5-T, the chemical compound that would constitute half of Agent Orange beginning in 1965 — the year the number of Ranch Hand sorties and gallons of herbicide sprayed expanded rapidly (figure 5).[16] MAAG had also received fifteen thousand gallons of cacodylic acid, or Agent Blue, an arsenical desiccant compound that remained the primary crop-destruction weapon for the duration of Operation Ranch Hand. Despite these sizable quantities, Brown sought the expedited arrival of an additional two hundred thousand gallons of Agent Purple (a 50:50 mix of 2,4-D and 2,4,5-T and near-identical predecessor of Agent Orange), procured by the Pentagon and en route from the Naval Supply Depot in Oakland, California, in anticipation of the arrival of the Ranch Hand crews.[17]

On January 7, 1962, at 9:00 a.m., the C-123s spray aircraft that formed the core of Operation Ranch Hand landed in formation at Tan Son Nhut airport, Saigon. It was the beginning of what one crew member recalled as "the most celebrated tour in history for a unit flying unarmed USAF aircraft," which would establish itself "as the most shot-up unit of the Vietnam venture."[18] In keeping with U.S. officials' overriding publicity concerns, the crews landed to no fanfare under the designation "Special Aerial Spray Flight."[19] Additionally, MAAG directed the crews to park the C-123 aircraft on a reserved lot designated for President Diem's personal fighter squadron. This area was closely guarded by the South Vietnamese Air Force and commanded by Lt. Col. Nguyen Cao Ky, who went on to become vice president of South Vietnam.

On January 8 herbicide drums en route from California had reached Saigon. Shortly afterward, MAAG conducted photographic aerial reconnaissance missions to determine optimum spray targets. Government agencies in Saigon concurrently spearheaded informational sessions with provincial leaders to explain the purpose of the spray missions. They peppered South Vietnamese officials with "talking points" regarding the vital necessity for herbicide operations. Such preparation anticipated the propaganda that the NLF and Hanoi would generate following spray missions.[20] Province chiefs distributed leaflets in the outlying areas of Saigon. One typical leaflet characterized herbicide operations — jointly executed by ARVN troops on the ground and the American pilots in the air — as a vital tool to stave off terrorist activities of NLF guerrillas. It also assured residents of the safety of the chemicals and promised compensation for any crop damage they might sustain as a result of spraying.[21]

Following two days of "psychological preparation" of local residents, Operation Ranch Hand conducted its first herbicide spray tests near Route 15, an important corridor northwest of Saigon vulnerable to guerrilla ambush. Nearly every aspect of this mission was experimental: the C-123, widely regarded for its long-haul transport capacities, was untested as a dispensary vehicle of liquids such as herbicides. So too was the MC-1, or "Hourglass," spray and nozzle system mounted under the aircraft. Furthermore, Brown had not tested Agent Purple on Vietnamese flora during his earlier field studies. Three days later, Ranch Hand launched its first large-scale mission.

On the morning of January 13, Capt. Carl Marshall and Capt. William F. Robison Jr., USAF, conducted two flights along Route 15, releasing nearly two thousand gallons of Agent Purple over an equal number of acres.[22] The beginning of herbicidal warfare demonstrated the kind of jointly executed mission that President Kennedy had envisioned upon committing to a strategy of counterinsurgency in South Vietnam. Given President Diem's personal enthusiasm for herbicidal warfare, RVN participation in Operation Ranch Hand would be politically and militarily useful to Saigon and Washington.[23] Persistent problems required matching cooperation at the tactical level, particularly because the lumbering and low-flying C-123s were vulnerable to ground fire from guerrillas. To meet this threat, ARVN dispatched ground forces along Route 15 to patrol and flush out NLF troops lying in wait. As further insurance, VNAF escort planes flanked the C-123s to bolster the surveillance activities on the ground.[24] The only fictive aspect of this joint effort was political, not military: to maintain the appearance that the chain of command for Operation Ranch Hand began with RVN military officials, all initial flights included a VNAF commanding officer who possessed no real authority over herbicide-related decisions.[25]

From an operational perspective, these preliminary herbicide flights struck Brown and the Ranch Hand crews as an unqualified success. The mission along Route 15 ended on January 16, at which point Adm. Harry Felt, CINCPAC, reviewed potential target areas for future operations.[26] The successful collaboration between Operation Ranch Hand and the VNAF offered a promising future for joint operations across a spectrum of counterinsurgency programs. The intricate synchronization required to get Operation Ranch Hand running — from the procurement of herbicides and their transpacific shipment, to the long transport of planes and crews from numerous bases in the United States, to calculations in Washington that sought a balance between tactical advantage and political fallout — coalesced in South Vietnam in mid-January 1962. Still, the most important questions that would decide the future viability of Operation Ranch Hand were not immediately apparent: Would aerial application of herbicidal chemicals sufficiently defoliate forest cover? Would defoliated areas weaken and alter the tactics of NLF guerrillas and ultimately weaken their influence on the perimeter of Saigon? Finally, would the local population accept official RVN assurances of the safety and necessity of herbicide operations in the long term?[27]

The most pressing question centered on the physiological effectiveness of the herbicide missions against their targets. Without reliable means to strip foliage from NLF-dominated areas, all peripheral issues would be rendered moot. Brown reported after observing the herbicidal effects following the January mission: "The chemicals used are sufficiently active to kill a majority of species in Vietnam if: (1) they are applied properly to the vegetation, (2) they are applied during a period of active growth . . . With respect to the timing of application, the chemicals are plant growth regulators and can only attack plants effectively during the active phases of the growth cycle" (figure 6).[28]

Brown also called attention to an ironic side effect of herbicide application atop the forest canopy: defoliation permitted sunlight to reach the forest floor, where it triggered dense vegetative growth at ground level, particularly bamboos and *imperata* (buffalo) grasses. Under these circumstances, the tactical utility of Operation Ranch Hand from an aerial reconnaissance perspective was indisputable. In many cases, however, the resulting ground-level growth inhibited lateral visibility along roadsides and military bases. Military assessment reports on the herbicide program repeatedly minimized this revelation. Later in the decade, critics of herbicidal warfare used this counterproductive effect to argue against military officials' assertions that the program saved the lives of U.S. soldiers.[29]

Brown was confident that the chemicals 2,4-D and 2,4,5-T would succeed both in stripping the forest of its foliage and in inhibiting future growth. He characterized the mission as valuable insofar as it would provide a spray schedule based on the seasonal growth cycle. In its review of Brown's report, the Agricultural Research Station of the Department of Agriculture advocated strongly for the expansion of herbicide operations on the basis that the effects of herbicides on one swath of land could not be extrapolated to understand herbicidal warfare's effect on the vast and diverse forests of South Vietnam. Although the review did not contradict Brown's basic findings, it ignored his suggestion to place the spray missions on hiatus. This position soon won the support of Secretary of Defense McNamara, CINCPAC Admiral Felt, and MAAG Lt. Gen. McGarr. Having already secured the support of Secretary of State Dean Rusk, McNamara laid out the case

Figure 6 James Brown, center, inspecting defoliation effects following the January 1962 mission. Reprinted from William S. Buckingham Jr., *Operation Ranch Hand: The Air Force and Herbicides in Southeast Asia, 1961–1971* (Washington, D.C.: Office of Air Force History, 1982), 40.

to President Kennedy: "The great variety of vegetation found in Vietnam includes species never treated in previous herbicide tests. The limited areas already sprayed do not include the variety of vegetation and conditions required for a full evaluation of the effectiveness of chemicals employed and possible operation concepts for their use. It is important that we test all conditions of vegetation, as well as the effectiveness of defoliant techniques in specific situations."[30]

McNamara went on to list six target areas selected by MAAG as suitable for herbicide missions, including defoliation of air bases and ammunition depots. The premise was that U.S.-RVN military installations in wooded areas were vulnerable to sabotage and ambush. President Kennedy authorized the new target areas, concurring that one isolated mission was insufficient to measure the defoliating capacity of Operation Ranch Hand. On February 8 sorties began to spray the authorized target areas, after which operations halted for five months to assess the value of herbicidal warfare for the broader U.S. and RVN counterinsurgency mission.[31]

On the same day McNamara issued his briefing, one of Ranch Hand's six C-123s crashed while on a training mission, killing its crew. Investigators never conclusively determined the cause of the crash. The deaths of Capt. Fergus C. Groves II, Capt. Robert D. Larson, and Sgt. Milo B. Coghill were the first sustained by the U.S. Air Force in Vietnam.[32] In a somewhat macabre reaction to the incident, Brown considered the fact that a forest fire did not erupt in unsprayed areas beyond the crash sight as "indisputable evidence" that the forests of South Vietnam could not be set ablaze with conventional methods, such as napalm, alone.[33] Later missions, dubbed Operation Pink Rose and Operation Sherwood Forest, demonstrated that incendiary projectile weapons such as napalm were far more effective when applied to previously defoliated forested areas.[34]

In April 1962, with nearly ten thousand acres sprayed by Operation Ranch Hand, the Pentagon's ARPA program spearheaded the first major evaluation of the program. The team, led by Brig. Gen. Fred J. Delmore, included representatives from the U.S. Army Chemical Corps and scientists from the Department of Agriculture. The report confirmed what plant physiologists had discovered in the 1940s: different plant species react to the same herbicidal chemicals in different ways. Contemporary surveys listed two major categories of vegetation in South Vietnam: mangrove forests located along the southern coast and the Mekong Delta and evergreen tropical forests spanning the central highlands from the demilitarized zone (DMZ) to the hinterlands surrounding Saigon in the south.[35]

Delmore's report, which he presented to McNamara in May, emphasized that if Operation Ranch Hand extended into the future, spray missions would have to account for uneven levels of defoliation. Also, meteorological conditions such as humidity and wind would repeatedly impede accurate targeting. Additionally, the effectiveness of the missions would be optimized only during the rainy season (May–October), when plant and tree growth was most active and thus most susceptible to chemical hormone regulation.[36] Delmore offset these logistical limitations with his analysis of the increased visibility afforded by the Ranch Hand spray missions, citing upward of 85 percent defoliation in mangrove forests in the southern tip of the country.[37] The most significant conclusion of the report held that any final judgment of the overall effectiveness of herbicidal warfare could not be reached for at least a year. To the extent that the ecological effects of herbicides had become well understood and could be "operationalized" into spray plans, no one could be certain how the NLF would respond.

More certain was that any perceptible limitation in NLF maneuverability and consequent shift in tactics as a result of defoliation would occur only if the United States embarked on a massive effort to denude South Vietnam's lush landscape of its forest cover. Given the size of the country — and the fact that the U.S. presence there was predicated on the assumption that the NLF operated unopposed across vast rural areas — military and civilian leaders would have to decide if Operation Ranch Hand should expand significantly or be scrapped altogether. A middle ground approach, which called for the "limited" or surgical style of operations initially approved by President Kennedy, would be more trouble than it was worth because it would fail to limit meaningfully the NLF's freedom of movement throughout the country. Under these conditions, no military officer would be able to justify the military expenditures and political liabilities generated by Operation Ranch Hand.

In August 1962 the White House offered the first sign that it was committed to expanding herbicide operations from its experimental phase to becoming a regular part of military operations in support of South Vietnam. Military Assistance Command, Vietnam (MACV), which military officials created in February 1962 to assist (and later absorb) MAAG, chose Ca Mau peninsula on the southernmost tip of Vietnam as a prime area for resuming large-scale spray missions. For the past several months, the area had become increasingly infiltrated by the NLF, while the mangrove forests in which they operated had already proved the most susceptible to herbicide applications. On McNamara's advice, President Kennedy authorized the "destruction" of the mangroves in the area, although he stipulated that Ranch Hand crews must avoid any accidental spraying of crops due to herbicide drift as far away as Cambodia.[38]

The spraying began in early September and lasted to the middle of October, covering nine thousand acres with nearly twenty-eight thousand gallons of Agent Purple. After action, reports tallied visibility improvement at 90–95 percent several weeks following the spraying.[39] Because a Ranch Hand attack left tree trunks and branches intact (which offered the possibility of future regeneration, not unlike the normal refoliation of deciduous trees in the spring), any figure approaching 100 percent indicated that herbicide applications succeeded in stripping almost every leaf from the plant in a given area. In October, at the tail end of the rainy season, Ranch Hand crews concentrated on the Laotian border in an area that came to be known as the Ho Chi Minh Trail, which was not a trail but a vast set of interconnecting overland routes that fed NLF forces military supplies from the north. Whereas the Ca Mau campaign aimed to help ARVN ground forces "search and destroy" guerrillas already in the country, herbicide missions to the north launched an "upstream" approach. They sought to break off contact between the NLF and its communist patrons in North Vietnam and China.[40]

At the conclusion of Ranch Hand's border operations, herbicidal activity went on hiatus until the following May. The U.S. Air Force reassigned Ranch Hand crews and aircraft to a number of troop and ammunition transport duties. Meanwhile, civilian and military commanders began to determine if herbicidal warfare aided the broader counterinsurgency mission upon which President Kennedy staked U.S. support of an independent and pro-American South Vietnam. Assessments were almost uniformly positive. At the most basic level—that is, the criterion that measures the effectiveness of defoliation in isolation from the political and strategic considerations that led to Kennedy's authorization and sensitivity to international back-lash—the chemicals 2,4-D and 2,4,5-T proved effective at killing plants.

In August 1962 Gen. Paul Harkins, commander of MACV, reported increased horizontal and vertical visibility in the range of 60 to 95 percent in areas following one or more sprayings.[41] At this early juncture, such figures vindicated the boosters of herbicidal warfare only in theory. Although military plant scientists demonstrated that agricultural chemicals could be formulated and applied toward a specific goal of clearing foliage in a variety of coastal and mountainous tropical settings, "hard" data correlating the incidence of NLF ambushes in sprayed areas remained elusive.[42] Even by the spring of 1963, the conflict was simply too young to yield precise statistical analysis upon which military tactics and policy could be adapted.[43]

Still, the lack of correlative data did not hinder the enthusiasm of subscribers to counterinsurgent theory. Kennedy, who continued to resist expanding U.S. involvement in the Vietnamese conflict, remained confident that technology would effectively substitute for manpower. The assessment period of early herbicide operations came at a crucial stage of the war. Senator Mike Mansfield's fact-finding mission to Vietnam in December 1962 and the Buddhist uprising against the Saigon regime several months later threw into question two pillars of Kennedy's Vietnam policy. First, Mansfield was among the first major politicians in Washington to demand evidence that the United States had clearly defined and achievable objectives in Vietnam. Second, Diem's dictatorial tendencies, brutally highlighted for worldwide consumption by a photograph of a self-immolated Buddhist monk in Saigon, challenged the view of Diem as a symbol of the United

States' commitment to defending freedom and democracy against communism.[44] Advisors within the Kennedy administration reflected on the criticism of U.S. policy at the highest levels. Fact-finding missions headed by the Departments of State and Defense respectively called for strengthening American support for Diem but warned that doing so would incite a Buddhist-Catholic civil war. In response to oral summaries of the missions presented by two officials in the Oval Office, Kennedy remarked, "You two did visit the same country, didn't you?"[45]

The paradox and simplicity of the strategy behind Operation Ranch Hand cut to the core of U.S. objectives in Indochina: If it were true, as Kennedy believed, that communist guerrillas operating in heavily forested rural areas represented the primary threat to the maintenance of a pro-American, "free" Republic of Vietnam, then the United States military had to take all steps to deny guerrillas their greatest tactical (if not political) advantage. The enemy's advantage likewise mirrored the major liability of American forces. Gen. William Westmoreland, successor to General Harkins as MACV commander and a proponent of herbicidal warfare, once likened the United States in Vietnam to a "giant without eyes." Westmoreland well understood that the American giant would remain more or less "blind" operating in the dense Vietnamese forest, whether represented by sixteen thousand advisors during the Kennedy administration or five hundred thousand ground troops stationed in South Vietnam at the height of the war under Lyndon Johnson in 1968.[46] The high-technology war-fighting solutions offered by Operation Ranch Hand served as a kind of harbinger of future wars that would increasingly substitute technology for manpower — what one historian has dubbed "technowar."[47]

Futuristic as Operation Ranch Hand might have seemed, its connections to the past ran deep. Fundamentally, the program picked up where E. J. Kraus left off during contingency planning against the Japanese in World War II. Further, as the environmental historian John McNeill has shown, the military imperative to control forests during battle is as old as war itself.[48] It was the means, not the ends, that made Operation Ranch Hand a new war tactic. Finally, the Kennedy administration emphasized repeatedly that the herbicidal chemicals used in South Vietnam were "similar to, and no more toxic than, weed killers which [were] widely used in the U.S., USSR and elsewhere" in an attempt to defuse charges of toxic warfare. This characterization played strongly into the assumption that the targets of herbicidal warfare — the Viet Cong — were not dissimilar to the pests and parasites that impede agricultural productivity.[49] As one American theorist wrote of the Viet Cong's rural strategy: "Like a disease, the revolutionary organism invades the body politic at the points of least resistance — in the peripheral or isolated communities less subject to government control. By the destruction of the government presence and the substitution of the Viet Cong's control in one village after another, the Communist area expands towards the centers of government power."[50]

For these reasons, to almost all observers at this early point the benefits of Operation Ranch Hand far outweighed its liabilities. At the official level, the case for the strategic importance of defoliation appeared prominently in a major assessment report, completed in September 1963 as an interagency project with the input of MACV and the U.S. embassy in Saigon. This review, known after its lead author as the Olenchuk Report, exhaustively studied the military and political effects of Operation Ranch Hand. Lt. Col. Peter Olenchuk and his colleagues noted bureaucratic obstructions encountered by peasants who sought compensation for crops accidentally destroyed by errant spray missions as the major defect of the program. Contextualized within the report's emphatic support of Operation Ranch Hand in all other regards, the bureaucratic defect appeared minor.

The authors of the report noted successes in "psyops" (psychological operations) designed to assure peasants that herbicides were harmful neither to them nor to their animals; that the time between authorization request for a particular mission and the execution of that mission was lengthy but orderly; and most important that herbicidal warfare was valuable at its current levels and would take on an even greater role should the broader war expand. In concluding remarks, the authors of the report stated: "Defoliation and chemical crop destruction have a direct and continuing favorable impact on military and civil activities in RVN."[51] By signing off on the report, Ambassador Henry Cabot Lodge Jr. and General Harkins ensured the escalation of Operation Ranch Hand from a research program to a routine and expansive military operation based at Da Nang Air Base.[52]

The more significant upgrades to the program included the State Department's decision to decentralize authorization for spray missions and the commencement of direct U.S. participation in the "food denial," or crop-destruction, program. The latter was once exclusively an American-supported VNAF mission due to the politically charged nature of the operation.[53] The herbicide of choice for such missions was an arsenical compound known as Agent Blue, which proved particularly effective against rice.[54] Military assessment reports from then on regularly cited food denial as a crucial component of the herbicide program to halt or hinder NLF activity. According to one after-action report, "the VC complained longer and more bitterly about the defoliation and crop destruction than any other weapon used against them. A significant reduction in their food supply and their shelter and concealment was caused by it."[55]

As the historian George Herring observes, in the last months of his life Kennedy refused "to face the hard questions," at a time when U.S.-RVN relations were in crisis. The assassinations of the American president and President Diem in November 1963 intensified the gulf between the two countries.[56] Diem, a victim of an ARVN generals' coup operating with tacit American support, had harmed U.S.-South Vietnamese efforts to subdue the NLF insurgency.[57] Insofar as the rebel generals were concerned, Diem's death offered the opportunity to reignite warm relations with Washington while refocusing the fight against the NLF and away from the Buddhists in the city of Hue — a prospect quickly embraced in the White House and the embassy in Saigon.[58] Kennedy, of course, would never learn if Diem's assassination would offer a new opportunity for the United States to achieve its anticommunist objectives in Indochina or if it would invite strategic disaster. Still, Kennedy died having put in place a counterinsurgency strategy that garnered enthusiasm among the political and military elite of both the United States and South Vietnam.

Any debate that considers what Kennedy would have done with respect to the situation in Vietnam and what was innovated by the slain president's successor, Lyndon B. Johnson, must take into account where each president sought to direct U.S. efforts amid a rapidly deteriorating situation in South Vietnam. Immediately upon assuming control and throughout 1964, the shaky government in Saigon could not counter significant NLF victories and the support its guerrilla fighters received from Hanoi. That the viability of South Vietnam seemed weakest just as the counterinsurgency strategies developed during the Kennedy years had reached a level of maturity begged two different lines of reasoning: either the techniques of herbicidal warfare, strategic hamlets, and development programs aiming to "win hearts and minds" of the rural peasantry were failing before their supporters were given the opportunity to implement them fully, or the United States had misdirected its efforts in South Vietnam without taking the fight directly to the North.[59]

As one political scientist observes, Kennedy tended to view the counter-insurgency mission in the hinterlands beyond Saigon as "the operational framework for designing 1960s containment strategies everywhere in the world."[60] The military theorist Robert Kipp adds, "The unparalleled, lavish use of firepower as a substitute for manpower is an outstanding characteristic of U.S. military tactics in the Vietnam War."[61] It is unlikely, then, that even in the worst of circumstances Kennedy would have adopted Johnson's parallel approach of maintaining the counterinsurgency program in rural South Vietnam (albeit with the direct and massive introduction of U.S. ground forces) while launching a sustained bombing campaign against North Vietnamese targets in 1965.

Kennedy had consistently rejected proposals calling for the deployment of combat forces to Vietnam. Moreover, the president simply had too much invested in his counterinsurgency strategy, at once a shining example of Flexible Response in action and a prototype to export the military experience gained in South Vietnam wherever U.S. allies faced the encroaching communist menace. John Gaddis's key observation that "the resulting Viet Cong gains led the Johnson administration by the end of 1964 to approve what Kennedy had rejected—a combat role for the United States in Vietnam" reinforces the idea that Kennedy's policies would not have radically changed course.[62] Indeed: the gathering strength of the NLF would have likely redoubled the president's faith in counterinsurgency's capacity to win the war without significant sacrifice of American blood and treasure.

With this approach, Kennedy understood better than his successor the extent to which Americans would tolerate an open-ended and ill-defined military commitment halfway around the world. After all, as Fredrik Logevall has painstakingly demonstrated, any "Cold War Consensus" that "whole-heartedly supported a staunch commitment to defend South Vietnam" had only *decreased* in 1964—to the extent that it existed at all with respect to Americans' desire to draw the line in Vietnam.[63]

What is the relationship between, on one hand, presidential decision making with respect to the escalating war in Vietnam and, on the other, the status of Operation Ranch Hand as it was inherited and expanded under Lyndon Johnson? It is impossible to understand the graphs presented in figure 7 in isolation from the major decisions that led to war.

Had Kennedy lived these graphs would likely look very different. Although it is apparent that the surge in Operation Ranch Hand activity followed the broader contours of the war (right down to the suspension of

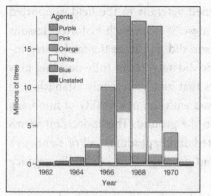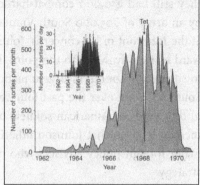

Figure 7 (a) Liters of herbicides sprayed over 1962–1971. (b) Time course of herbicide sorties. Reprinted by permission from Macmillan Publishers Ltd: *Nature*, Jeanne Mager Stellman et al., "The Extent and Patterns of Usage of Agent Orange and Other Herbicides in Vietnam," copyright 2003.

almost all spray missions during the Tet Offensive of 1968), the correlation between the prevalence of ground troops operating in South Vietnam and the magnitude of the defoliation mission obfuscates the original purpose of herbicidal warfare as a key component of Kennedy's strategy of counterinsurgency: the substitution of high-technology solutions for ground troops prepared for the decisive combat that Russell Weigley has famously termed the "American Way of War."[64] In one of the most authoritative conclusions on the legacy of Kennedy's counterinsurgency policy in Vietnam, the historian William Duiker argues that "Kennedy's actions and comments about Vietnam throughout his presidency suggest the agonized ambivalence that he experienced in grappling with the problem. Unlike many of his advisors, who saw no alternative to the defense of South Vietnam, Kennedy was clearly tortured by doubts about the wisdom of involvement there, while at the same time fearful of the high price of withdrawal."[65]

President Johnson experienced no less "agonized ambivalence" when it came to Vietnam, and he was certainly no less sensitive (although less responsive) than Kennedy to the dangers of history repeating itself. In the run up to the massive ground-troop deployment to South Vietnam in July 1965, Under Secretary of State George Ball—who enjoyed close access to Johnson—warned the president, "A review of the French experience more than a decade ago may be helpful. The French fought a war in Vietnam, and were finally defeated—after seven years of bloody struggle and when they still had 250,000 combat-hardened veterans in the field, supported by an army of 205,000 South Vietnamese."[66] With such historical lessons at the forefront of his concerns, Johnson did not make the fateful step toward war easily. More to the point, he did so without fully deciding how to square the counterinsurgent tactics that had been firmly established in South Vietnam over the past four years with the new reality of hundreds of thousands of American soldiers on the ground. This indecision seems incredible given that Johnson inherited and kept almost all of Kennedy's major foreign-policy advisors who had developed the counterinsurgency strategy.

The result, as it pertains to herbicidal warfare illustrated in the graphs presented here, was a snowball effect of epic proportions. The massive deployment of ground forces in South Vietnam, without any substantial overhaul or top-level review of the defoliation program, negated Kennedy's built-in guarantee to prevent what would soon become known as ecocide in South Vietnam by mandating the limited scope of operations under his watch. Despite the best efforts of the USAF and its strategic bombing of North Vietnam, American forces would never sever the support infrastructure from Hanoi to the NLF. Its leadership steadily ramped up guerrilla-style ambushes against U.S. ground troops in virtually every area of South Vietnam, from the southernmost areas of the Mekong Delta up to the demilitarized zone north of Hue.[67] Well-supplied guerrillas facing huge numbers of American soldiers thus guaranteed the chance of surprise attacks at any time and place in the country. The NLF's capacity to operate countrywide generated this typical call for greater budgetary support of herbicidal warfare during congressional testimony in April 1965:

> Right now our biggest problem in Vietnam is uncovering the Communist guerrilla forces who find sanctuary in the jungle areas of both Vietnam and Laos . . . [Chemical defoliants] would lay bare the whole terrain or area sprayed. This could be one of the most effective ways of stopping the communists from coming into South Vietnam and carrying on their aggression.[68]

Because the purpose of Operation Ranch Hand was to track NLF movements (either as a preventive measure to protect soldiers on foot patrol or in swift boats, or as an offensive tactic in identifying NLF strongholds in defoliated areas previously opaque to aerial reconnaissance),[69] often one of the first after-action responses was to call in a C-123 Ranch Hand sortie to spray that area. Although the authorization process became more streamlined following the routinization of Operation Ranch Hand in 1964, lag time between request and execution could stretch from days to several weeks. The process originated with either a U.S. ground commander or his ARVN counterpart, whose request went to MACV and then on for final approval at the U.S. embassy. During the review period, one or more MACV representatives would board Operation Ranch Hand reconnaissance flights to verify that the geographic coordinates matched the original request.[70] The "workhorse" of the Operation Ranch Hand Fleet, the C-123 Provider, was fitted with a one-thousand-gallon tank and pump located on the craft's underbelly.[71] The lumbering and low-flying C-123 — among the most shot-at aircraft in the Air Force fleet — was often supplemented by helicopter spray missions in areas known to be hot spots for ground fire and in times when air force commanders reassigned Ranch Hand C-123s for transport duty (figure 8).[72]

The explanation for the expansion of Operation Ranch Hand from 1966 to 1968 can be explained by the following passage from an herbicide assessment review: "The availability of adequate alternative locations sometimes places limitations on the benefits derived by Allied forces from defoliation of bases or enemy troop locations. VC in the spacious vegetated areas of the highlands often express little concern about the possibility of defoliation. Although some inconvenience will occur, they feel they can easily move to another area in the immense jungle."[73]

In other words, spray missions begot spray missions. As soon as the United States committed to direct combat in Vietnam, where a guerrilla war deprived American troops of fixed boundaries to defend and advance on, commanders called on the crew members of Operation Ranch Hand to spray vast areas of highland forest, rice paddies, and coastal mangrove swamps. In purely military terms, the mission was self-perpetuating: conduct herbicide operations to ensure a given area would remain free of guerrilla activity, and repeat that process wherever guerrillas in the previous area had moved.

This strategy, which ultimately led to Operation Ranch Hand spraying approximately five million acres of South Vietnam, 12 percent of the entire country, could not meaningfully distinguish between enemy and civilian areas. In some cases, that was the point. At the earliest stages of the program, in fact, MACV authorized defoliation missions as part of the broader "rural pacification" program. Civilians in defoliated areas were moved to strategic hamlets. The sequence of one mission in the southern province of Tay Ninh,

Crew members of C-123 defoliation aircraft return to Tan Son Nhut air base after mission, above, prior to debriefing, at left, on success of flight and any Viet Cong reaction. "Ranch Hand" aircraft normally are accompanied by strike fighters to counter any Communist fire directed against the slow-moving converted transports. Below, a C-123 is loaded with spray for a defoliation flight. Canal-laced, swampy area of the South Vietnamese delta region is evident from panoramic view beneath a flight of three C-123 spray aircraft in picture above on facing page. Single "Ranch Hand" aircraft flies low over paddy fields, below, opposite page, during course of defoliation mission. In close-up views of C-123s, note Vietnamese air force insignia carried by all USAF "Ranch Hand" aircraft to counter Viet Cong charges of U.S. "chemical warfare."

Figure 8 Operation Ranch Hand in action. This page appeared as part of an article in a popular aviation magazine in 1967.

as described in an after-action report, illustrates the symbiotic relationship between defoliation and pacification:

Defoliate the Boi Loi Forest, thereby precluding further use of the area by the VC as a concealed redoubt.

Kill crops growing in the area, thereby severing the food supply of the population and forcing the people to seek GVN assistance.

Relocate the population living within the Boi Loi Forest into hamlets in pacified areas under GVN control.[74]

The process of rendering forested areas unfit for civilian habitation led the political scientist Samuel Huntington to identify an overarching goal of the United States' counterinsurgency strategy in South Vietnam as it had evolved by 1968. At that juncture, more Americans were beginning to demand an explanation of U.S. military objectives for the war. Huntington provided his own theory:

In an absent-minded way the United States in Viet Nam may well have stumbled upon the answer to "wars of national liberation" . . . It is instead forced-draft urbanization and modernization which rapidly brings the country in question out of the phase in which a rural revolutionary movement can hope to generate sufficient strength to come to power . . . In the short run, with half the population still in the countryside, the Viet Cong will remain a powerful force which cannot be dislodged from its constituency so long as the constituency exist.[75]

Was this indeed the state of counterinsurgency strategy five years after Kennedy's death? No government official — and certainly no serviceman connected to Operation Ranch Hand — couched the United States' purpose in Vietnam in these terms. The closest approximation of Huntington's analysis may be found in Walt Rostow's 1952 work *The Process of Economic Growth: A Non-Communist Manifesto*, in which he argued that societies failing to progress from a traditional/rural to an advanced/technological social system are vulnerable to communist subversion. In Vietnam Rostow believed he had discovered the perfect expression of his theory. He described the United States' goal in that country to halt NLF attempts to wreck South Vietnam's natural progression toward modernity.[76] There is no evidence that Rostow's theories on economic development became operationalized during the Vietnam War, as Huntington correctly observed. But that is precisely the point. This lack of accounting explains why the scope of Operation Ranch Hand at the height of the war bore little resemblance to the origins of the defoliation program and the strategic assumptions that propelled it. The extant record indicates that, in stark contrast to John Kennedy, Lyndon Johnson limited his direct involvement in Operation Ranch Hand to rejecting Barry Goldwater's call for "nuclear defoliation" and awarding the Presidential Unit Citation to the Twelfth Air Commando Squadron for "extraordinary gallantry" during defoliation operations in 1966 and 1967.[77]

President Johnson, who shared none of his predecessor's appetite for counterinsurgency theory as an antidote to escalation, effectively allowed Operation Ranch Hand to grow unchecked. Johnson's interests lay elsewhere—particularly in the bombing campaign of North Vietnam—illustrated vividly when he once boasted, "They [the USAF] can't even bomb an outhouse without my approval."[78] Had Kennedy lived to continue managing counterinsurgency missions in Vietnam, Operation Ranch Hand likely would not have escalated into one of the greatest chemical warfare operations in history. Sensitive as Kennedy was to international condemnation of the defoliation program, it is equally likely that protest against herbicidal warfare would not have gained sufficient momentum to halt the program in its tracks. Yet Kennedy was worried about such condemnation emanating from Hanoi, Moscow, and Beijing. That the greatest protest came from American citizens and from U.S. allies in Europe was a development that never garnered serious consideration by the military and political planners of herbicidal warfare.

CHAPTER SIX

SCIENCE, ETHICS, AND DISSENT

THE SCIENTIFIC CONTROVERSY over Operation Ranch Hand picked up where the controversy over atomic radiation had left off. A 1964 article in the *Bulletin of the Atomic Scientists* launched the decade-long scientific movement to terminate herbicidal warfare.[1] That same year, Lyndon B. Johnson declared ecological victory ten years in the making. In a nationally televised broadcast, the president celebrated the end of atmospheric testing of nuclear bombs, declaring: "The deadly products of atomic explosions were poisoning our soil and our food and the milk our children drank and the air we all breathe ... Radioactive poisons were beginning to threaten the safety of people throughout the world. They were a growing menace to the health of every unborn child."[2]

As a political statement, Johnson's was hardly risky. By overwhelming margins, the public supported the ban, and the real work to end atmospheric testing had been completed by John F. Kennedy and Soviet Premier Nikita Khrushchev, culminating in the Limited Test Ban Treaty of 1963.[3] The origins of this agreement, widely hailed as Kennedy's greatest achievement in the area of cold war détente and nuclear disarmament, began not in the halls of America's elite foreign-policy establishments but in the laboratory of Barry Commoner, a biologist at Washington University in St. Louis. Commoner, regarded by many admirers as the "father" of modern environmentalism, became a key player in the scientific protest against defoliation in Vietnam following his work on atmospheric testing.[4] The scientists who protested Operation Ranch Hand worked to replicate Commoner's success in the political arena.

In 1953 Commoner became one of the first American scientists to view nuclear weaponry as having a more pernicious role than guarantor of post-war American security. In April of that year, the Atomic Energy Commission exploded a nuclear bomb at the Nevada test site. The following day, a huge thunderstorm across the country rained radioactive debris on Troy, New York.[5] To Commoner, who had spent his early career studying the effects of cancer and free radicals in human tissue, this was alarming news; over the next five years he attempted in vain to extract information from federal authorities on all aspects of the nuclear testing program. Commoner encountered a wall of silence, buttressed by a steady rejoinder from federal officials, including President Dwight D. Eisenhower, that radioactive fallout posed no health danger to humans.[6] Fears of atomic espionage and the Soviets' launch of Sputnik in 1957 further undermined Commoner's efforts. In a sweeping editorial in *Foreign Affairs*, Edward Teller, the "father" of the hydrogen bomb, suggested that Sputnik was only the beginning of an ominous trend toward Soviet scientific superiority, and any attempt to ban nuclear testing would further the trend.[7] In response Commoner exhorted his colleagues to keep in mind that scientific certainty is "a direct outcome of the degree of communication which normally exists in science . . . What we call a scientific truth emerges from investigators' insistence on free publication of their own observations. This permits the rest of the scientific community to check the data and evaluate the interpretations, so that eventually a commonly held body of facts and ideas comes into being. Any failure to communicate information to the entire scientific community hampers the attainment of a common understanding."[8]

The "problem," as the title of Commoner's piece, "The Fallout Problem," suggested, was double-edged: the elevation of secrecy above ecological health for the sake of national security remained a political and a scientific problem; in his analysis the two were inseparable because the political repression of scientific collaboration rendered deductive discovery impossible. To circumvent this dilemma, Commoner created the Committee for Nuclear Information (CNI) and initiated a baby-tooth survey that subsequently became famous. Commoner was convinced that radioactive fallout, particularly the radioactive isotope strontium 90, which had been deposited over fields on which cows grazed, had worked its way into the human food supply. He was right: after an enthusiastic response from the greater St. Louis community, netting CNI some seventeen thousand teeth in two years, Commoner and his colleagues demonstrated that even the remotest areas "sacrificed" for nuclear testing could not adequately shield American citizens from radioactive contamination. This was precisely the position that President Johnson staked in 1964 with the support of anxious parents all over the country.[9]

Building on his success as both political organizer and scientific populist, in the late 1960s Commoner took the cause of scientific openness and citizen involvement to its broadest concern: saving Earth from ecological doom by questioning the wisdom and motives of the "military-industrial complex." By then — and in no small part because of Commoner's work — ecology had become as much a political platform as a branch of science.[10] In one of his many invocations of the global ecological crisis, Commoner intoned, "The planet has become a kind of colossal, lightly triggered time bomb."[11] In the late 1970s, when the issue of Agent Orange and its impact on the health of Vietnam veterans was at its apex, Commoner argued that herbicidal warfare in Vietnam was itself a time bomb as a public health catastrophe in the making.[12]

The similarities between Commoner's populist activism and the later organized opposition to herbicidal warfare, the way he articulated the perils of elevating cold war expedience above ecological caution, and his successful bid to change minds at the highest levels of government place Commoner squarely within the story of herbicidal protest. His work and the work of the scientists who protested and ultimately terminated herbicidal warfare in Vietnam must be understood as parts of a continuous whole.[13] Their efforts and that of all scientists in the 1960s who explicitly rejected the status quo and couched their ecological worries in planetary terms — those labeled by one historian as "guerrilla scientists" — had antecedents as least as far back as the 1930s.[14] As the historian Peter Kuznik observes, "Virtually every important study of scientists and politics wrongly assumes that, in the quarter century prior to Hiroshima, American scientists were either politically apathetic or blindly supporting the status quo."[15] Even before atomic weapons or Agent Orange, for some scientists the dangers of military weaponry demanded introspection and political action.

On the eve of World War II, the specter of trench warfare and the poison gas attacks of the Great War loomed large for scientists on both sides of the Atlantic. J. D. Bernal, a professor of physics at the University of London, lamented in 1939 that science was no longer "the noblest flower of the human mind and the most promising source of material benefactions." Since the Armistice, he explained, events had "done more than cause a different attitude towards science by people at large; they [had] profoundly changed the attitudes of scientists themselves towards science."[16] In the late 1930s, Britain's Parliament allocated nearly the same amount of funds to poison gas as to medical research. To Bernal this parity was illustrative: "In almost every country," he warned, "scientists are being pressed into the service of war industries and classified for various military occupations if that war comes."[17] The years following World War II saw a surge of concern among scientists regarding new and frightening applications of science. Addressing a Christian social-action group, Theodor Rosebury, a professor of medicine at Columbia University, argued that science itself is morally neutral, but how humans apply it is literally a matter of life and death: "We can choose to save the world for ourselves or our children, with science as our servant . . . or we can choose the easier road, the road of hate and fear that would lead us to destroy our neighbors because we don't like the way they live and because we are sure they are threatening to destroy us."[18]

For Rosebury only a concerted international effort to curb or preferably ban weapons proliferation offered a reasonable hope for peace. Writing at the same time was William Vogt, an American ornithologist who saw the marriage of war making and science as emblematic of the gravest threat posed by modern technology to the natural world: consuming and destroying Earth's resources at rates unsustainable for the rising human population. Long before George Kennan theorized and called for an international environmental policy regime, Vogt called on the nascent UN to regulate and ultimately reverse nations' tendencies toward war and ecological destruction as problems that demanded resolution in tandem.[19] Vannevar Bush, director of the U.S. Office of Scientific Research and Development, who more than any other American was responsible for the creation of the "military-industrial complex" after World War II, anticipated Barry Commoner's ruminations on military weaponry and the democratic process. In 1949, even as the fears of a Soviet nuclear bomb were becoming confirmed, Bush warned that the threat of planetary destruction during war was just "over the horizon." The antidote was precisely the openness, accountability, and citizen participation that distinguished dictatorships from democracies.[20]

Enter Rachel Carson. Her celebrated work *Silent Spring* (1962) foreshadows and hovers above the herbicide controversy — if only its author had lived to write a second edition. Carson, a biologist and longtime staff writer at the U.S. Fish and Wildlife Service (1936–49), is widely credited as a (if not *the*) founder of modern environmentalism.[21] Like Barry Commoner,

Carson is best known for her social critique of American politics, science, and weaponry. Although *Silent Spring* is nominally about the dangers of DDT, her fears expressed in the book centered on an imagined apocalypse resulting from America's profligate — indeed reckless — use of chemicals. Why was the spring silent? We must intuit from her question: "The birds, for example — where had they gone?" Carson did not know, for the setting of this spring season is an imaginary town, whose hypothetical residents are equally puzzled. Although Carson's town is in "heartland" America, it might be described as an ecological necropolis: from berries to cattle, wrens to ferns, everything was dead. The tale is an omen: "A grim specter has crept upon us almost unnoticed, and this imagined tragedy may easily become a stark reality we all shall know."[22]

Carson devoted a sizable portion of her study to herbicides. Her characterization of them as "a bright new toy . . . [which gives] a giddy sense of power over nature to those who wield them" was somewhat misleading. If their quixotic effects as tamers of nature were debatable, their newness was not. DDT was only one of several chemicals designed for environmental control, but America's massive use of herbicides for forest management and agricultural weed killers was emblematic of Carson's central point: in the postwar era humans had achieved a technological sophistication and capacity to change environments without fully understanding the ecological consequences of their actions.[23]

Carson was no Luddite; she did not call for the abolition of insecticides, pesticides, and herbicides, and in fact she highlighted their benefits. It was the *scope* of chemical applications that caused her concern.[24] She was convinced that the complexity of natural life — including the human body — virtually precluded our full understanding of what poisonous chemicals do once released into an ecological system. If, for reasons we do not understand, DDT killed mosquitoes but then birds ended up dying, or if 2,4-D and 2,4,5-T decimated ragweed but also poisoned bee colonies, then humans had reason to fear the worst for their own health and for that of the natural environment. This was the logic of *Silent Spring*, and Carson positioned her work as the antithesis to the worldview and business plan of chemical manufacturers and their customers. The companies themselves objected vehemently to this negative attention. The Monsanto Corporation, one of the major agricultural herbicide producers (and later a primary supplier of Agent Orange to the U.S. military), shot back at Carson with its own apocalyptic vision: a world *without* pesticides and herbicides. "The bugs

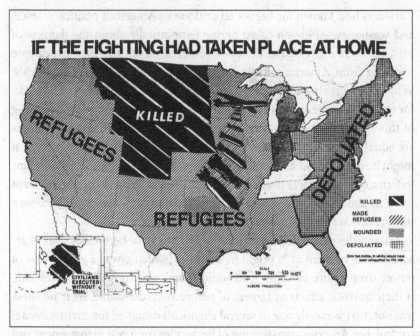

Figure 9 Carson's America in the antiwar era? The boundaries are based on mathematical ratios of Vietnamese population and land factored into U.S. proportions. This graphic appeared in the radical GI newspaper *Broken Arrow*, May 30, 1970. Folder A–E, GI Publications, Swarthmore College Peace Collection, Swarthmore, Pa.

were everywhere: unseen. Unheard. Unbelievably universal. Beneath the ground, beneath the waters, on and in limbs and twigs and stalks, under rocks, inside trees and animals and other insects — and yes, inside man."[25]

Carson died before the herbicide controversy in Vietnam began in earnest. She spent her final two years totally absorbed in the sensation (and uproar) caused by *Silent Spring* — all the while battling terminal cancer.[26] Although the timing of early news reports of herbicidal warfare could have reached Carson, there is no record of her commenting on the matter.[27] Still, Operation Ranch Hand manifested virtually all the warnings laid out in *Silent Spring*. By the end of the decade, it reached a scope even Carson could not have imagined, and it did so in a land far removed from rural America (figure 9).[28]

Operation Ranch Hand was an immense chemical warfare operation, and one directed explicitly at killing the flora of vast areas of land. By 1969 academic scientists began to denounce herbicidal warfare as an act of "ecocide," a word closely associated with "biocide," the word Carson leveled against "non-selective chemicals that have the power to kill every insect," with unknown effects on the larger ecosystem.[29] The scientists who studied and ultimately forced the termination of Operation Ranch Hand carried Carson's message forward into the era of Vietnam antiwar protest.[30]

The origins of explicit protest (rather than the implicit variety offered by Carson) against herbicidal warfare began almost as soon as the experimental defoliation missions in Vietnam became public. President John F. Kennedy authorized the herbicide operation with serious concern over the international repercussions that would likely arise in the communist orbit.[31] The concern was well founded: Moscow, Beijing, and almost all the world's communist foreign ministries issued statements decrying the "imperialist poison war" against the revolutionaries, or some variation of the theme. But the cold war's bipolar divide did not neatly contain such protest, as the president had assumed. Wilfred Burchett, an Australian journalist who worked for and identified with communist governments and their regional patrons, issued the first recorded denunciation of herbicidal warfare in *Novoe Vremia* (New Times) of Moscow. Titled "South Viet-Nam: War against the Trees," Burchett's article offered a unique perspective because he was "embedded" with Viet Cong guerrillas[32]: "To wage war against Nature as well as against the Vietnamese people adds a macabre element to the American intervention in Vietnam. Using Asians as victims for tests of new weapons fits into an all-too familiar picture which stretches from Hiroshima to the present nuclear weapons tests in the Pacific."[33]

Burchett, playing the "race card," emphasized the parallels between herbicidal and atomic warfare. He implied that the willingness of the United States to use these weapons stemmed from racism. The historian John Dower argues powerfully that racism explains the ferocity of fighting between Japan and the United States in the Pacific war, but his analysis cannot be transplanted to the case of Agent Orange.[34] No official U.S. document or statement on herbicidal warfare suggests anything hinting of racism. The analogy to Japan breaks down at another crucial point as well, as noted earlier: the South Vietnamese government was centrally involved in Operation Ranch Hand. Its leaders detested the NLF and were willing to deploy a number of fearsome weapons against the guerrilla fighters in order to remain in power. Burchett had to overlook this fact because it conflicted with his portrait of race war in Vietnam.

Not long after Burchett's early reporting, politicians in the United States raised their own concerns. Robert Kastenmeier, Democratic representative from Wisconsin and a longtime critic of chemical warfare, led a growing chorus of politicians to question the cost-benefit calculus of the defoliation program.[35] The congressman's letter to Kennedy in March 1963 also framed the "lessons" of World War II as central to American prudence with respect to herbicidal warfare in Vietnam. By citing President Franklin D. Roosevelt's famous denunciation of chemical and biological warfare in 1943, Kastenmeier reminded Kennedy that the United States did not use herbicides against the Japanese and urged him to cease defoliation operations on legal and moral grounds.[36] William Bundy, a State Department advisor to Kennedy and one of the key architects of the U.S. strategy of counterinsurgency in Vietnam, replied to Kastenmeier that there was no cause for concern: "Over 400,000,000 acres of land have been sprayed in the United States with 2,4-D and 2,4,5-T since 1947."[37] Although there is no record of Kastenmeier's response to Bundy, this figure may have given the congressman additional cause for concern.

Two weeks later, the *New Republic* produced the first editorial critical of herbicide operations. It explicitly rejected the "home use" theory, which government officials and scientists invoked to justify defoliating large swaths of land in South Vietnam. Government assurances that Operation Ranch Hand was safe and carefully controlled are "only true if one postulates an essential difference between something poisonous and something highly toxic." Domestic applications of herbicides, the editorial argued, are an insufficient analog because "they are hardly ever used in the concentrations and over the wide areas in which the large C-123 transport aircraft spray them over the Vietnamese countryside." Again the specter of nuclear weapons loomed ominously:

> Does not the use of such chemicals, particularly on Asians who already feel that the A-Bomb, too, was used only because Asia rather than Europe was the target, not outweigh in political adverse reaction whatever slim gains one might hope from their dubious military effectiveness?[38]

This early denunciation of herbicidal warfare from an "establishment" political journal reverberated through the scientific community. The board of the Federation of American Scientists (FAS) and its in-house journal, *Bulletin of the American Scientists*, were the first to raise the issue. In the October 1964 issue of the *Bulletin*, the FAS board implored its readers not to lose sight of apocalyptical dangers beyond nuclear weaponry. The FAS demanded that the U.S. government restrain itself from causing or fostering global catastrophe: "In view of the potential danger to our entire civilization from the development of biological and chemical weapons and in view of the specific disadvantages to the security of the U.S. . . . the [FAS] urges: that the President declare a policy of 'no first use' of chemical and biological weapons; that all mass production of biological weapons be abandoned; and that development of new biological and chemical weapons be stopped."[39]

The editorial surveyed the state of U.S. CBW research, questioned the overall military value of such weapons, and ended by condemning herbicidal warfare. Unlike government attorneys and military officials, the FAS considered defoliation in Vietnam an act of chemical warfare or a "proving ground for chemical and biological warfare."[40]

The following year, the AAAS took up the issue. The AAAS, whose representative scientists helped to force the termination of herbicidal warfare in 1971, was uniquely suited to support such an endeavor. From the organization's inception in 1848, AAAS members debated policy as much as scientific theory. Alexander Dallas Bache, AAAS president and great-grandson of Benjamin Franklin, declared in his 1851 address, "Science without organization is without power."[41] By the turn of the century, the AAAS was articulating its platform in the classic Progressive Era vocabulary of human health and lobbied the government for greater industrial regulation. After the atomic attacks on Japan in August 1945, the AAAS devoted much of its organization and political influence to two interrelated goals: checking American militarism and promoting "human welfare" through science. The organization's in-house journal, *Science*, provided a key forum for the debates sparked by Barry Commoner and others. These debates approached the nuclear controversy as part of a broader scientific "revolution" of technological domination of nature — one in which the boundaries between "peace" and "war" were increasingly blurred. In 1960 Commoner chaired the AAAS Committee on Science in the Promotion of Human Welfare. It was a misleadingly optimistic title, for the committee's guiding premise was grim: science can produce miracles, but in the wrong hands it can doom all life on the planet. Among the most disturbing of postwar scientific trends identified by the committee was the merger of science and the cold war:

The conscious exploitation of science for military advantage continues at an accelerating rate. But in recent years this process has merged with another, equally important trend; science is being pressed into the service of international politics. Scientific accomplishment per se has become an accepted — and at present dominant — factor of prestige among nations. The philosophy of "getting ahead" of the Russians (or Americans), which once referred only to military matters, now includes scientific achievements as well. This rivalry has strongly motivated the recent intensification of government support for scientific research.[42]

Commoner and the committee were denouncing government officials for co-opting science, and in doing so, they argued, the government was degrading the moral worth of scientific discovery. That the committee report ignored the fact that war and technology had coevolved for millennia suggests that the destructive capacity of nuclear weaponry represented unknown threats for which the past offered no guide. Further, the report stressed that the advent of nuclear, chemical, and biological weapons was symptomatic of a broader ethical lapse in the scientific community. Cold war nationalism had run roughshod over a human endeavor that should remain aloof from such considerations.[43]

Within the AAAS community, Commoner's human welfare committee made a lasting impression. Over the next five years, *Science* became the premier American forum for discussing all matters relating to science and ethics. Commoner's concerns over nuclear weapons, combined with Carson's critique of the chemical industry, spawned a cottage industry. Scientists from every discipline weighed in with articles and letters addressing such issues as poverty, military grants for university research, animal testing, government secrecy, and environmental degradation.[44] As a result of the herbicide controversy, the AAAS added a sister committee to the Human Welfare group called the Committee on Environmental Alteration.[45]

In 1965 the AAAS turned its attention to the Vietnam War. Scientific misgivings about the war represented a logical progression of the AAAS platform. Even at that early juncture — a time characterized by one authority as "confused or indifferent" about American actions in Vietnam — for many scientists the war was simply the next phase of a postwar trend toward technological militarism.[46] At the AAAS annual meeting in 1965, the Committee on Council Affairs released a resolution titled "Settlement of the Vietnam War." The last two paragraphs made the resolution unique among early antiwar platforms:

Prolongation of the Vietnam War, with its increasing danger of universal catastrophe, threatens not only the lives of millions, but the humanitarian values and goals which we are striving to maintain.

Beside this concern which we share with all citizens, we bear a special responsibility as scientists to point out the large costs of war for the continued vigor of scientific research. Like all scholarship, the sciences cannot fully flourish, and may be badly damaged, in a society which gives an increasing share of its resources to military purposes.[47]

Vietnam thus merged the two great concerns among politically active scientists over the previous twenty years. First, as an actual war — as opposed to the hypothetical one that mandated frequent nuclear testing in the preceding decade — the threat of escalation from regional (or "subtheater" in national security parlance) to general strategic war involving the Soviet Union, China, or both was inherently greater.[48] Second, even if the United States managed to avoid an escalation of the war to a global conflagration, the resources required to "win" — meaning the maintenance of a pro-American and capitalist South Vietnam — guaranteed ever more expenditures and an expansion of power for the "military-industrial complex."

In the summer of 1966, Bert Pfeiffer, a professor of wildlife biology at the University of Montana, raised the issue of herbicidal warfare as a topic of concern for the AAAS. A former Marine during World War II and the son of a wealthy Wall Street lawyer, Pfeiffer launched the scientific protest movement against Operation Ranch Hand. His earlier work followed a trajectory similar to Barry Commoner's. After completing his PhD at the University of California, Berkeley, Pfeiffer taught at Utah State University and the University of North Dakota. Both locales offered Pfeiffer an opportunity to study the fallout effects of nuclear testing. Utah's close proximity to Nevada's atomic-testing sites created widespread anxiety about nuclear fallout, while in North Dakota the agricultural sector voiced concerns over the exposure of farmland to strontium 90. Pfeiffer's widow recalled that in both states the problem was not merely academic: throughout the 1950s the Pfeiffers had powdered milk shipped in from California to feed their two young children.[49]

Pfeiffer first became aware of Operation Ranch Hand through newspaper accounts, not from government sources or scientific contacts. The key passage from his resolution reads: "Whereas, the effect of these [herbicidal] agents upon biological systems in warfare is not known to the scientific community, and . . . Whereas the scientific community has a responsibility to be fully informed of these agents and their use in warfare because they are a result of scientific research."[50] Pfeiffer's approach to herbicidal warfare mirrored Commoner's political platform: in the face of government secrecy and a myopic prioritization of cold war expediency over ecological wisdom, scientists had a duty to act. Although Pfeiffer protested the "Americanization" of the war from the start and actively cultivated the mantle of a scientific antiwar activist throughout the Vietnam era, his resolution was measured in the subdued tone of scientific concern.[51]

This was a tactical move — Pfeiffer well understood that adopting a more strident antiwar stance could kill the resolution at the committee level; further, the ultimate goal of conducting an independent investigation of the ecological effects of herbicides in Vietnam required the support and participation of U.S. military officials. Still, the resolution underwent substantial revision before reaching the executive council at the end of the year. Several AAAS members, including government scientists, rejected out of hand the idea of investigating and perhaps shutting down a wartime operation characterized by the U.S. military as instrumental to protecting American soldiers in Vietnam.[52] The executive council played down Pfeiffer's characterization of the matter as urgent, and most important, the council rejected his call for direct AAAS involvement to study herbicides and other CBW in Vietnam.[53]

As consolation the AAAS made sure that Pfeiffer's concerns reached the highest levels of government. In September 1967, Don Price, a dean at the Kennedy School of Government at Harvard and AAAS president, wrote a letter to Secretary of Defense Robert McNamara. Price explained that AAAS members

agreed that it would be in the public interest if more were known about the effects on the natural environment (and thus indirectly on the populations) of the agents employed to destroy crops and to defoliate jungles in the course of military operations in Vietnam. The directors do not consider the AAAS to be equipped to conduct such a study, and do not believe that any effective scientific study of the effects of such agents could be carried out in an active theater of war without military or other official permission and sponsorship. The Board of Directors therefore respectfully recommends that the Department of Defense authorize and support a study by an independent scientific institution or committee of both the short and long-range effects of the military use of chemical agents which modify the environment.[54]

The institution that Price had in mind was the National Academy of Sciences (NAS). His characterization of the NAS was half-right: compared to the AAAS the NAS was the "establishment" institution; membership was more exclusive, and the organization's mandate was far removed from the political activism central to the AAAS mission.[55] From a financial perspective, Price was correct; the NAS easily could have dipped into its discretionary funds to support a scientific mission to Vietnam. But the premise that the NAS was an independent or disinterested scientific body vis-à-vis CBW research was suspect. Since World War I, the academy had taken an active role in the development of America's chemical and biological weapons arsenal. More to the point, the herbicide research conducted at Fort Detrick during World War II likely would not have been operationalized without active input from the NAS.[56] The science journalist Philip Boffey has assessed the curious logic behind Price's suggestion, which appeared to elevate financial resources above impartiality: "The [NAS] was not, after all, serving as an adviser to the Vietnam spray campaign. But to the extent that there was an institutional bias at the Academy, it would tend to support a program that the Academy helped to foster."[57]

The letter McNamara received from the AAAS was not the first of its kind to reach a high-level government official. Although E. W. Pfeiffer was the initial scientist to push for an institutional protest of herbicidal warfare, other scientists through more informal means challenged the long-term wisdom of the program. In January 1966, twenty-nine scientists from Harvard University (including Matthew Meselson, who would chair the AAAS mission to Vietnam in 1970) and other Boston-area institutions sent a petition to the White House denouncing herbicidal warfare and calling for its termination. The petition labeled the program "barbarous" and tantamount to an "attack on the entire population of the region where the crops are destroyed, combatants and noncombatants alike."[58] The statement's attention to the apparent inability of Operation Ranch Hand to distinguish civilians from soldiers foreshadowed the term "ecocide" as Arthur Galston and others would use it later in the decade.

The White House did not respond to the petition. Following early critiques in the New Republic and among members of Congress, both Secretary of State Dean Rusk and Defense Secretary Robert McNamara had drafted stock answers in an NSC memorandum titled "For Use *Only* If Asked." The responses (some of which Rusk had delivered during a press conference in March 1965) would remain unchanged during the Nixon administration, when the herbicide controversy reached its apex: (1) the U.S. government does not consider herbicides to be in the same category as antipersonnel weapons, and they are therefore not prohibited by the Geneva Protocol of 1925; (2) herbicide sprayings in Vietnam are far more carefully controlled than the scientists assert; (3) the administration is actively reviewing the entire CBW program.[59]

According to a memo from White House aide Joseph Califano to Walt Rostow, Lyndon Johnson personally instructed his staff to ignore the scientists' petition.[60] We can only guess why the president chose not to address these concerns, but if his hope was that the issue would fade away on its own, Johnson badly misjudged. In early September 1966, twelve plant physiologists led by Arthur Galston sent a letter to the White House again urging Johnson to reconsider the herbicide program. The letter anticipated the president's likely agitation at being lectured on national security matters by academic scientists — a not unreasonable supposition given the president's proclivity to lash out at anyone who stood in the way of his agenda.

> We are aware that the issues in Vietnam are complex . . . There are deep divisions of opinion concerning the correct course of events for us to follow in that tragic part of the world. Thus, we do not presume to give you either political or military advice. We wish to address you only as socially concerned biologists with some claim to special knowledge of the effects of chemicals on plants.[61]

This prelude was too modest. As Galston later recalled, the real message was that government assurances of the overall ecological safety of Operation Ranch Hand had no scientific basis as long as the very biologists who knew the most about herbicide science were kept in the dark about the program.[62] The letter went on to explain ecological interconnectedness to the president:

> We would assert in the first place that even the most specific herbicides known do not affect only a single type of plant. Thus a chemical designed to defoliate trees might also be expected to have some side effects on other plants, including food crops. Secondly, the persistence of some of these chemicals in soil is such that productive agriculture may be prevented for years into the

future, possibly even after peace has been restored. Thirdly, the toxicology of some herbicides is such that one cannot assert that there are no deleterious effects on human and domestic animal populations. It is safe to say that massive use of chemical herbicides can upset the ecology of an entire region, and in the absence of more definite information, such an upset would be catastrophic.[63]

If the image of a catastrophe — one designed to conjure parallels to a nuclear catastrophe — was not enough, the letter concluded on a particularly poignant note. The scientists suggested that the food-denial component of the herbicide program would harm the weakest members of a society first; in other words, women and children would likely face starvation as a result of Operation Ranch Hand.[64]

Two weeks later, Galston received a terse reply from an assistant secretary of state stating that his concerns were unfounded. The scientists could not understand the situation because they were not in Vietnam to witness the effects of herbicide operations.[65] Given Johnson's original directive to ignore the petition, the president probably felt his choice to acknowledge it was sufficient to end the matter. The scientists, of course, lobbied for more than Johnson's attention. The White House response apparently missed the point that the scientists had attempted to convey. E. W. Pfeiffer's reason for lobbying the AAAS in the first place was to secure institutional (and less biased) heft to correct scientists' government-mandated ignorance of Operation Ranch Hand. The rebuff only steeled the scientists' determination to achieve peaceful solutions through scientific prudence.[66]

What can we make of the Johnson administration's stance? The most transparent answers are grounded in competing notions of sociopolitical priorities. First, in the middle part of the decade, scientists remained at the cutting edge of global environmental activism. As scholars have noted, environmental concerns framed at the planetary level did not begin until the late 1960s. This shift, which has been explained as a response to the NASA space program or Malthusian perceptions of global population growth, must also be understood in part by the confluence of rising antiwar protest and the shock of the "ecocide" wrought by herbicidal warfare.[67]

The Johnson administration did not conceive of a "global environment" as did scientists who connected Vietnam and the United States in ecological as well as political relationships. Further, Washington's official stance was in keeping with mainstream American thought.[68] Even Rachel Carson's

Silent Spring remained a warning rooted in nationalist sentiment propelled by visions of saving the American environment. To Johnson, who believed that refraining from nuclear warfare in Vietnam was prima facie a significant achievement for the cause of peace, the use of herbicides was an insignificant issue.[69] Unlike the strategic bombing of North Vietnam, Operation Ranch Hand had always been one of Johnson's inherited programs — and therefore beyond his purview. And so long as military commanders in the field extolled its virtues, dissenting voices would remain background noise.[70] Further, the protesting AAAS scientists were in the minority *within their own profession*. In one AAAS poll, only 5 percent of the respondents indicated that they would not participate in any research or development if the work was "directly relevant to [the] conduct of military operations."[71] In another survey, 89 percent of the scientific respondents called for the continuation of CBW research, and 81 percent supported the defoliation program in Vietnam.[72]

In a final attempt to satisfy the minority without offering what the scientists actually wanted — access to sprayed war zones — Defense Secretary McNamara contracted the Midwest Research Institute (MRI) of Kansas City to conduct a review of herbicides, which the NAS would review on completion. If the White House response was blunt, the Pentagon's plan suggested a wrongheaded assumption about what the critics of herbicidal warfare wanted. MRI was a private-sector research firm whose workers engaged almost strictly in library work. McNamara's mandate was for MRI to conduct a comprehensive review of secondary and unclassified literature relating to herbicide science; there would be no field work.[73] Meanwhile, the NAS would be saved from a potentially embarrassing conflict of interest; its assessment of the MRI final report would concentrate only on how well MRI gathered and assessed the extant literature.[74] John S. Foster, the Pentagon's director of the Defense Research and Engineering division, explained why the government assumed a positive outcome: "Qualified scientists, both inside and outside our government, and in the governments of other nations, have judged that seriously adverse consequences will not occur. Unless we had confidence in these judgments, we would not continue to employ these materials."[75]

Government officials and academic professors — even those who shared subspecialty research interests — were working at cross purposes when it came to herbicidal warfare in Vietnam. But on domestic issues the opposite was true. Foster's assessment was exactly right: in the five years since Rachel

Carson warned of herbicides and other agricultural chemicals in apocalyptic terms, there was no evidence that anything like what Carson imagined had occurred.[76] On this point, the academic scientists readily agreed. Arthur Westing, a forester and former professor at Windham College who became director of the AAAS herbicide mission to Vietnam, had admired the labor- and cost-saving benefits of herbicide use since the 1950s. Long before the herbicide controversy in Vietnam, Westing had worked for the U.S. Forest Service in Michigan, where he conducted forest-management experiments with compounds developed and supplied by Dow Chemical (a major producer of Agent Orange). When pressed to explain his general views of chemical control of agriculture and forests, Westing, also a former Marine, minced no words: "I had no problem at the time and no problem now."[77]

But the AAAS scientists contended that Operation Ranch Hand was different. First, the chemical companies such as Dow and Monsanto that supplied the U.S. military were operating around the clock to satisfy quotas for the domestic market and the Department of Defense.[78] By operating at full capacity, the chemical plants could not credibly guarantee the chemical purity of their product, with the result that dioxin, a toxic by-product that occurs during the production of 2,4,5-T, began to appear in Agent Orange as early as 1965. Hence that herbicidal compound became the most infamous among the "rainbow" herbicides and the reason for ongoing concerns about Agent Orange exposure and human health effects.[79] Second, the astounding rate of aerial application of herbicides in concentrations upward of ten times stronger than herbicides intended for domestic use ensured a tabula rasa understanding of the ecological effects of herbicidal warfare in Vietnam. Vietnamese flora and ecological characteristics, located on the other side of the planet, were entirely distinct from American farms and forests.

Arthur Galston explained the questionable value of the MRI review and any other substitute for onsite investigation: "When we spray a synthetic chemical from an airplane over a mixed population of exotic plants growing under uninvestigated climatic conditions — as in Vietnam — we are performing the most empirical of operations."[80] Subsequent to the publication of the report, Barry Commoner, who had been following the issue closely, was less subtle. At the 1968 annual AAAS meeting, he said the MRI report was "put together in sixty days by people who know nothing about herbicides."[81] Despite the official line being pushed by Pentagon spokesmen and the White House, John S. Foster of the Defense Department could not help but agree with virtually every point that AAAS members raised against the report. In a letter to AAAS president Don Price, Foster conceded that the long-term effects of Operation Ranch Hand were impossible to know and that it was certain that MRI reviewers would not have the last word on the subject.[82]

MRI hurriedly completed its two-month project in December 1967. The report offered a comprehensive review of all domestic and international uses of herbicides, which gave the overall impression that Ranch Hand was merely a military extension of established and accepted domestic practices of weed control. The authors offered an extremely mild and brief assessment of the ecological consequences of herbicidal warfare in Vietnam. The report devoted sixteen of three hundred pages to the issue and introduced the section on Vietnam by quoting a U.S. forestry official who observed, "The forests of South Vietnam have been devastated for many centuries. First nomadic or semi-savage people occupied the land and destroyed the forests without discrimination for centuries."[83] Of the effects of herbicidal warfare, the report cited Department of Agriculture and military assessments that argued that sprayed forest areas would experience a pause in plant succession "similar in some respects to that found in abandoned forest clearings."[84]

Because the NAS had agreed to review the MRI report exclusively in terms of what it was (a literature review, not a primary-source scientific investigation), its approval amounted to little more than an endorsement of MRI's capacity to gather and analyze secondary material and summarize the pertinent (and politically useful) writing on the topic.[85] Frederic Seitz, one NAS member assigned to review the report, explained why it was destined to leave AAAS members unsatisfied: "The [NAS] reviewers were not asked to consider the specific issue of how well or how fully the report responds to the questions expressed in the AAAS resolution of December 1966. Also they were not asked to endorse, approve, or reject the report."[86] Predictably, the report inflamed scientific opinion and confirmed suspicions that the military would rather mute the controversy than respond to it with a legitimate scientific undertaking.[87] Individual members of the AAAS complained that the MRI report offered no new substantive information. They again called for an independent investigation, this time emboldened with evidence that the government's main interest was to keep the scientists at arm's length. The AAAS board of directors issued a statement in *Science* on July 19, 1968: "Because large-scale employment of herbicides has taken place in Vietnam, and because questions of the long-term welfare of all the peoples of Vietnam are of great importance to the United States and other countries, we urge that steps be promptly undertaken to initiate long-term, on-the-spot studies of the regions of Vietnam affected by the use of herbicides."[88]

The statement called on the military to open its records on Operation Ranch Hand to independent researchers and urged the United Nations to lead a scientific mission to Vietnam. The Pentagon rejected both requests. It had no intention of declassifying its records in the midst of the war, and the UN was unprepared to take an active role beyond its numerous resolutions on the Geneva Protocol.

Again E. W. Pfeiffer pushed the AAAS to take the active role he had envisioned two years earlier. At this point, he approached the issue with a mixture of exasperation and satisfaction driven by evidence that his instincts had been right from the beginning. Based on the official response to the scientists' queries, Pfeiffer and his colleagues had every reason to believe that the military, with White House support, at the least did not want to bother with scientists conducting field research in active war zones and probably more perniciously, wanted to hide the true extent of the damage wrought by Operation Ranch Hand.[89] In late November 1968, Pfeiffer sent a letter to AAAS headquarters urging the board to reconsider his original proposal. As events of the past two years demonstrated, he wrote, only the AAAS boasted an untainted stance toward the herbicide controversy and the political connections in Washington to see a scientific mission through to completion.[90] This time the executive council accepted Pfeiffer's resolution. At the annual AAAS meeting in Dallas, the board passed the "Resolution Concerning the Study of the Use of Herbicides in Vietnam." The resolution

> determines that it shall be the purpose of the Association to bring into being the most effective possible field study of the potential long- and short-term risks and benefits to the ecology of Vietnam through the use of herbicides, and . . . specifically directs the AAAS staff to convene, as soon as possible, an ad hoc group involving representation of interested national and international organizations . . . to prepare specific plans for conduct of such a field study and with the expectation that the AAAS would participate in such a study within the reasonable limits of its resources.[91]

Why had the AAAS come around to support this unprecedented trip? On a prosaic level, the executive council arrived at the decision by default; no other organization could do what Pfeiffer had been demanding for the last two years. But in a broader sense, the council recognized a sea change in two interrelated social developments that converged around the herbicide controversy: antiwar protest and rising anxieties related to the massive destructiveness of modern war. As the historian Lawrence Wittner concludes in his expansive study of the American peace movement in the twentieth century, protestors had consistently mobilized based on "the realization that warfare had progressed to the point where it threatened global survival."[92] Even at the dawn of the nuclear age, some Americans were more concerned about the dangers of chemical and biological survival. Writing in 1947 in the UN journal *World*, retired Adm. Ellis M. Zacharias warned of impeding disaster: "There are today in the arsenals of several of the great powers, other absolute weapons, chemical, biological, and climatological, more devastating than the atom. They are capable of exterminating the last vestige of human, animal, and even vegetable life from the face of the earth. *These weapons exist. They are being manufactured right now* . . . Furthermore, unlike the atom bomb, they are of such a nature that smaller nations with limited industrial facilities are in a position to develop them."[93]

Twenty years later, this hyperbolic scenario was reincarnated from global dystopia to real, urgent focus on a particular region.

E. W. Pfeiffer and his colleagues had repeatedly emphasized that Vietnam proved this calamity could happen even in the absence of nuclear weapons. Supporting a scientific mission to Vietnam thus offered the AAAS the opportunity to parlay rhetoric on scientific ethics into political action. In so doing, the executive council — well aware of rapidly expanding scientific concern on CBW research — decided finally to throw its support behind Pfeiffer and his colleagues. Ad hoc committees and authors in the United States and Europe devoted to stopping CBW proliferation would be watching the herbicide commission closely (figure 10).[94]

The scientists who protested herbicidal warfare must be understood within the broader spectrum of antiwar protest in the United States. We might call them "boutique" protesters because they concentrated their efforts not on the war in general but on a particular battlefield tactic. By contrast, Students for a Democratic Society and members of the New Left in general took the opposite tack: they sought to cast the Vietnam War in its entirety as a moral and political disaster.[95] Unlike Martin Luther King Jr. or George Kennan, the scientists did not frame their activism in opposition to broader socioeconomic inequalities. Nor did they paint the American war in Vietnam as a criminal, neo-imperialist enterprise, as did radical writers

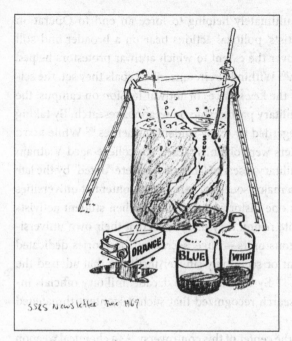

Figure 10 Anticipating the AAAS mission: South Vietnam dunked in Agent Orange. Reprinted from *Science and Social Responsibility Bulletin*, June 1969.

such as Gabriel Kolko. This is not to say that the protesting scientists did not share these sentiments to varying degrees. As professors on university campuses, the scientists were not oblivious to the widely felt antiwar sentiment among their students.[96] None of the scientists were willing to associate their work with more extreme or violent student activism relating to Vietnam and the "hijacking" of science.[97] But they were heartened to see environmental activism flourishing on college campuses, where numerous groups seamlessly critiqued domestic environmental problems and defoliation in Vietnam.[98]

As one student put it during a special congressional session on antiwar upheaval, "The campus unrest has many problems at its base: war in Southeast Asia; poverty; environmental pollution; racism; and the endless rhetoric. None of these by itself would find any broad support on campus but the coalition of them together has brought many students into campus dissent."[99] Even the Sierra Club, once focused exclusively on domestic environmental issues, weighed in on the herbicide controversy. Shortly after the scientists returned from their AAAS mission in Vietnam, the Sierra Club published a statement urging Congress to halt herbicidal warfare and end production of other chemical warfare agents.[100]

By challenging and ultimately helping to force an end to Operation Ranch Hand, the scientists' political actions bear on a broader and still hotly contested debate over the extent to which antiwar protestors helped to end the Vietnam War.[101] Within the circumscribed goals they set, the scientists addressed one of the key sources of antiwar tension on campus: the full-blown university-military partnership on weapons research. By taking this stance, they were regarded by many students as heroes.[102] While ROTC and CIA campus recruiters were obvious targets for college-aged Vietnam War protestors, secret military research laboratories were "outed" by the late 1960s and had become a major source of campus discontent at universities all over the country. As one historian has noted, "When student activists peered into this recondite realm, they discovered that their own universities contained incongruous units — huge, secretive laboratories dedicated to weapons development or seemingly sinister institutes that advised the Pentagon war machine."[103] By the end of the decade, military officials involved with campus research recognized that such discontent threatened the entire enterprise.[104]

Agent Orange was at the center of this controversy. As a chemical weapon employed by the U.S. military in Vietnam in staggering quantities, herbicides provided a bridge between weapons in actual use and those being developed for hypothetical future wars. Despite government assurances that herbicides should not even be considered part of America's CBW arsenal, student activists on campus saw no such distinction. In the fall of 1965, students at the University of Pennsylvania learned that top administrators had been collaborating with the U.S. military to develop a wide array of counterinsurgent weapons, including incapacitating agents (riot gas), biological weapons, and more-potent herbicides under the code name Spicerack. The ensuing student protest, organized in part by the radical Gabriel Kolko, demanded that the university divest itself of all CBW contracts with the military.[105] If antiwar protest in general suffered from a lack of specificity, students at Penn were able to direct their energy toward a precise target: their own university, as opposed to the more elusive "military-industrial complex" or the impossibly vast federal government. In a foreshadowing of the herbicide scientists' fortunes upon their return from Vietnam, students at Penn forced the termination of the Spicerack program in 1967.[106]

As "boutique" protestors on campus, the scientists also focused attention on the herbicide manufacturing industry, particular Dow Chemical of Midland, Michigan. In addition to manufacturing Agent Orange, Dow was the principal supplier of napalm to U.S. forces in Vietnam, and it was that weapon that first made Dow one of the most notorious members of the "military-industrial complex" in the eyes of antiwar protestors. Napalm is as simple a weapon as herbicides are complex. Developed at Harvard during World War II, it is a jellied gasoline that is ignited and heaved at its target; those caught in its path suffer horrific burns.[107] There was (and still is) no international law prohibiting its use or the use of any type of incendiary weapon in war. Yet this was an unimportant distinction to those who viewed Dow Chemical as the corporate embodiment of American atrocities in Vietnam. In 1967 the leftist historian Howard Zinn succumbed to an irresistible pun with a pamphlet titled *Dow Shalt Not Kill*. Citing Dow's onerous record of supplying U.S. forces with napalm and herbicides, the pamphlet was an impassioned defense of the civil liberties of students to keep Dow research and job recruiters off campus.[108]

Beginning in 1967, students at MIT, the University of Pennsylvania, and elsewhere routinely protested Dow's presence on campus. In Washington, D.C., that year, college students ransacked the offices of Dow. This act of vandalism symbolically linked Dow with draft-board offices that were similarly vandalized around the country.[109] Dow officials strenuously objected to such treatment. Dow president Herbert Doan noted that it supplied chemicals to the U.S. military as a patriotic duty, not for profit. "As long as the U.S. is involved in Viet Nam," he declared in November 1967, "we believe in fulfilling our responsibility to this national commitment of a democratic society."[110] For the "military-industrial complex," or at least representative officials of that amorphous entity, the goal was to win the Vietnam War with the best available weapons. It was a rationale inimical to the protestors' worldview: to the herbicide scientists and those who supported their work, the question of what it would take to win in Vietnam was no longer answerable. By the late 1960s, the political and military benchmarks traditionally used to end war — such as those that concluded the war in the Pacific against Japan — seemed inapplicable in Vietnam.[111] For those concerned about the proliferation of chemical and biological weapons, a more immediate question loomed: what damage had herbicidal warfare wrought in Vietnam?

Since 1964 the question of the effects of herbicidal warfare remained an ecological curiosity — and fear — among a small but growing group of academic scientists. After years of bureaucratic stalemate and government resistance, those scientists were ready to find out for themselves.

CHAPTER SEVEN

SURVEYING A
CATASTROPHE

THE AMERICAN WAR IN VIETNAM was not the first to create widespread ecological damage in that country. The Japanese occupation during World War II devastated Vietnamese forests. In keeping with Japan's main goal to extract the maximum amount of natural resources from Indochina, Imperial soldiers clear-cut fifty thousand hectares of tropical hardwoods from South Vietnamese forests. Additional destruction caused during the period of anticolonial resistance against the French (1945–54) led one American observer before the U.S. war to liken the state of Vietnam's forest and its human dependents to "a very sick patient which we must save and tend with great care."[1] For the protesting herbicide scientists, such sentiment sharpened in the wake of herbicidal warfare in a biodiverse (and largely unstudied) region.

The dominant ecological characteristic of South Vietnam (today, the southern area of reunified Vietnam) is the Mekong Delta, a region of tributaries and alluvial (silty) floodplains that boast fantastically fertile soil, earning the region's nickname as "rice basket" of Southeast Asia. Below Saigon (Ho Chi Minh City as of 1975), the Mekong River empties into the Pacific Ocean, completing a 2,700-mile trek beginning in the Tibetan plateau of China, winding through Burma, Thailand, Laos, and Cambodia before reaching Vietnam's delta floodplains. To the north and east are a wide variety of evergreen and more humid deciduous forests. To the coastal south of the Mekong lie vast tracts of swampy mangrove forests (figure 11).

In drier regions, pine dominates.[2] The humid areas north of Saigon host a great diversity of flora, which is typical of equatorial forests around the

Figure 11 Vam Sat Mangrove Sanctuary, Vietnam, refoliated after herbicide attacks. Author's photo.

globe.[3] South Vietnam belongs to a larger monsoonal system of the South China Sea. The rainy season, which can produce up to eighty inches of rain, extends from May to November, followed by a dry period that ends the following spring. Seasonal and regional moisture variation creates red, yellow, and gray soils throughout the region with differing levels of acidity and fertility. In tilled lands, these soil varieties can support hundreds of staple crops and fruits.[4] To the north, near the ancient imperial city of Hue and the former demilitarized zone at the seventeenth parallel, lie the central highlands. The mountain ranges run north to south and host many of the region's densest tropical forests, which have been cut back over thousands of years to make room for terracing (hill farming) peanuts and corn. The area also produces commercial products for export such as rubber and coffee.[5]

Official figures estimate that southern Vietnam is home to 2,500 unique species of fish, reptiles, birds, and mammals.[6] The diversity of South Vietnam's flora and fauna ensures that no ecological generalizations can be made of the region. Or rather, the only generality is that South Vietnam's environment is atypical with respect to the astonishing diversity of its ecosystems as expressed in land area relative to other regions.[7] Vietnam's biodiversity is more impressive when one considers the human imprint on the country's environment. The region has not been "pristine" for the last four thousand years. As a recent study notes, many areas in Vietnam "are among the oldest continuously modified environments in the world."[8]

The scientists who protested herbicidal warfare knew this well. They were not motivated by a desire to "save" some imagined ecological Eden devoid of human influence.[9] It was the very *presence* of human (or civilian) habitation of massively sprayed areas that exercised the scientists' collective conscience over the danger posed by Operation Ranch Hand. Arthur Galston, the Yale biologist, underscores the point in his statement that introduced the term "ecocide" to the modern lexicon:

> It seems to me that the willful and permanent destruction of environment in which a people can live in a manner of their own choosing ought similarly to be considered as a crime against humanity, to be designated by the term *ecocide* . . . At the present time, the United States stands alone as possibly having committed ecocide against another country, Vietnam, through its massive use of chemical defoliants and herbicides.[10]

Toward the end of the 1960s, U.S. Army officials decided on a different approach to assuage mounting scientific concerns about herbicidal warfare. This development emerged by default; earlier attempts to stonewall or even mislead the scientists who feared an ecological catastrophe had failed to deflect attention from Operation Ranch Hand. If anything, the strategy backfired. Military officials thus offered to authorize ecological analyses of the herbicide program conducted by government scientists. In January 1968, C. E. Minarik, director of the plant science laboratory at Fort Detrick (a longtime site of military herbicide research), presented a paper at the annual northeastern weed control conference. The presentation anticipated the publication of the MRI report by several days.

Minarik's paper strongly emphasized the military value of herbicidal warfare and discounted the possibility that Vietnam would sustain long-term ecological damage. Minarik also cited some unforeseen benefits of defoliation: he claimed that Operation Ranch Hand helped boating purveyors who could spot potential clients along defoliated riverbanks. The paper also emphasized the safety of Agent Orange and other herbicides for human contact and characterized Ranch Hand almost as a civic or development project in the works: dead trees would make excellent charcoal (the main cooking fuel in rural areas); defoliated areas could be plowed under; and cleared brush could improve conditions for communication and electricity lines.[11]

The respected industry journal *Chemical Week*, citing an unnamed source in the Pentagon, wrote that Minarik's bosses in the Defense Department had rejected his original paper in toto.[12] Although this information could not be verified elsewhere, there is little reason to doubt its authenticity. Minarik's original assessment likely doubted or contradicted the Pentagon's repeated assurances of the ecological safety of Operation Ranch Hand. John Foster, director of the Defense Research and Engineering Program at the Pentagon, summarized this position: "Qualified scientists, both inside and outside our government, and in the governments of other nations, have judged that serious adverse consequences will not occur. Unless we had confidence in these judgments we would not continue to employ these [herbicidal] materials."[13] Foster did not identify these scientists; certainly Bert Pfeiffer and his colleagues did not know of them. The problem with the statement was that Pentagon officials lacked confidence in their judgments. If they had been certain, the protesting scientists would have gained access to the sprayed areas in 1968, not 1970.

Internal communication between the NAS and the AAAS in May suggested the dubiousness of the Minarik report. Harold J. Coolidge, executive director of the NAS, wrote to Dael Wolfle, AAAS executive officer, regarding a trip he took to Vietnam in January. The official purpose of the trip, led by a scientific education mission of the U.S. Agency for International Development (USAID), had nothing to do with herbicide research. But Coolidge independently discussed the matter in private with his Vietnamese colleagues who worked for the Government Forest Service and the Ministry of Agriculture. "I was made strongly aware," he wrote to Wolfle, "of the deep concern over the fact that thousands of acres of forest and crop land are being affected . . . No one knew what the long-term effects of these poisons would be, *and no one was aware of any scientific research studies being made in South Vietnam to determine these effects.*" Coolidge went on to encourage the AAAS to support an independent research mission. Although RVN scientists would risk termination or worse by embracing such an investigation, they were receptive to the idea if it were to happen.[14] Since 1966 E. W. Pfeiffer had been motivated largely by suspicion. Now it was becoming clearer that Pentagon assurances of ecological safety were baseless if there were no studies that could reliably support the claim. The executive officer of the AAAS had reason to vindicate Pfeiffer's calls for investigation.

For Wolfle, Coolidge's revelation was all the more disconcerting when military officials disclosed that herbicide spray craft were using a rice-killing compound that contained pentavalent arsenic (Agent Blue, in Ranch Hand's rainbow schema). The chemicals that comprise Agent Orange, 2,4-D and 2,4,5-T, had proven less effective as killers of grassy, or non-broadleaf, plants. In July the AAAS demanded that the Pentagon cease spraying Agent Blue for two reasons. First, the large-scale destruction of the staple of the Vietnamese diet struck the scientists as a particularly odious threat to civilian sustenance; second, arsenic — unlike Agent Orange — was a confirmed poison. The Pentagon rejected the AAAS call, citing the use of arsenical herbicides on American cotton and tobacco farms and sticking to the Kennedy-era assumption that NLF guerrillas could not be defeated as long as they had reliable sources of food.[15] A board of directors meeting in October suggested a major shift since E. W. Pfeiffer's original resolution had been met tepidly by AAAS members. At this later juncture, twelve of the board's thirteen members supported a resolution stating that the Pentagon had no basis for its claims of the overall safety of Operation Ranch Hand.[16]

One of the key factors that propelled the herbicide controversy was a lack of communication between civilian scientists and the military. This problem was symptomatic of a broader divide between the military-political decision making in Vietnam and domestic society.[17] The scientists were not simply demanding access to sprayed areas in South Vietnam; they wanted to know what ecological accounting the U.S. military had conducted to support their safety assurances. Until the fall of 1967, there was no credible basis to such claims. Only then did officials in the U.S. embassy and in the military agree to conduct an ecological survey, which would be delayed five months by the Tet Offensive.[18]

To be sure, MACV kept precise logs and analyses of Operation Ranch Hand. In conjunction with the U.S. embassy, military officials commissioned exhaustive herbicide reviews and statistical and narrative analysis to determine the mission's military worth.[19] Additionally, the Pentagon contracted RAND and other defense corporations to provide socio-statistical analyses and herbicide data sets — essentially information that could be fed into a computer.[20] Although these studies were useful to mathematicians, anthropologists, and military theorists, they were of little value to biologists. The protesting scientists' beliefs about the tactical value of Agent Orange remained outside their professional purview.[21] What they wanted to know about the effects of herbicidal warfare, as Barry Commoner explained in a letter to the editor of *BioScience*, existed at the cellular level of plants, animals, and humans.[22] Commoner also took the opportunity to reformulate his nuclear politics in accord with the herbicide controversy. For those who claimed that Operation Ranch Hand saved the lives of U.S. soldiers, Commoner questioned why nuclear weapons could not be used for the same purpose.[23]

In January 1968, the U.S. ambassador to South Vietnam, Ellsworth Bunker, created the interagency Herbicide Policy Review Committee, the first to examine ecological effects as an explicit category for analysis. At the behest of the State Department, the task fell to Fred Tschirley, a tropical ecologist and assistant chief of the Crops Research division of the USDA. Tschirley was an expert in the field who enjoyed respect among his academic colleagues, and his strong public critique of the MRI Report suggested he would not allow his government employment to influence his scientific assessment.[24] Tschirley spent a month in the field beginning in mid-March 1968. Even before the results of his trip became known to the AAAS, the fact the trip took place at all was something of a victory for Pfeiffer and his colleagues — it demonstrated that the military had the logistical capacity and political willingness to support a scientific mission in hostile areas.

MACV civil relations officers shared portions of Tschirley's report with the press the following fall, and in January 1969 the full report appeared in the AAAS's own *Science*.[25] The basic conclusions of an advance story and the full report were identical, suggesting that Tschirley's findings accorded with the Pentagon's official assessments. The report was comprehensive, heavily footnoted, and above all a *biological* study of herbicidal warfare based on Tschirley's examinations from the air, land, and sea in many of South Vietnam's most heavily sprayed areas. The principal findings of the report are paraphrased below:

1. Due to high levels of atmospheric humidity, widespread denuding of ground vegetation would likely not result in a catastrophic loss of soil moisture; therefore a transition from rain forest to semiarid plain or even desert was unlikely.

2. Soil laterization (or hardening), which leads to soil erosion, is a real threat to any tropical soil that is exposed to excessive solar radiation and wind — as was the case in defoliated areas. Approximately 30 percent of soil in South Vietnam was experiencing this process at various stages.

3. Compromised soil, in conjunction with sunlight that can hit the forest floor after triple canopy rainforests become defoliated, are ideal breeding

grounds for bamboo, *imperata* grasses, and other invasive species that thrive in soil too poor for dominant species. Thus, it was not the herbicides themselves that would prevent forest regeneration but rather the ecological process that an herbicide attack unleashes. This was the case in both inland semideciduous forests and mangrove swamps, where even weedy species had trouble regenerating and thus more complete devastation resulted.

4. Soil, plant, and animal samples measuring the toxic prevalence of herbicides suggested no long-term impact on health for humans or animals. Tschirley concluded the report emphasizing the preliminary nature of his findings and hedging: "The defoliation program has caused ecologic changes. I do not feel the changes are irreversible, but complete recovery may take a long time."[26]

The report neither vindicated nor dismissed the scientists' concerns; Tschirley's analysis provided ammunition for both the staunchest critics and the strongest supporters of herbicidal warfare. It galvanized more scientists to support an AAAS mission.

Shortly before Tschirley's report became public, the AAAS received encouraging news from the State Department. In response to the AAAS statement in July calling for independent scientific investigation, Charles (Chip) Bohlen, an undersecretary of state, expressed his almost wholesale support for the AAAS position: the ecological effects of herbicidal warfare remained unknown and therefore deserved investigation. Bohlen was influenced by the logistical success of the Tschirley mission to move through the region's dense and war-torn sprayed areas. The State Department and the AAAS disagreed only on timing. The State Department wanted to delay a mission until some ill-defined future date; the scientists, seeing no foreseeable end to the war, advocated that studies begin immediately.[27] Dael Wolfle followed this communication by cultivating relations with the Department of Defense.[28] In October the AAAS board hosted a panel featuring Tschirley, Minarik, and other military scientists, and Wolfle gained a contact in the Pentagon's Defense Research and Engineering division whose duties included oversight of the herbicide operations in Vietnam. As Wolfle well understood, no amount of politicking within the AAAS would influence actual policy without improved military-scientific relations.

E. W. Pfeiffer considered this progress too slow. For Pfeiffer, the scientist responsible for launching AAAS involvement in the herbicide controversy, patience was not a virtue. The urgency of the matter was central to Pfeiffer's entire platform — and 1968 was already shaping up to be the most intense period of herbicide spraying to date. Operation Ranch Hand had doubled expenditures over the previous year.[29] Pfeiffer's continuing insistence had won him the chance to go to Vietnam a year prior to the AAAS herbicide commission. After Pfeiffer wrote several letters to the USDA criticizing the herbicide research it had conducted in Vietnam, one exasperated official challenged him to conduct his own field study to find shortcomings in the government studies.[30] With the tepid support of the Departments of State and Defense, Pfeiffer took up the challenge along with Gordon Orians of the University of California at Berkeley. Supported by the Bala Cynwyd, Pennsylvania-based Society for Social Responsibility in Science (SSRS) and Barry Commoner's Scientists' Institute for Public Information, Pfeiffer and Orians commenced their trip one year after the Tschirley mission.

Pfeiffer and Orians spent two weeks in Vietnam, the maximum their budget and academic responsibilities allowed. Their report, published in the SSRS *Bulletin*, differed from Tschirley's analysis in several respects. Pfeiffer and Orians agreed that the evidence thus far could not correlate direct evidence of herbicide toxicity to animals. Yet they tempered this uncertainty (which continues to the present day), observing that it would be difficult to determine a correlation, let alone causality, of herbicide toxicity to humans in a battlefield environment that offered no scientific controls for determining exposure and subsequent linkage to various illnesses.[31] As the SSRS editors noted in their accompanying analysis, Vietnamese scientists did not even know the chemical composition of the herbicides. More obvious was the catastrophic toll taken on wildlife in areas particularly sensitive to herbicide attacks, particularly the coastal mangrove forests. There Pfeiffer and Orians observed severely diminished or absent populations of bird and terrestrial wildlife. One of the few animals they found thriving were tigers. The great carnivores had learned over decades of war to associate gunfire with dead bodies to be scavenged.

The scientists also noted extreme variance of forests based on the number of times a given area was sprayed. A single spraying allowed for fairly quick regeneration of the dominant species, but following multiple sprayings vulnerable seedlings and weakened trees experienced massive die-offs. These dead zones, some hundreds of acres across, were unexceptional — the point of Operation Ranch Hand, after all, was to keep the leaves off the trees. Pfeiffer and Orians also found that areas surrounding defoliation targets sustained significant ecological damage as well, thus offering solid evidence

Figure 12 E. W. Pfeiffer with Vietnamese colleagues Le Anh Kiêh and Le Chi
Tanh, Saigon, 1969. Original photo in E. W. Pfeiffer papers, Missoula, Mont.

that herbicide drift spread the chemicals well beyond areas thought to be
under NLF control. The evidence was particularly strong on rubber plantations (some along the Cambodian border), whose valuable products ensured that those areas were off limits to direct herbicide attack.[32]

The report suggested that overall assessments of the ecological effects of herbicidal warfare defied precise (or objective) quantification.
Where Tschirley — who had toured many of the same areas as Pfeiffer and
Orians — saw "little" evidence of long-term damage, the latter claimed the
total effects were *"very* severe." These conclusions, based on expert infer-
ence, brief assessments, and a hurried aggregation of data, were colored by
the unique perspective of the scientists.

For Pfeiffer, the brief trip was a positive step toward strengthening international scientific collaboration (figure 12). In a sense, he went to swap
knowledge: Americans scientists knew the precise chemical makeup of the
herbicides but little about their effect on ecosystems. Their Vietnamese colleagues had it the other way around. Pfeiffer concluded that continuing lack
of interest or outright criticism among scientists at home and a policy of
military secrecy abroad were an embarrassment to the United States.[33]

Pfeiffer returned to the United States and almost immediately found himself embroiled in a scientific debate about his activities. At a news conference at the New York Hilton, Pfeiffer described how he had come under fire during a river trip. He estimated that without the improvements of lateral visibility afforded by defoliation, he likely would have been killed.[34] Given Pfeiffer's extreme interest in ending herbicidal warfare, it was an inauspicious way to introduce his findings. After several highly critical letters to the editor in *Science* needled Pfeiffer on the point, the zoologist from Montana finally put the issue to rest in February 1971. He pointed out that the AAAS herbicide mission of August 1970 had also come under heavy fire in a completely defoliated mangrove swamp. Pfeiffer backpedaled, suggesting his press account was anecdotal and did not offer a demonstrable correlation between herbicide spraying and the diminished ability of NLF fighters to launch attacks.[35]

At the end of the decade, the protesting scientists had made significant inroads among their departmental and research colleagues. In step with dwindling domestic support for the Vietnam War, what had seemed radical in 1966 was steadily evolving toward centrism in 1970. At the end of that year, for example, Senator Charles Goodell of New York—once considered an "establishment" Republican—famously sponsored legislation to cut off all funding for the war.[36] But did the newly available evidence vindicate the scientists' concerns? In addition to disagreements over the military effectiveness of herbicidal warfare—which Pfeiffer had repeatedly insisted remained beyond his purview—fellow scientists attacked his methodology, questioned the validity of his findings based on merely two weeks of field work, and suggested that an academic scientist had no business protesting wartime tactics, especially in wartime.[37] Fred Tschirley was subjected to none of this criticism—not because his research was demonstrably more solid than Pfeiffer's, but because his purpose did not defy government policy.

One critic shared Pfeiffer's moral qualms but challenged his investigative focus. In July 1970, William Haseltine, a graduate student in biology at Harvard (who went on to found Human Genome Sciences, Inc.) wrote to *Science* accusing Pfeiffer of failing to study the greatest potential danger posed by herbicidal warfare: massive genetic mutation and cancer among human populations exposed to Operation Ranch Hand sprays.[38] It was not a fair critique: Haseltine based his concerns on disconcerting data relating to the potential toxicity of Agent Orange, about which Pfeiffer knew nothing before or during his research trip.[39]

In 1969 Haseltine became privy to information suggesting that government officials were suppressing information about the teratogenicity (a cause of birth defects) of 2,4,5-T — the compound that comprised half of Agent Orange. During the fall semester, Haseltine ran a lecture series in his department at Harvard, where he hosted Anita Johnson, a young law student and a member of "Nader's Raiders," Ralph Nader's consumer advocacy group in Washington, D.C. In the summer of 1969, Johnson had received a secret report titled "2,4,5-T: Teratogenetic in Mice" from Dr. Marvin Legator, chief of the Genetic Toxicology Branch of the Food and Drug Administration.[40] In September Johnson passed the report to Haseltine, who shared it with Matthew Meselson, professor of molecular chemistry at Harvard and soon to be director of the AAAS Herbicide Commission. Haseltine recalled thinking, "If this stuff causes teratogenesis in animals, it's probably very bad for people. If we can get this story out, maybe that will stop the use [of Agent Orange]."[41] With this straightforward logic, Haseltine helped end the use of Agent Orange in Vietnam.

For Haseltine the story came full circle on a personal level; he had grown up on a military base in California where his father worked on weapons technologies. Through Matt Meselson, Haseltine connected with Michael Klare, a young scholar affiliated with the American Friends Service Committee (AFSC) and founder of the National Association on Research of the Military-Industrial Complex (NARMIC).[42] With Klare's input, Haseltine embarked on a speaking tour around the country. As a self-described New Leftist, Haseltine espoused a platform that melded CBW and antiwar protest more fluidly than his academic mentors did. "I knew about the defoliation program," Haseltine recalled, "but nobody knew it was harmful to people; they knew it was harmful to trees. But any edge I could get to try to turn people against the war and to understand that they were supporting it through their own activities — taxes — and they knew that science was being misused, I used."[43]

In January 1970, Haseltine broke the story in the *New Republic*, in an article cowritten with Arthur Galston and Robert Cook, one of Galston's graduate students at Yale. The story was a bombshell: if it was disconcerting that government officials had information suggesting the human health dangers associated with Agent Orange, the depth of the cover-up was damning. In June 1966, Bionetics Research Laboratories, a private company working under government contract, informed the National Cancer Institute (NCI) that female lab mice injected with small doses of 2,4,5-T gave birth in very high ratios to offspring with birth defects.[44] The NCI sent the results back to Bionetics, where workers made another disturbing finding: in massive doses 100 percent of female rats produced stillborn or mutated babies. At this point, the NCI involved the surgeon general, the National Institutes of Health, representatives from the National Academy of Sciences, and government liaison officials from Dow and other chemical corporations. Everyone involved agreed to sit on the report.

It is not clear if representatives at the meeting agreed to make a concerted effort to keep the findings private, or if they merely assumed that a leak was inevitable.[45] More certain is that Dow and other chemical executives rejected out of hand the Bionetics findings, arguing that the laboratory doses were of far higher concentrations than was the case in any "real-world" applications. As Dow vice president Julius Johnson asserted, "If we thought 2,4,5-T was harming anybody we'd take it off the market tomorrow."[46] Five months later Dow claimed that dioxin, a toxic by-product created during the production of 2,4,5-T, was likely responsible for the mutations — not the herbicide itself.[47] As a preventive move against the company's liability, this was a key distinction, albeit one that made little difference to American soldiers and Vietnamese exposed to Agent Orange.[48] For the time being, available data in Vietnam suggested no correlation between the incidence of birth defects and Agent Orange exposure.[49]

Matthew Meselson was well positioned to force government action before Haseltine's story broke. His work with fellow biochemist Franklin Stahl in the late 1950s on DNA replication effectively launched the field of modern genetics.[50] In 1963 President Kennedy invited Meselson to join the Arms Control and Disarmament Agency. With the help of his friends and fellow Harvard colleagues Henry Kissinger and McGeorge Bundy, Meselson quickly became one of Washington's best-connected scientists. Initially Meselson's supervisors assigned him to study tactical nuclear weapons — a topic about which he "knew nothing" — as he recalled, and so he turned his attention to chemical and biological weapons. His bosses soon learned that he had no interest in contributing to their proliferation. Meselson was motivated to protest CBW by a simple proposition: "Modern war should be kept as expensive as possible." Unlike nuclear weapons, CBW were relatively cheap and easy to produce and therefore strong candidates for unchecked proliferation.[51]

Back at Harvard in October 1969, Meselson called Lee A. DuBridge, a physicist and science advisor to President Richard M. Nixon. Meselson asked for an explanation for the apparent Bionetics cover-up. DuBridge promised that he would look into the matter. Meanwhile, Bryce Nelson, a reporter for the *Los Angeles Times*, had learned of the story, and somehow the White House had learned of Nelson's plans to publish his findings. In an attempt to preempt a major embarrassment before Nelson's article appeared, DuBridge released a White House statement promising "a coordinated series of actions . . . by the agencies of Government to restrict the use of the weed-killing chemical, 2,4,5-T . . . The actions taken will assure safety of the public while further evidence is being sought."[52] In Vietnam DuBridge vaguely pledged that Operation Ranch Hand planes would use Agent Orange in "areas remote from population."[53] Yet government policy did not move as swiftly as DuBridge's statement suggested: 2,4,5-T applications in Vietnam and domestically continued unabated until the following spring. A letter from a USDA official to the AAAS provides insight into the sluggish official response:

> As you know, the herbicide 2,4,5-T is a major production tool, which has increased food production in the United States and abroad. Farmers use this herbicide to protect their crops against the devastation caused by weeds and brush, and to increase the production of pastures, rangelands, and grain crops. These increased yields have been used to reduce hunger in some of the developing countries, and to contribute to our "Food for Freedom" program. We believe it would be extremely unfortunate to permit those opposed to the war in Vietnam to center their anxiety in the defoliation program, and through the improper use and interpretation of the results of such a preliminary toxicological study, achieve cancellation of the use of an important agricultural tool, which has been so effective in increasing food supplies in the world, and in reducing the loss of lives through enemy ambushes in Southeast Asia.[54]

Bureaucratic slowness notwithstanding, many government officials believed that the threats posed by Agent Orange did not justify a forfeiture of the benefits (real or perceived) it created. The chemical industry agreed.[55] So continued the decades-long debate between proponents of scientific ethics and advocates of the short-term expedience of business and politics. For the herbicide controversy, the critics of Operation Ranch Hand would soon prevail. Reminiscent of Barry Commoner's public health victory against atmospheric radiation, the Bionetics cover-up and subsequent health scare associated with Agent Orange set the course for the end of herbicidal warfare.

In April 1970, the federal government moved in a concerted effort to limit human exposure to 2,4,5-T, both in the United States and in South Vietnam. The secretaries of Agriculture, the Interior, and Health, Education, and Welfare jointly announced the "immediate suspension" of the herbicide "for uses around the home and on lakes, ponds and ditch banks . . . [and] on all food crops intended for human consumption." The suspension did *not* affect the domestic use of 2,4,5-T for control of weeds in managed forests and range lands or other areas remote from sustained human contact.[56] The domestic ban closely paralleled restrictions on herbicidal missions in Vietnam. Initially the Department of Defense claimed that Operation Ranch Hand aircraft never sprayed Agent Orange in populated areas and therefore herbicide tactics would be unaffected.

But the claim was absurd: there was no way to draw neat boundaries between sprayed and civilian-inhabited areas. By distinguishing the areas suspected of NLF activity from those known to be occupied by people — as if the guerrilla soldiers were not human — the Pentagon was implicitly suggesting that NLF exposure to a potentially toxic chemical conformed to official U.S. policy. Such reasoning raised the problematic question of whether Agent Orange was a type of chemical weapon banned by the Geneva Protocol of 1925. As will be examined in the following chapter, the AAAS scientists successfully convinced the SCFR to follow this line of reasoning. In anticipation of further problems, the Department of Defense changed its policy on 2,4,5-T in Vietnam in accord with the April announcement. Deputy Secretary of Defense David Packard ordered a total suspension of Agent Orange "pending a more thorough evaluation of the situation."[57]

What had changed in the six months since the Bionetics cover-up to force the policy shift? In the interim, scientists at the National Institute of Environmental Health Sciences determined that pure 2,4,5-T was also found to cause deformities in lab mice subjected to massive and repeated doses.[58] This meant, potentially, that it would be harder to blame the health scare on isolated "bad batches" of 2,4,5-T that contained dioxin due to workers' failure to follow safety protocols. Still, Dow continued to defend its product.[59] On a philosophical level, nevertheless, the finding was a major vindication of the protesting scientists, whose main contention had always cited lack of knowledge as sufficient cause to end herbicidal warfare.[60]

At this point, the AAAS found itself in a unique position: the U.S. government was following (or at least acting in accordance with) AAAS lobbying efforts with respect to Vietnam. A resolution written by E. W. Pfeiffer for the

AAAS annual meeting in December 1969, titled the "Scientists Committee on Chemical and Biological Warfare," read almost identically to Lee DuBridge's statement in October calling for the restriction of 2,4,5-T.[61] This shift was reflected at the institution's highest levels as well. A draft letter from AAAS president Walter Orr Roberts to Ambassador Ellsworth Bunker the previous January omitted Roberts's original assurance that herbicides "appear to provide significant military advantages."[62] In a political atmosphere supported by a degree of convergence between the scientific protestors and government officials, such niceties were unnecessary and likely counterproductive to the AAAS mission to end herbicidal warfare. Most promising was Ellsworth Bunker's positive response to the proposed AAAS research trip. As Roberts reported to the AAAS board, the U.S. embassy in Saigon had taken to heart Fred Tschirley's proposal for a large-scale ecological study of herbicidal warfare, thus assuring AAAS leadership that the AAAS was the only institution capable of supporting such a mission.[63]

The logistics that would make the AAAS Herbicide Assessment Commission (HAC) come to fruition began at the AAAS annual meeting in December 1969. By then Matthew Meselson had agreed to lead the mission. The position was more political than scientific. Meselson, a biochemist, had no expertise in tropical ecology, but his handling of the Bionetics controversy and demonstrated capacity to command attention in Washington made him an obvious choice for the job. Walter Roberts had praised Meselson's "statesmanship" in support of his appointment. Meselson requested and received, "with enthusiastic support," fifty thousand dollars for HAC start-up costs.[64] A widely respected scientist traded on his political capital by securing total autonomy over the HAC mission in South Vietnam. In a letter to Dael Wolfle, Meselson laid out the terms of his chairmanship of the mission: "I will have complete authority over the conduct of the work and over staff and consultants; that I may involve persons in this study without regard to nationality or affiliation; that I expect to obtain cooperation of the Department of Defense; that I also hope to obtain information and assistance from Vietnamese on both sides; and finally, that my responsibilities will end after twelve months."[65]

Almost immediately Meselson demonstrated his capacity to forge cooperation over a highly sensitive issue. On the one hand, he appointed Arthur Westing — among the most determined and outspoken critics of Operation Ranch Hand and its corporate suppliers — as chair of the HAC; on the other, Meselson obtained assurances of cooperation from officials at Dow.[66] In keeping with Meselson's agenda, in March the Pentagon formally announced its decision to support the HAC — likely because of Ambassador Ellsworth Bunker's keen interest in seeing the mission through. At this point, Defense Department officials abandoned spurious claims that military assessments of herbicidal warfare had sufficiently demonstrated the ecological safety of the program; in light of the Bionetics imbroglio claims to the contrary would have appeared preposterous or cynical. As an assistant secretary of defense acknowledged, the HAC would be the first "systematic study" of the damage wrought by Operation Ranch Hand.[67]

By June 1970, the HAC had made significant progress in preparation for its Vietnam trip in August. The first goal was to ensure a smooth and comprehensive trip. Coordinated by the U.S. embassy in Saigon, the Departments of State and Defense navigated the logistical maze required to get the scientists into the country and then to sprayed areas.[68] The second was to amass all available information on herbicides. To that end, Meselson convened a conference at Woods Hole, Massachusetts, in mid-June, to which he invited American and European academic, private industry, and government authorities on all aspects of herbicide ecology and potential human health effects. The conference assembled a comprehensive research plan for the HAC. Meselson asked John Constable, a French-speaking surgeon at Massachusetts General Hospital, to join the mission and spearhead the commission's health-effects studies in Vietnam. Constable put together a questionnaire to distribute to village leaders in sprayed areas to determine when and where locals had come into direct or secondary contact (through consumption of plants and animals) with herbicidal chemicals. Other conference working groups devised a research plan to study ecological effects on forests (with particular emphasis on the highly susceptible mangrove stands), soil nutrition and composition, and the crop-destruction program, with special emphasis on the sociological and economic impact sustained by farming communities targeted by Operation Ranch Hand.[69]

Although it was never the official intent of the HAC to lobby for the end of the herbicide program, this was the result. It would take the impassioned congressional testimony of the protesting scientists following the HAC trip to create a formal mechanism to end herbicidal warfare for all time. To prevent such a prohibition, the U.S. military took steps prior to the HAC mission to minimize the scope of Operation Ranch Hand. Officials cited budgetary constraints as the reason for cutting Ranch Hand spray sorties and diverting C-123 and other spray aircraft to other duties.[70] The timing of

MACV's decision vis-à-vis the planned HAC mission was too convenient in a period of wartime de-escalation — and inconsistent with earlier rumors relating to the phase-out of the program.[71] If the U.S. military could no longer keep the effects of herbicidal warfare from public scrutiny, it could at least minimize the program and perhaps temper the scientists' reactions. This was not to say that military officials lost their appetite for the tactical benefits afforded by herbicidal warfare. As Operation Ranch Hand sorties decreased, they were replaced by Rome plows, massive bulldozers that leveled vast forest areas — essentially an extreme form of defoliation with none of the controversy associated with chemical warfare.[72]

On July 27, 1970, the HAC departed Boston for Paris. Meselson, Constable, and Westing were joined by Robert Cook, a graduate student of Arthur Galston's and self-described "gopher" of the HAC. Cook, who coauthored the *New Republic* article with William Haseltine, would go on to become the director of the arboretum at Harvard. He had an academic pedigree that positioned him well for the job: he had first met Meselson as an undergraduate at Harvard, and Arthur Galston recommended him for the position.[73] In Paris, thanks to arrangements made by E. W. Pfeiffer, the group was met by Alexandre Minkowski, a prominent French biologist, and Buu Hoi, science advisor to President Ngo Dinh Diem, who had fled South Vietnam after Diem's assassination. Buu Hoi had first supported Diem's decision to approve herbicidal warfare but had since come to regret that decision. The HAC members spent three days in Paris talking with Vietnamese expatriates and French scientists familiar with the herbicide controversy.

On August 1, the group landed in Saigon, where they were greeted by officials from USAID. Over breakfast the following morning, Meselson underscored the sensitive (and apolitical) nature of the mission. He told his team to avoid all contact with antiwar Buddhists, "left-wing subversive types" of any nationalities, and the press.[74] As a guest of a consortium of official American agencies in Vietnam, Meselson wanted to distance the HAC from all overtly antiwar activities. If the HAC was operating at least implicitly on an antiwar platform, Meselson wanted to avoid any embarrassments that could impede the scientific investigation. In a meeting with Ellsworth Bunker two days later, Meselson was relieved to hear the ambassador reiterate his interest in and support for the mission. Still, Bunker's interest was hardly a golden key; MACV officials, although cordial, would not give the scientists the "time of day." The scientists had requested and were denied the opportunity to fly on a Ranch Hand mission. They also failed to access

Figure 13 Matthew Meselson (left) and Arthur Westing touring destroyed mangroves in a swift boat under ARVN guard, south of Saigon, August 1970. Herbicide Assessment Commission slides, Matthew S. Meselson Papers, Department of Biological Sciences, Harvard University, Cambridge, Mass.

Ranch Hand documents relating to all aspects of the program, including flight logs and types and concentrations of herbicidal chemicals sprayed in a given area. MACV officials claimed legitimately to be caught in a chain of command that made declassifying materials on an ad hoc basis virtually impossible.[75] To make matters more difficult, the scientists found their Vietnamese colleagues willing to help, yet they were woefully uninformed about even basic facts relating to herbicidal warfare.

If the scientists met a wall of silence regarding military documentation of Operation Ranch Hand, government agencies (South Vietnamese and American, including the transport outfit Air America) more than compensated by facilitating transportation logistics and providing letters of introduction and invaluable advice about how to navigate throughout the war-torn country. By plane, helicopter, jeep, and swift boat, over the next month the scientists surveyed nearly every major region that had sustained herbicide attacks (figure 13). Given the scope of Operation Ranch Hand, whose planes had sprayed a seventh of the entire country, the scientists prepared for a month-long tour of most of the country. The HAC objective valued breadth over depth. In the allotted time, and under the assumption

Figure 14 Dr. John Constable interviewing hamlet chief, Tay Ninh Province. Herbicide Assessment Commission slides, Matthew S. Meselson Papers, Department of Biological Sciences, Harvard University, Cambridge, Mass.

that the research would only begin the monumental task of a full ecological and epidemiological study of herbicidal warfare, the scientists moved about quickly. In several sprayed areas beyond Saigon, they harvested soil and animal samples, interviewed village chiefs, and took lateral and aerial photographs of the environments most dramatically affected by herbicide sprays (figure 14).

In Saigon the scientists spent most of their time investigating potential causation of the high incidence of human stillbirths and malformations. The chasm they discovered between anecdotal evidence of adverse effects on animals in rural sprayed areas and hard data suggesting the same for humans continues to this day. Robert Cook's meticulous diary detailing an interview with rural farmers starkly suggests that the Bionetics report had indicated the real ramifications of actual herbicide use.

August 13, 1970

We drove up to Phu Cuong where we met the cantonment [ARVN military] forester, Nguyen Tri Phuong, very nice man who spoke English quite well and who escorted us most of the day. We drove north up to Beu Cat where we spoke with the deputy administrative chief, Nguyen Cao Tuan. He spoke of the spraying of Lai Kai hamlet, Lai Kai village, Beu Cat district. He said it was sprayed several weeks ago. Of the 10,000 chickens in the hamlet, 5,000 were subsequently sick and about 1000 chicks died. Of the 200 pigs, 100 pigs were sick and 15 died. The chickens did not eat and, upon death, they ran in circles. We drove to the village and saw that defoliation had taken place. Five weeks ago because many dried leaves were still hanging on trees. About 10–20% of the trees were defoliated, all *Autocarpus integrifolia* (jackfruit) looked defoliated. They were still alive, but it was too soon after the spraying to tell if the trees would die. We had Coke in the village and then walked to the home of a lady whose chickens had been affected. She had lost 80 or so. Some of the lower leaves of the banana [trees] were dead, the leaves of mangos were shriveled, and her vegetables were affected. We estimated that the plane flew high because the swath was 500 meters wide. We looked at her chickens; they were all in cages, well covered, and we found that they always remained in these cages. The sides were open to the air. She showed us a separate cage in which were sick chickens, one of which could not stand. I inspected it closely; its feathers were in poor shape and it could have had any disease. Thus we were left with the impression that everything we could verify was verified and the chick-pig situation had to be taken on their word. We thanked the lady and left.[76]

What did the reported catastrophic losses in farm animal populations mean for human beings? As far as the scientists could tell, the reports meant little from a human epidemiological perspective. As the HAC report noted in its section on herbicide toxicology in South Vietnam, stillborn rates over the past ten years had actually *decreased*, while the incidence of congenital deformities, even in the most heavily sprayed areas, did not appear to correlate with exposure to Agent Orange.[77] Conversely, the findings did not vindicate oft-repeated assurances of the safety of herbicidal chemicals to human exposure. If anything the trailblazing work conducted by the HAC highlighted how little data existed to support any view of the health effects of Agent Orange. Hospital record keeping in the chaos of war-torn Vietnam was neither modern nor well organized. Available data and actual data were simply not the same. Compounding the confusion was the Pentagon's steadfast refusal to disclose what Meselson later called "the most basic information we need[ed] — a list of areas sprayed, and when, and with what."[78] Without this information, evidence of the health effects of herbicidal warfare would be no more solid than the claims of the chicken farmer who complained to Robert Cook.

The scientists did confirm that, whatever the actual health effects of Agent Orange, the U.S. military had failed to isolate spray missions from civilian-occupied areas. The attempt to do so assumed such distinctions were feasible in a war with no fixed fronts and against an enemy whose entire strategy centered on the guerrillas' ability to operate among village populations. It was civilian exposure to herbicides that most offended the HAC: if the question of human health effects remained fuzzy, the collateral damage sustained by Vietnamese exposed to Operation Ranch Hand attacks was obvious, particularly the crop-destruction program's impact on civilian nutritional needs.[79] Upon returning to the United States with soil samples and human breast milk in tow, Meselson and his team wrote letters to high government officials, including MACV Commanding General Creighton Abrams, Ambassador Bunker, and Secretary of State William Rogers. The letters included detailed information that challenged stated military policy of conducting Ranch Hand missions only in areas devoid of civilians.[80]

The controversy surrounding the Bionetics report weighed heavily on the HAC report. E. W. Pfeiffer's calls four years earlier for independent scientific investigation centered on his concerns for the long-term impact of herbicidal warfare on the Vietnamese environment, not its people. But the HAC mission took on a new urgency when not merely plant life but a potential human health disaster was at stake. Even if the mission ended inconclusively with regard to human health effects, its members confirmed the massive and potentially irreversible damage sustained by the ecology of South Vietnam. The journal *Science* outlined the mission's principal findings, as reported at the 1970 AAAS annual meeting in Chicago:

- One fifth to one-half of South Vietnam's mangrove forests, some 1400 square kilometers in all, have been "utterly destroyed," and even now, years after spraying, there is almost no sign of new life coming back.

- Perhaps half the trees in mature hardwood forests north and west of Saigon are dead, and a massive invasion of apparently worthless bamboo threatens to take over the area for decades to come.

- The Army's crop destruction program, which seeks to deny food to enemy soldiers, has been a near total "failure," because nearly all the food destroyed would actually have been consumed by civilian populations, particularly the Montagnard tribes of the Central Highlands.[81]

The greatest potential damage discovered by the scientists was a phenomenon they dubbed "nutrient dumping." When triple-canopy forests experience a massive die-off of leaves following a defoliation mission, the soil on the forest floor becomes saturated with decomposing matter and is unable to absorb nutrients supplied by leaves when they fall at normal rates. In monsoonal forests, rainfall ensures runoff and soil leeching and erosion, thereby compounding the difficulty of floral refoliation and the survival of animal species dependent on the surrounding plant life.[82]

With the HAC report, media attention to the herbicide controversy reached a new level. Protest against Operation Ranch Hand, which began almost immediately following the program's launch, focused on the murky details of herbicidal warfare and consequent need for greater understanding. In lieu of the U.S. military's willingness to open its activities to independent scrutiny, critics international and domestic, lay and scientific, based their concerns on assumed rather than confirmed dangers. The HAC report shifted the criticisms toward defiant confidence. The science reporter for the *Boston Globe* called Ranch Hand — even in its period of decline — a "juggernaut out of control."[83] A reporter for the *London Times* called the herbicide sprays "rains of destruction."[84] *New York Times* columnist Anthony Lewis railed against Pentagon assertions of the economic benefits created by herbicidal warfare as "grimly cynical and factually incorrect."[85] An underground socialist newspaper deployed a disturbing sexual metaphor to describe herbicidal warfare.[86] A group of biology professors and students at Stanford went so far as to extrapolate herbicidal warfare as tantamount to the "destruction of Indochina."[87] Aerial photographs taken by the HAC showing before-and-after views of forests targeted by Ranch Hand, which appeared in the *Washington Post*, the *New York Times*, and the *Los Angeles Times*, seemed to confirm these characterizations (figure 15).

By far the greatest efforts to publicize and denounce the "ecocide" of Vietnam came from the scientists themselves. This work has engaged the scientists throughout their careers and into retirement. Their long interest in the controversy conforms to their earliest beliefs that a full reckoning of the legacy of herbicidal warfare would be a decades-long process. Arthur Westing, HAC chair and the most prolific scientific critic of herbicidal warfare, immediately began publishing about his experiences after his return home. Although his main research interests were in forestry studies, his articles examined the effects of Operation Ranch Hand with titles that often suggested a flair for the dramatic.[88] In the early 1980s, Westing became

Figure 15 Before and after: unsprayed (top) and sprayed (bottom) mangrove forests. Herbicide Assessment Commission slides, Matthew S. Meselson Papers, Department of Biological Sciences, Harvard University, Cambridge, Mass.

a fellow at the Stockholm Institute for Peace Research Studies, where he wrote two books on the subject and helped create the nascent study of environmental warfare.[89] Today in retirement, Westing continues to work as a consultant on issues relating to international conflict and the environment.[90] E. W. Pfeiffer, who pioneered the involvement of the AAAS in the herbicide controversy, never participated in herbicide research as an official representative of that organization. Pfeiffer was the most overtly antiwar scientist among the group, and the AAAS board thus viewed him as too polarizing a figure and kept him at arm's length. As his widow, Jean, recalls, the AAAS never considered Pfeiffer to be "one of their own people."[91] Yet Pfeiffer remained interested in the subject until his death in 2005. With Westing and other colleagues, Pfeiffer authored the book *Harvest of Death* in 1972, which detailed the impact of herbicidal warfare in Vietnam, and in subsequent years he published frequently on the topic. In 1982 Pfeiffer directed the documentary *Ecocide: A Strategy of War*, which included much of his own footage of sprayed areas.[92]

Matthew Meselson and John Constable coauthored one article in the Sierra Club's *Bulletin* on their work in Vietnam; both then moved on to other pursuits.[93] Meselson agreed to chair the HAC mission on the condition that his appointment would end in twelve months. He made good on that agreement. Constable, a plastic surgeon by training, has since become one of the field's leading skeptics regarding the correlation of Agent Orange exposure to the dozens of life-threatening health ailments that Vietnam veterans and Vietnamese nationals have blamed on that herbicide. Constable, whose involvement in the controversy began with his expectation to find such causation, has concluded that the data simply does not correlate — even though recent studies have demonstrated conclusively the persistence of dioxin-contaminated 2,4,5-T "hot spots" throughout South Vietnam.[94] As Constable emphasized when pressed to recognize *any* Agent Orange–related illness as is the policy of the U.S. government: "You have to remember, when the Vietnam Veterans came back to the country, they were not the heroes of World War I and II; they got a pretty raw deal . . . The least we can do is bend over backwards to help them medically, to give them the benefit of the doubt, even if a proper scientific study doesn't have a doubt to give."[95] In Constable's view, there is no meaningful evidence that proves a human's death or life-threatening illness can be blamed on Agent Orange, yet causation and medical support are *not* mutually exclusive.

Among the protesting scientists, Arthur Galston engaged with Operation

Ranch Hand primarily on a philosophical and political level. It was Galston, coiner of the term "ecocide," who most systematically positioned the herbicide controversy within the broader Vietnam-era debate of science and social responsibility. Galston felt special concern as an educator working within a broader higher-education debate over the moral interaction of science and politics. In his 1969 presidential address to the Botanical Society of America, he stressed this point as an entrée to explaining his interest in the herbicide controversy:

> To anyone teaching in a university or college in the United States or anywhere in the Western world, one of the key words of everyone's conversation has come to be *relevance*. Students are questioning as never before the relevance of their studies to the real world outside the academy . . . Should we be concerned by a generation "turned off" by science? . . . Must we in any way respond to the cries of those who are disaffected with the present order? I suggest that to ignore the requests for dialogue from a large or even small group of our student colleagues in educational adventure is not only impolite, possibly arrogant, but also dangerous. For when discontent is not channeled into proper constructive pathways, violence and destruction frequently occur.[96]

Galston, a self-proclaimed admirer of the "middle way" of Scandinavian socialism, made good on his pronouncements and worked hard at transnational scientific cooperation across the cold war divide. His trips to China and Vietnam in the 1970s yielded long-term educational partnerships between American scientists and their Asian colleagues beyond the herbicide controversy.[97] Galston liked to joke that he, not Richard Nixon, was actually the first American to "open" China in 1972. Back home in New Haven, in 1977 he developed Yale's curriculum on bioethics, for which the introductory course remains among the most popular on campus.[98]

In 1964, when scientists first learned of Operation Ranch Hand, they understood immediately that the unprecedented scope of the program — both in terms of the use of chemicals in war and as a variant of agricultural and forestry weed control — would ensure that the ecological and epidemiological legacy of herbicidal warfare would remain a source of scientific curiosity long after the war's end. But in 1970, upon the return of the HAC to the United States, its representative scientists and their colleagues faced a far more urgent matter: stopping Operation Ranch Hand and preventing herbicidal warfare for all time. Such a feat required the scientists to step fully into the political arena to face down both the Nixon administration and a Pentagon bureaucracy intent on retaining Agent Orange for future conflicts. The scientists, well aware of the novel role they were assuming, saw an opportunity to make amends with the scars of the Vietnam War, both abroad and at home. They also began to see themselves as historical actors, presented with a special opportunity to change for the better the course of America's "military-industrial complex." Jeffrey Race, a political science professor and a former U.S. Army officer, captured well the scientists' mood — and their own sense of importance — as imagined in an eco-political dystopia set one hundred years in the future:

> Reflective investigators in the year 2072 will draw the following propositions: that the richest and most powerful nation of the late 20th century used the resources of modern science to frustrate the social revolution in a poor and distant land; that, with little protest from men of science, many of the discoveries intended to advance health and agriculture production were turned to the purposes of human misery and crop destruction; that chemical substances, whose long term effect on human life is unknown, were loosed in staggering and heretofore unprecedented quantities by whites upon Asians; that the political — and presumably moral — leaders of the powerful nation, when questioned about their actions pursued a policy of lies, half-truths, and studied evasions.[99]

Thanks to a major miscalculation of Richard Nixon's new policies on chemical and biological warfare, the scientists seized an opportunity to halt this imagined future of "studied evasions." Following a battle between the U.S. Senate and the White House over the next several years, ecocide would become prohibited under international law.

CHAPTER EIGHT

AGAINST PROTOCOL

FORTUITOUS TIMING allowed the protesting scientists to help end herbicidal warfare for all time. The HAC members and their colleagues found an unwitting ally in President Richard M. Nixon. By attempting to ratify the Geneva Protocol of 1925, the president aimed to showcase American global leadership to stop the proliferation of chemical and biological weapons. Fresh from their trip to Vietnam, the HAC scientists and their colleagues pivoted off Nixon's policies by demonstrating that Operation Ranch Hand made the United States not a leader but a pariah. The question came down to whether herbicidal warfare constituted chemical and antipersonnel warfare and was therefore prohibited by the Geneva Protocol. The Nixon administration, fixated on the grand designs of Great Power politics and contemptuous of its domestic critics, did not initially give the issue much thought: previous administrations considered herbicidal warfare outside the prohibitions of international law, including the protocol. To the bafflement of Nixon and his advisors, the scientists rebuked the legal rationale that separated antiplant from antipersonnel weapons. Arthur Galston and his colleagues convinced a sympathetic SCFR that ecocide violated the letter and the spirit of the Geneva Protocol. To gain the Senate's consent to ratify, U.S. policy would first have to renounce the first use of herbicides in war.

In his first foreign-policy report to Congress in 1970, President Nixon declared, "The postwar period in international relations has ended." He then proceeded to lay out his plan for American leadership in a period of global flux. Nixon sought to overhaul the assumptions that had guided U.S. cold war policy since the Korean War. Rising tensions between the Soviet Union and China, along with the war in Vietnam and waning influence within the Atlantic Alliance, convinced Nixon and his national security advisor Henry Kissinger that the cold war could no longer be defined as a global struggle waged by two monoliths.[1] Kissinger's realist approach to foreign affairs, combined with Nixon's long-standing reputation as an anticommunist hardliner, heralded an opportunity for the United States to foster cooperation and political dialogue with cold war allies and enemies alike.

In the strategy that Nixon termed "a structure of peace," a budding détente with the communist world could offer a way out of Vietnam by enhancing U.S. diplomatic and military flexibility and thereby diminishing the war against communism in Vietnam as the dominant symbol of American resolve in the cold war.[2] Central to this strategy was disarmament, which the administration defined on two levels: (1) international reduction in strategic stocks of nuclear, chemical, and biological weapons; (2) massive withdrawal of American troops from Indochina to be replaced by the American-supported Army of the Republic of Vietnam and a new round of negotiations with the North to end the war.

In recognition of the Soviet Union's achievement of "strategic parity," or capability to inflict unacceptable damage to the United States and its allies, the president initiated an ambitious plan to slow the nuclear arms race with the Soviets by shrinking existing stocks and pledging limits on the development of new weapons systems. Nixon was equally intent on curbing America's chemical and biological weapons arsenal, which had proliferated since the 1950s when Pentagon strategists had looked to bolster the deterrent value of nuclear weapons.[3] At this relatively late juncture in the superpower competition, the Nixon disarmament initiative recognized the United States' limited capacity to contain communism abroad and accepted that it was safer to accommodate rather than challenge Moscow's strategic and political power on the world stage.[4] Thus the cold war would continue, albeit in a way that would militate against a crisis that could erupt into strategic nuclear war.

On November 25, 1969, the president issued a sweeping statement on U.S. policy on chemical and biological warfare based on a major interagency review (the first undertaken in fifteen years) by the NSC, the Departments of State and Defense, and the Arms Control and Disarmament Agency (ACDA). Nixon reaffirmed the long-standing policy that the United States would not be the first nation to introduce chemical weapons in war, but he vowed to keep a chemical arsenal solely for retaliatory (and hence, deterrent) purposes. Citing the "massive, unpredictable and potentially uncontrollable consequences" of biological weapons, the president renounced all forms of biological warfare and directed the Department of Defense to dismantle its offensive bacteriological program.[5] Finally, the president pledged to submit the Geneva Protocol of 1925 to the Senate for its advice and consent to ratification. The White House regarded the Geneva Protocol as a political and strategic capstone to its disarmament initiative; it was the premier international treaty prohibiting the use of chemical and biological weapons in war. By taking bold policy moves in the field of nuclear, chemical, and biological disarmament, the Nixon administration hoped to establish the executive branch as the sole government entity with the authority to interpret the Geneva Protocol. Nixon sought to frame its ratification as a symbol of American leadership for global peace and security.[6]

Yet as an unintended consequence, Nixon's resubmission of the protocol for ratification generated a congressional referendum for U.S. policies on chemical and biological warfare, including the military use of chemical herbicides in Vietnam. Letters to the White House praised Nixon's initiative while at the same time urging the president to include herbicides under the prohibitions mandated by the Geneva Protocol.[7] Some observers assumed that Nixon's initiative would spell a quick end to herbicidal warfare in Vietnam.[8] The impact was broader than that: by opening up the CBW debate, Nixon accidentally set the stage for the intersection of two major political formations in which herbicidal warfare stood front and center. Launched under Kennedy earlier in the decade as part of the United States' determination to enforce cold war containment by any means necessary, to its critics Operation Ranch Hand had come to symbolize the failings of containment and the importance of recognizing new forms of security beyond the cold war divide. By the late 1960s, the United States' massive and ecologically destructive use of Agent Orange in Vietnam had engendered an effective campaign to halt herbicidal warfare for all time. At the forefront were the AAAS-affiliated scientists lobbying in Congress, who were offended by the war in general and disturbed by their newly acquired firsthand knowledge of the deleterious effects of herbicides on the people and nature of Vietnam.

During hearings before the SCFR, the protesting scientists indicted the environmental destruction of Vietnam's forests and cropland as a shortsighted and counterproductive endeavor. Rather than containing communism in Indochina, it would only harm and alienate the very people whose "hearts and minds" the United States had hoped to win. More important, they argued, the United States must recognize that banning herbicidal warfare would help maintain the precarious balance between global population growth and the natural resources required to sustain it.

If the protesting scientists were careful to limit their lobbying efforts to nonmilitary analysis, they displayed no such hesitation when it came to interpreting international law. Before Matthew Meselson accepted the job as HAC mission chair (seven months prior to Nixon's CBW announcement), the Harvard professor had proved to be a strong leader on CBW issues on Capitol Hill. J. William Fulbright, chairman of the powerful SCFR and outspoken opponent of the Vietnam War, invited Meselson to Washington in April 1969 to share his views on the subject with the committee. Meselson testified that chemicals designed to be nonlethal could threaten catastrophe simply because they are cheap and easy to produce. He further argued that the first step toward meaningfully preventing CBW proliferation must begin by self-enforcement. U.S. ratification of the Geneva Protocol would serve the cause of disarmament only after the United States halted chemical warfare in Vietnam and renounced the use of chemical weapons in future wars. Meselson knew that herbicides and other chemicals had proved destructive on their own; in future wars — with or without U.S. participation — they could be a prelude to even greater devastation:

> As long as wars continue to be fought with high explosive weapons and napalm, what sense does it make to maintain special constraints on CBW? . . . We realize that special rules are required for nuclear weapons. The distinction between conventional weapons and nuclear ones of any size is a real one, and the importance of maintaining it is generally understood. Chemical and biological weapons share with nuclear ones potentially overwhelming destructiveness . . . Once developed [they] can be exceedingly cheap, relatively easy to produce, and quick to proliferate. They would threaten civilians especially.[9]

In testimony before the Senate committee, Meselson went on to link the inherent danger of CBW proliferation and the "myth" that the nonlethal chemicals employed by the U.S. military in Vietnam were humane. First, in his view the designation of a nonlethal chemical bore no relation to what is "humane" — one need not die to suffer. Second, the parsing of terms and interpretations eroded the enforcing capacity of the Geneva Protocol and other international legal agreements to prevent the proliferation of *lethal* CBW agents.[10]

Since his days at the ACDA, Meselson had found himself at odds with many government and military officials on CBW policy. In 1964 retired Brig. Gen. J. H. Rothschild published *Tomorrow's Weapons*, a ringing endorsement of chemical and biological weapons as benevolent alternatives to their nuclear and conventional counterparts. In this formulation, CBW were humane because they could either destroy the enemy's capacity to fight or kill surgically the fewest people to achieve maximum tactical advantage. Meselson's review of the book dismantled the logic of "humane" CBW by demonstrating that, even if wars could be won using novel weapons that neither kill people nor destroy cities, the success of such tactics could just as easily ensure the proliferation of CBW among smaller powers (and rogue states) eager to acquire cheap and easily deployable weapons.[11] As Meselson saw it, by 1970 Rothschild's dreams were becoming a reality in Vietnam. J. W. Fulbright accepted Meselson's logic. In February 1970, the senator wrote to Nixon urging the president to break from his predecessors on the conduct of chemical warfare in Vietnam.[12]

The preemptive move did not work. In an attempt to minimize and deflect rising political attention from opposition to chemical warfare in Vietnam following Nixon's announcement, the administration affirmed that the scope of the Geneva Protocol did not extend to herbicides or chemical riot-control agents (another name for tear gas, used widely by the U.S. military in Vietnam). The White House sought to sidestep debate in the United Nations and at home on the United States' adherence to international law, while officials in the Pentagon sought to retain the capacity to kill plants and subdue combatants with chemicals that they deemed tactically useful and relatively harmless in Vietnam and possibly elsewhere in the future.[13] Nixon's policies crystallized the sentiments of Meselson and his colleagues — with the White House demonstrating its preparedness to hold fast to its interpretation of the Geneva Protocol, the scientists positioned their own views as the polar opposite.[14] Before the HAC departed for Vietnam, its members alerted influential members of Congress about their trip and suggested that their findings could prove useful later to challenge the White House.[15] The scientists understood well that the fissures between Nixon and the Democrat-controlled Congress could be exploited to good effect. As one historian noted of the president's congressional relations, Nixon "proceeded as if there were a guerrilla war on the Potomac as well as the Mekong."[16]

The White House strategy presented a strange logic that almost immediately created the opposite effect from the one it intended: Nixon sought to push the United States to the fore of global disarmament by ratifying an international treaty with the understanding that the United States had not violated it.[17] The ensuing ratification process thus offered a stark legislative choice to assess the nation's place in the world: Did the United States stand on the cutting edge of peace and cold war disarmament? Or did the Vietnam War signal the reintroduction of widespread chemical warfare unseen since World War I and "ecocide," with herbicidal chemicals aimed against the people, cropland, and forests of Vietnam?

A declassified CIA intelligence report for the president offers insight into the White House strategy. In August 1969 — two months before the administration's major announcement of its CBW policy — the CIA assessment demonstrated an existing, well-entrenched assumption that political issues relating to CBW were tainted by a broader antiwar (and nonlegal) political activism: "Recent international interest, while generating considerable CBW debate, has nevertheless failed to stimulate attitudes that are sufficiently forthcoming to force new international agreements. The basic disputes over existing constraints no longer appear to hinge on philosophic interpretations of the 'unnecessary suffering' principle or technical legal argumentation. Instead they have become political issues in the larger context of general and complete disarmament."[18]

In this formulation, the Geneva Protocol, to borrow Nixon's crude way with words, was a tool for domestic and international critics of American policies in Vietnam to "stick it" to the president. Denunciations of herbicidal warfare from international communist news organs strengthened the Nixon administration's suspicions throughout the Geneva Protocol controversy.[19] This helps explain the near-total disconnect between the goals of the scientists and those of the White House regarding the purpose of ratifying the Geneva Protocol.

The scientists insisted that any discussion of CBW begin with Vietnam. But Nixon saw a political opportunity to shape a post-Vietnam future of global détente; what was actually happening in Vietnam was irrelevant to this vision. In the protocol, the scientists recognized a legal opportunity to halt the decimation of Vietnamese landscapes and prevent the same from happening elsewhere. In step with an increasingly antiwar congressional and international body politic, and despite the Nixon administration's efforts to circumvent the issue, the scientists commanded the political dialogue surrounding CBW. Back from Vietnam, the scientists and their colleagues reframed the Geneva Protocol as a treaty that bound the United

States to refrain from environmental warfare and destruction. This goal, they emphasized, transcended cold war national security policy.

President Nixon's resubmission of the Geneva Protocol and the controversy over chemical warfare in Vietnam reignited an American debate that had lain dormant since the 1920s. Following World War I, the United States led efforts to ban the first use of chemical and biological weapons in war as a reaction to worldwide public horror over the grisly effects of poison gases used by the major belligerents.[20] In the Versailles Treaty of 1919, the victorious Allies reaffirmed the prohibition against poison gases, as stipulated by the First and Second Hague Peace Conferences of 1899 and 1907, and forbade Germany from manufacturing and importing chemicals or other materials necessary to produce such weapons (figure 16). The United States convened the Washington Naval Disarmament Conference in 1922, where the Americans proposed a ban on the use of poisonous gases. The U.S. Senate unanimously ratified the treaty, but France's objection to provisions relating to submarine warfare prevented the agreement from taking force.[21]

Still, the conference succeeded in pushing chemical weapons disarmament as a universal ideal shared among the Great Powers and provided the diplomatic foundation for the 1925 Geneva Conference for the Supervision of the International Traffic in Arms. Again the United States proposed a ban on gas warfare, and with a proposal offered by Poland banning bacteriological warfare, the conference created the Geneva Protocol, signed on June 17, 1925, and ratified by all the European powers by 1930. Despite support in the Senate Committee on Foreign Relations, a strong lobbying campaign coordinated by the Army Chemical Warfare Service and the chemical industry prevented the protocol from reaching a vote in the Senate.[22] Almost two decades later, President Harry Truman in 1947 officially withdrew the protocol from the Senate.

Although the United States remained through 1970 the sole major power not a party to the Geneva Protocol, statements made by U.S. officials regularly characterized the United States as a strong adherent to its prohibitions.

In 1966, however, a major international challenge to the U.S. position arose when Hungary accused the United States of violating the Geneva Protocol by using herbicides and tear gas in Vietnam. U.S. delegates to the United Nations denied the charges on the grounds that the protocol prohibited only antipersonnel weapons. The debate generated General Assembly

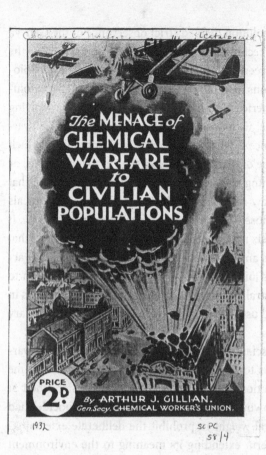

Figure 16 Early fears of CBW: Interwar pamphlet from Great Britain. Box 4, RG 58, Swarthmore College Peace Collection, Swarthmore, Pa.

The MENACE *of* CHEMICAL WARFARE *to* CIVILIAN POPULATIONS

PRICE 2D

By ARTHUR J. GILLIAN. *Gen.Secy.* CHEMICAL WORKER'S UNION.

Resolution 2162 B (XXI), which called for "strict observance by all States of the principles and objectives" and condemned "all actions contrary" to the objectives of the Geneva Protocol, but made no mention of its scope with regard to specific weapons. Because the American military was engaged in chemical warfare in Vietnam, the vagueness of the resolution worked in the United States' favor. The resolution passed 90 to 1 with one abstention, but more significantly it expressed widespread support for an inclusive interpretation of the protocol and marked the first time that the United States was forced to defend its military policies in Vietnam in the United Nations.[23]

The UN General Assembly continued debate on this issue. Over the next two years, the General Assembly passed a string of resolutions urging all states to adhere to a broad and inclusive interpretation of the Geneva Protocol. Finally, Resolution 2603 (XXIV) of December 16, 1969 (brought to a vote by the Swedish ambassador to the UN) targeted U.S. policy in Vietnam on two levels. First, the resolution defined strict observance of the Geneva Protocol "regardless of any technical developments," thus characterizing the protocol as an evolving agreement capable of prohibiting a variety of biological and chemical weapons that did not exist in 1925. Second, the resolution circumscribed the American interpretation of the protocol as applying only to lethal antipersonnel weapons by defining chemical agents of warfare as a "chemical substance — whether gaseous, liquid, or solid — which might be employed because of the direct toxic effects on man, animals, or plants."[24] By an overwhelming vote, the resolution offered a clear sign that customary international law regarded the distinction between chemicals toxic to humankind and those toxic to the environment an artificial one. It passed 80 to 3, with thirty-six nations abstaining largely on the grounds that the General Assembly was an inappropriate forum for interpreting treaty law. The United States was joined by two nations that had good reason to protest the resolution: Australian forces took part in herbicidal missions in Vietnam, and Portugal had used chemical herbicides against revolutionary insurgents in Angola.

A key strategy among scientists who were appalled by herbicidal warfare in South Vietnam was to link the protection of nature as a wartime goal similar to the protection of civilian noncombatants established at the Nuremberg trials following World War II. If the term "genocide" had come to command a moral weight to prohibit the deliberate extermination of a people, then a term extending its meaning to the environment might be able to do the same for nonhuman casualties of war.[25] As the legal scholar Richard Falk asserted, rather breathlessly, "Surely it is no exaggeration to consider the forests and plantations treated by Agent Orange as an Auschwitz for environmental values."[26] By the early 1970s, the protesting scientists — now armed with firsthand knowledge of the effects of Operation Ranch Hand — were able to advance this view in congressional hearings, where an increasing number of legislators were eager to bolster the movement to end the war as quickly as possible.[27] To these scientists, the question of whether herbicides belong to the category of weapons prohibited by the Geneva Protocol should not be answered solely on the legal — and largely arcane — merits of treaty law interpretation. So long as the end of the Vietnam War remained an elusive goal, the banning (through any available means) of at least one cruel and environmentally destructive tactic could bring to an end at least one aspect of the war that had made it unpopular in the first place.

The notion of ecocide as a criminal and indiscriminate wartime tactic became a common theme in congressional debate. Senator Stephen Young of Ohio was one of many legislators who explicitly linked environmental warfare and the indiscriminate killing of innocents: "Often lost amid the statistics of our war dead and wounded and those of the Vietcong and North Vietnamese is the fact that more than half a million women, children, and old men have been killed or maimed for life by our artillery, our napalm bombing, and our use of chemical defoliants."[28]

On December 26, 1970, the AAAS released the "Resolution on Chemical Defoliants," which called on the government "rapidly to phase out the use of all herbicides in Vietnam."[29] On the same day, the Nixon administration announced its plans "for an orderly, yet rapid phase out of the herbicide operations."[30] While the end of Ranch Hand had been a fait accompli since October, upcoming Senate deliberations on the Geneva Protocol required a display of initiative from the White House.

The AAAS had initially set out to understand the ecological and human health effects of an unprecedented chemical attack on plant life in Indochina. U.S. military strategy conceived of Vietnamese nature as a tactical liability to be dominated. It did not want either to relinquish its immediate plans to counter the guerrillas' strategy or to risk its long term flexibility to plan for future communist insurgency wars. A leaked report prepared by the U.S. Army Corps of Engineers in 1971 indicated that the Pentagon considered herbicidal warfare an integral component of strategic planning in a variety of potential theaters of war. Code-named SPECTRUM, these war-game scenarios deemed herbicides essential to counterinsurgency operations in Cuba, Ethiopia, and Venezuela and in conventional operations on the Korean Peninsula and against Warsaw Pact forces in France and the Benelux countries. SPECTRUM suggests that the political goals of détente had not penetrated the military ethos in the wake of Vietnam; despite Nixon's rhetoric about fostering a "structure of peace," the Pentagon was clearly planning to fight future wars not unlike Vietnam.[31]

The report helps to explain why the Pentagon was unwilling to consider the protection of Vietnam's environment a valuable goal. More important, it contextualizes military officials' congressional testimony before the SCFR in which they bridled at the notion of civilian outsiders (aside from established defense contractors such as the RAND Corporation) to have a say in strategic decision making.[32] By default, then, the AAAS found itself leading the herbicide investigation, which quickly confirmed the fears of the scientists who had first called for the ecological study. The key achievement of the AAAS was its ability to publicize the immense chemical destruction of nature in Vietnam as a war crime unjustifiable under any circumstances. In an alliance with a Congress increasingly receptive to the environmental movement and critical of the war in Vietnam, the AAAS ensured that the Nixon administration could not ratify the Geneva Protocol on the terms it sought.[33]

The move to undertake a major review of CBW culminating in Nixon's dramatic November 1969 announcement was initiated by Secretary of Defense Melvin Laird seven months earlier. Laird, a longtime and influential congressman from Wisconsin, was tapped by Nixon to head the Pentagon because of his reputation as a highly skilled politician and bureaucrat. True to form, Laird called for the review with an eye to Capitol Hill; he predicted that a comprehensive review headed by the NSC would stave off mounting antiwar sentiment and clarify U.S. policy on CBW with respect to international norms (figure 17).[34]

Henry Kissinger agreed to lead the study, the findings of which formed the basis of Nixon's major policy directive of November 25. In large part, the NSC resolved most of the outstanding CBW issues. The initiative was politically and strategically useful: Nixon's unilateral renunciation of the use of toxins (poisonous chemical substances produced by living organisms) and biological methods of warfare aligned U.S. policy with the Geneva Committee on Disarmament, which began negotiations in July 1969. The resulting resolution was signed by the United Kingdom, the United States, and the Soviet Union in May 1972.[35] Much like the Geneva Protocol, this document recognized and aimed to mitigate a new and horrifying era of biological weapons capable of uncontrolled self-regeneration that could wreak havoc across vast areas of land. The president's affirmation of no first use of chemical weapons rounded out his disarmament initiatives, which quickly received solid bipartisan support. The reaction of Congressman Robert Kastenmeier, a Democrat from Wisconsin, was exemplary: "The President's announcement [of] November 25 on our future chemical and biological warfare policy has uniformly been well received throughout the Nation and the world. I think this is an important step on the road to disarmament, and its timing at the commencement of the SALT talks is particularly appropriate. Our total renunciation of the use of biological warfare is a practical demonstration of a reversal in the trend toward harnessing our technological skills for more efficient means of destroying ourselves."[36]

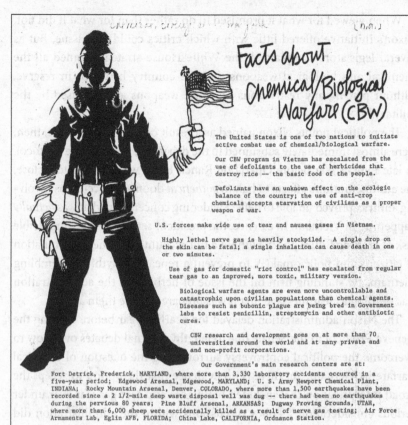

Facts about
Chemical/Biological
Warfare (CBW)

The United States is one of two nations to initiate active combat use of chemical/biological warfare.

Our CBW program in Vietnam has escalated from the use of defoliants to the use of herbicides that destroy rice -- the basic food of the people.

Defoliants have an unknown effect on the ecologic balance of the country; the use of anti-crop chemicals accepts starvation of civilians as a proper weapon of war.

U.S. forces make wide use of tear and nausea gases in Vietnam.

Highly lethal nerve gas is heavily stockpiled. A single drop on the skin can be fatal; a single inhalation can cause death in one or two minutes.

Use of gas for domestic "riot control" has escalated from regular tear gas to an improved, more toxic, military version.

Biological warfare agents are even more uncontrollable and catastrophic upon civilian populations than chemical agents. Diseases such as bubonic plague are being bred in Government labs to resist penicillin, streptomycin and other antibiotic cures.

CBW research and development goes on at more than 70 universities around the world and at many private and and non-profit corporations.

Our Government's main research centers are at:

Fort Detrick, Frederick, MARYLAND, where more than 3,330 laboratory accidents occurred in a five-year period; Edgewood Arsenal, Edgewood, MARYLAND; U. S. Army Newport Chemical Plant, INDIANA; Rocky Mountain Arsenal, Denver, COLORADO, where more than 1,500 earthquakes have been recorded since a 2 1/2-mile deep waste disposal well was dug -- there had been no earthquakes during the pervious 80 years; Pine Bluff Arsenal, ARKANSAS; Dugway Proving Grounds, UTAH, where more than 6,000 sheep were accidentally killed as a result of nerve gas testing; Air Force Armaments Lab, Eglin AFB, FLORIDA; China Lake, CALIFORNIA, Ordnance Station.

Many physicians, scientists and scientific groups are speaking out against chemical and biological warfare.

LEARN where this research is going on in your area and confront it. INITIATE projects to inform the public of the nature of CBW.

For more information contact: Mid-Atlantic Committee on Fort Detrick
2140 P Street, N. W.
Washington, D. C. 20036

SPC
6 I / A - E   (facts from Chemical & Biological Warfare by Seymour M. Hersh, publisher Bobbs-Merrill)

Figure 17 Anti-CBW flier appearing in the radical GI newspaper *Broken Arrow* (1969). Files A–E, GI files, Swarthmore College Peace Collection, Swarthmore, Pa.

When viewed for what it promised to do rather than for what it did not, Nixon's initiative offered little with which critics could take issue. But as several legislators complained, the White House strategy banned all the chemical and biological weapons that the country had kept in reserve, without placing any restrictions on those weapons actually used by the military.[37]

The political points Nixon gained as a result of the CBW initiative, then, were almost immediately subsumed in the debate over the Geneva Protocol. In late 1969, a year before Operation Ranch Hand was drawing to a close, the administration's efforts to halt *hypothetical* doomsday scenarios involving anthrax proved unable to deflect widening concern for what was *actually* happening in Vietnam. In essence, the president set himself the impossible task of crafting future policy without a full accounting of the determination of citizens and policy makers to prevent a repeat of anything resembling Vietnam. By standing firm on the issue of herbicides, the administration was sending a clear message that it was prepared to use them again.

The Nixon administration delayed for nearly a year before sending the Geneva Protocol to the Senate due to lengthy internal debates over how to overcome the political controversy surrounding the question of chemical warfare in Vietnam. Yet there is no evidence that the option to accept the broad interpretation that included herbicides and tear gas was ever under serious consideration.[38] Policy discussions within the administration did not focus on *if* the chemicals used in Vietnam violated the Geneva Protocol, but rather *how* this sensitive issue could be avoided altogether. The fact that the United States was not a party to the Geneva Protocol and therefore technically not bound to observe its dictates was of little use to a president who sought to portray the United States as a guarantor of international law, global peace, and disarmament. Moreover, recognition by the White House of the illegal use of chemicals in the Vietnam War would have demolished the long-standing government assertion that the United States had always adhered to the Geneva Protocol.[39] At the least such an admission would have amounted to an act of contrition that the country was unprepared to make in the midst of an ongoing war. Worse, it would have exposed the Nixon administration to the excruciating question of why it was employing wartime tactics that it considered illegal.

Getting around this political conundrum required a labyrinthine strategy. The administration sought to convey its unpopular legal position in a way that would encourage the Senate to ratify the protocol. A joint memorandum to Nixon by the Departments of State and Defense and the ACDA laid out three options:

1. Provide an explicit written statement to the Senate and countries party to the Geneva Protocol that the United States did not consider chemical herbicides and tear gas to be prohibited by the protocol.

2. Provide verbal communication to the Senate and parties to the protocol on the White House interpretation but omit any language to the effect of option 1.

3. Same as option 2 except only the Senate would receive verbal communication while parties to the protocol would be offered no explanation of the unique American interpretation.[40]

The memo acknowledged that protest against the restrictive view of the protocol was already overwhelming. Hence, the goal was to present the resubmission of the Geneva Protocol in such a way as to avoid outright rejection of the White House stance. Both in the Senate and among extant parties to the protocol, the likelihood of this happening was high. The Senate could simply tack onto the protocol resolution the position taken by the White House that the protocol excluded herbicides. On the international stage, moreover, nations already party to the protocol could refuse to accept the United States' membership in that club and/or refer the matter to the ICJ for an authoritative ruling on customary international law.[41]

The Nixon administration wanted all the prestige associated with the Geneva Protocol but none of the restrictions that had made the issue controversial in the first place. For this reason, its protocol strategy became wholly concerned with style over substance. Because the phase-out of Operation Ranch Hand was already well under way, the administration's decision-making process regarding formal versus informal reservations and verbal versus written communications had become oddly detached from the actual use of herbicides in Vietnam.

The president decided that a formal communication of the administration's narrow interpretation of the Geneva Protocol only to the Senate offered the best chance to minimize political liabilities and to retain the option of first use of herbicides in future wars. The communication stated that any such use would require direct presidential authorization and conformity to domestic standards governing safe herbicide use.[42] This was a two-pronged strategy, formed a week before the submission of the Geneva Protocol to the

Senate, intended to demonstrate that any decision to resort to herbicides in the future would not be delegated to low-level military officials, and no chemicals harmful to human beings (such as Agent Orange) would be employed in war.

On August 19, 1970, Nixon sent the Geneva Protocol to the Senate with a message that restated the goals of his November policy initiative, namely, the renunciation of all biological weapons and the restriction of a chemical-weapons arsenal solely for its deterrent effect against a chemical, biological, or nuclear attack on the United States. In an attempt to secure ratification of the protocol, Nixon had met with Senate leaders the previous day.[43] In an attached report, Secretary of State William Rogers detailed a formal reservation, already shared by France, Britain, and the Soviet Union, that would permit (i.e., release the country from its treaty obligations regarding) chemical retaliation in the event of an attack on U.S. soil using chemical weapons. Rogers reaffirmed the president's declaration that "the United States always has observed the principles and objectives of the protocol." He also underscored the need for the United States finally to become a party to the "basic international agreement" that prohibited chemical and biological warfare. On the issue of the administration's narrow interpretation, Rogers explained, "It is the United States' understanding of the Protocol that it does not prohibit the use in war of riot-control agents and chemical herbicides. Smoke, flame, and napalm are also not covered by the Protocol."[44]

The SCFR began hearings on the Geneva Protocol the following March in an atmosphere largely predisposed against the administration's position. The committee assembled a list of witnesses that included legal scholars, scientists, and politicians known to be critical of the White House interpretation.[45] Additionally, Operation Ranch Hand and the controversy surrounding 2,4,5-T had already received considerable negative attention in the mainstream media. The previous month, Senator Gaylord Nelson of Wisconsin, who founded Earth Day in 1970 and had become a major voice for environmental issues in Congress, proposed that if and when the Senate ratified the Geneva Protocol, the declaration should conclude with the statement: "It is the understanding of the Senate, which understanding inheres in its advice and consent to the ratification of the protocol, that the terms of the protocol prohibit the use in war of chemical herbicides."[46]

In testimony administration officials repeatedly touted the global significance of Nixon's disarmament strategy only to have the issue invariably shift to the Vietnam War. Senator J. William Fulbright of Arkansas, chair of the SCFR, tried to corner Assistant Secretary of Defense G. Warren Nutter in similar fashion:

THE CHAIRMAN: Do you know if any other nations view our use of these weapons as an international criminal act?

MR. NUTTER: View these weapons as criminal?

THE CHAIRMAN: Yes; do any of them make that assertion?

MR. NUTTER: No, sir. I am not familiar with any list of nations that would view the use of riot control agents and herbicides as criminal acts.

THE CHAIRMAN: I thought I read several articles that there had been great revulsion about the effect, particularly of herbicides, with our growing concern about the pollution of our planet. The stories about these tended to view that the destruction of forests and crops was thought to be a very serious matter, including many Americans. That is true; isn't it?[47]

The senators at the hearing demonstrated almost no patience with either the interpretive legal views of the administration or avowals of the tactical necessity from military officials. The rest of the witnesses, however, enjoyed a far more sympathetic atmosphere; this was particularly true for the testifying scientists, Arthur Galston and two members of the AAAS herbicide mission, Matthew Meselson and Arthur Westing. All urged ratification of the Geneva Protocol without any restrictive interpretation. Westing promoted his scientific expertise as a forester and botanist and direct experience with herbicides, both in field studies in Vietnam and as an herbicide specialist with the U.S. Forest Service, to bolster his own interpretation of the protocol. In Westing's view, herbicides had proved to be "at least as pernicious in their effects upon human beings and other living things" and for that reason should be banned as an antipersonnel weapon explicitly prohibited by the Geneva Protocol.[48] Arthur Galston again declared that the ecocide of Indochina must be confronted in a manner similar to the way in which the Nuremburg trials confronted genocide. Then he undertook an ecological soliloquy summoning the technological humility urged by Rachel Carson in

Silent Spring and the doomsday entreaties of Paul Ehrlich in *The Population Bomb*:

> Let me tell you why, as a botanist, I am so convinced of the necessity of banning herbicides and defoliants as weapons of war. These days it is convenient for man to consider himself as master of all he surveys. His ability to reach the bottom of the sea or the surface of the moon, to fly at supersonic speeds, to split the atom, and to construct sophisticated computers makes him feel that there is no problem requiring scientific or technological expertise that he cannot overcome . . . But the attitude that I describe I consider a dangerous fallacy which could lead man to overlook his own Achilles' heel.
>
> For man lives in this world only by the grace of vegetation. He is totally dependent on and cannot substitute for that thin mantle of green matter living precariously on the partially decomposed rock that we call soil . . . In view of the present population of about 3.5 billion people on Earth and the estimated doubling of the population in about 30 years, it ill behooves us to destroy with profligacy the ability of any part of the earth to yield food for man's nutrition, fiber for his clothes, wood to build and heat his houses, and other useful products, too numerous to mention.[49]

Shortly after Senator Fulbright told Galston that his testimony "ought to be brought to the attention of everybody in the country," the mutual admirers engaged in a lengthy and philosophical dialogue covering Louis XIV, humankind's vanity, and the foreign policy of Sweden, among other topics.

In addition to enlivening the hearings — which otherwise would have depended largely on an arcane debate over the ambiguous wording of treaty law — the inclusion of an ecological perspective provided the Senate committee with a logic militating against a restrictive interpretation for which the Nixon administration had no rebuttal. Arthur Galston and his colleagues had effectively reimagined the meaning of herbicidal warfare in a way that transcended the anticommunist objectives for which military strategy had designed it. The scientific objection to herbicides in war framed the issue as one of unmitigated human and natural devastation, and in so doing, upstaged the rhetoric of utilitarian tactical expedience advanced by the defenders of Operation Ranch Hand. The stakes surrounding the ratification of the Geneva Protocol thus contained elements of one of the key debates of the subsequent decade: could a balance be struck between technological innovation, economic growth, and environmental protection? There were, of course, no easy answers to this question. Yet as a legislative matter, the Geneva Protocol offered the committee members a clear choice on both.

On behalf of the SCFR, Senator Fulbright wrote to the president on April 15, 1971, urging the White House to reconsider its restrictive interpretation of the Geneva Protocol to avoid either its rejection or total modification in a Senate vote. Although Fulbright offered his admiration to Nixon for the great strides he had already taken in the field of disarmament — and for resubmitting the protocol in the first place — he made clear that the administration was isolated: it ran against the grain of world opinion as expressed in the UN and was counterproductive to the basic goal of weapons nonproliferation. Fulbright admitted that the legal merits of interpreting the scope of the Geneva Protocol were ambiguous. Still, he observed, what was totally clear was that herbicides as weapons were utterly frightening from an environmental perspective and should be banned absolutely and for all time. Fulbright closed the letter with an appeal to Nixon's ego and political instincts: "If the administration were to take the longer and broader view of our own interests, I cannot imagine any serious opposition to that decision, either here at home or abroad. On the contrary, I personally believe that were you to take this initiative your action would be regarded as truly courageous and possessed of real moral force."[50]

The White House offered no immediate response to Fulbright. It was silent on Senate resolutions and various calls from members of Congress to abandon its interpretation for a speedy ratification of the protocol.[51] History was poised to repeat itself: the standoff between Fulbright and Nixon meant that once again the United States would fail to become a party to the Geneva Protocol. Instead the administration chose retrenchment until it could counter with a new round of fact-finding missions already under way at the time of the Senate hearings. Following the standoff, the president ordered the NSC to review all chemicals used in the Vietnam War with regard to military utility, environmental effects, and international and domestic political liabilities. The NSC completed the report in September 1971.[52] Although Congress had ordered the NAS to conduct its own survey of herbicidal warfare in October 1970, the White House wanted an internal report before the completion of the NAS study, scheduled for release in 1974.[53] The NSC report again underscored the military utility of herbicides and tear gas while acknowledging the political liabilities associated with the use of any chemicals in war. It was also the first memorandum to explore seriously the pros and cons of consenting to Fulbright's urging, although the administration gave no indication as such either publicly or in private consultation with the SCFR.[54]

Senate hearings are customarily printed and available to the public shortly after they conclude. But Fulbright delayed publication until the following August, when it no longer seemed likely that the administration was willing to budge from its position. The release of the hearings thus became a political act in itself; Fulbright hoped to reignite the debate, especially because the Geneva Convention on Disarmament had recently concluded, and the White House had submitted the convention treaty to the Senate for ratification.[55] Although the destruction of U.S. bacteriological stocks as announced in Nixon's policy initiative of November 1969 aligned U.S. policy with the convention, the SCFR linked its ratification with a solution to the Geneva Protocol impasse. By late 1972, then, the Nixon administration's entire strategy on chemical and biological weapons was stalled, where it would remain until the president's resignation in August 1974. The Geneva Protocol languished in committee while Nixon turned his attention to withdrawing the last U.S. troops from Vietnam and trying to contain the Watergate scandal. Rather than serve as a beacon of Nixon's détente policies, the Geneva Protocol had become an early sign of a presidency in crisis.

In late 1974, President Gerald R. Ford renewed efforts to find common ground on the protocol issue with the SCFR as part of a larger initiative to move beyond what the new president famously termed "our long national nightmare." Significantly Henry Kissinger, as secretary of state, was not the administration official sent to the SCFR to represent the White House; as the main symbol of Nixonian continuity, Kissinger was too polarizing a figure for this sensitive matter. Instead Ford dispatched Fred Ikle, the director of the ACDA, to strike a compromise. Ikle presented an option that actually had been developed by the NSC in April 1974, when Nixon was still in office.[56] On December 10 Ikle informed the SCFR that the White House was prepared "to renounce as a matter of national policy" first use of chemical herbicides and riot-control agents in war, with the reservation that herbicides could still be used to clear vegetation around the perimeter of U.S. military bases.[57]

These reservations signaled that the Pentagon had never reconsidered its long-standing faith in the tactical utility of these weapons no matter the political costs their use entailed. The phrase "matter of national policy" avoided explicitly affirming that the Geneva Protocol prohibits the first use of herbicides and riot-control agents. The Ford administration was not prepared to radically reinterpret the Geneva Protocol—and with it a de facto ruling that past U.S. policy violated it. Further, military officials indicated that the United States' overall chemical warfare program would remain unaffected.[58]

Although the phrasing deliberately avoided legally binding language, Fred Ikle convinced skeptical SCFR members that the White House position would "be inextricably linked with the history of the Senate consent to ratification of the protocol with its consent dependent upon its observance. If a future administration should change this policy without Senate consent whether in practice or by a formal policy change, it would be inconsistent with the history of the ratification, and could have extremely grave political repercussions and as a result [was] extremely unlikely to happen."[59]

The committee agreed with this political forecast and voted unanimously to bring the resolutions on the Geneva Protocol and the Biological Weapons Convention before the Senate, according to Fulbright's directive to link the two treaties. On December 16, the Senate also unanimously approved both. On January 22, 1975, Ford signed the instruments of ratification of the Geneva Protocol nearly fifty years after the United States first proposed it. Two years later, the U.S. military transferred the remaining stocks of Agent Orange to Johnston Atoll, one of the most isolated islands in the Pacific Ocean, where they were subsequently incinerated.[60] Since then herbicides have played no major role in any war.

As in many international treaties, the vague language of the Geneva Protocol acts as an incentive for states to agree to abide by its provisions. This arrangement enhances a signatory state's national security under the umbrella of the protocol. At the same time, the state enjoys a degree of leeway to pursue military objectives. Consequently the price over time of the increasing number of ratifying nations has been the degradation of the protocol's capacity to establish clear guidelines for what is and is not acceptable international behavior with regard to chemical and biological weapons. The negotiating history of the Geneva Protocol demonstrates that the American experience was dramatic but not unique: a majority of nations party to the treaty have issued reservations that have diminished the protocol's absolute ban on "asphyxiating, poisonous or other gases, and of all analogous liquids, materials or devices."[61]

From a purely legal perspective, the question about the prohibitory scope of riot-control agents and herbicides in war was essentially a dead end. John Norton Moore, author of the definitive legal analysis of the Geneva Protocol (written in the middle of the legislative impasse), concluded:

It is important for the Executive and the Senate to reach agreement on a policy for riot-control agents and chemical herbicides as soon as possible. As a starting point both might candidly admit that there is no authoritative interpretation on whether riot-control agents and chemical herbicides are included in the protocol . . . Both the Administration and the Senate might also agree that in view of the importance of promoting widespread international agreement on the interpretation of the protocol, the United States will support international consideration of the issues, preferably through an international conference but if that proves impractical, through submission through the International Court of Justice.[62]

Moore's point is that legal positions on binding international agreements, such as that proffered by the Nixon administration, tend to focus narrowly (but not illegitimately) on a given treaty's stated prohibitory parameters to the exclusion of the political context in which that treaty came into being. This nuance meant little to Senator Fulbright and his colleagues on the SCFR. Their decision to block ratification was rooted in disenchantment with the Vietnam War and respect for the scientists' articulation of herbicidal warfare in Vietnam as an omen of global environmental catastrophe.

The negotiating parties that convened in Geneva in 1925 recognized the need for an international mechanism to place limits on both the production of chemical and biological weapons and the willingness of states to unleash them in war. Likewise, the scientists who first demanded that the AAAS investigate Operation Ranch Hand came to a similar conclusion. To them, whether or not the use of chemical herbicides violated the Geneva Protocol was tangential to their insistence that herbicides — like all CBW — were horrifying weapons that should be banned by any means necessary. As a result of the misguided political assumptions of the White House, in 1975 the Geneva Protocol became that mechanism, resulting in victory for those scientists and their allies in Congress who considered the phrase "No more Vietnams!" a battle cry for ecological protection in times of peace and war.

CHAPTER NINE

CONCLUSION
Ecocide and International Security

BY THE END of the 1960s, the cold war "consensus" among the Washington political establishment had collapsed.[1] In the words of Senator Mark O. Hatfield, Republican from Oregon, as the decade drew to a close, "the disposition of Congress began to shift, almost imperceptibly. National economic strains appeared, generated by the inflationary financing of the Vietnam War. The Soviet Union was recognized as approaching parity with the United States in numbers of strategic weapons. The myth of the world communist monolith had been convincingly dispelled. Slowly these facts exerted their weight on Congress and some calls for rethinking were heard."[2] The Vietnam War destroyed Lyndon Johnson's presidency and his dreams to complete the Great Society, an updated New Deal for the 1960s. John Kennedy's soaring but vague pledge to "pay any price" to support cold war allies bore little resemblance to the disaster in Vietnam. Richard Nixon's grim yet equally vague declaration that he had achieved "peace with honor" in the United States' chaotic exit from Vietnam ended the era of liberal interventionism. The war began as a low-level counterguerrilla conflict — a small but determined display of technology and cold war resolve. Johnson's tortured determination to "Americanize" the war negated the strategic salience of fighting to prevent the spread of communism. To increasing numbers of disaffected citizens in the United States and around the world, there was simply too much destruction of human and natural life and too little explanation for what the U.S. government hoped to accomplish.

The success of the movement against herbicidal warfare can be directly attributed to the unpopularity of the war and its negation of the strategy of containment. The ecological concerns that first exercised the collective conscience of the protesting scientists would have otherwise dead-ended in the mid-1960s. Indeed, the Johnson administration, the Pentagon, and many in the scientific community made strong efforts to kill the campaign before it gained traction. But the scientists persisted. They were offended and deeply concerned about the ecological effects of herbicidal warfare, both as an actual crisis unfolding in Vietnam and as a hypothetical calamity that could spread wherever forests and war intersected. The scientists succeeded because they capitalized on a particular credibility gap between what the U.S. government *could* know and what it *did* know regarding the damage caused by herbicidal warfare. Government assurances of health safety and short-term environmental effects actually had no basis in fact; indeed the 1974 NAS study concluded that a century could pass before full ecological recovery was complete. The magnitude of Operation Ranch Hand was unprecedented in the history of herbicides, and thus it was logically impossible to assess precisely its damage by extrapolation. If herbicidal warfare had remained the small and carefully controlled program that John Kennedy had authorized, scientific protest almost certainly would have been nonexistent. But this is only a historical "what if"; as this book has demonstrated, the massive intensification of Operation Ranch Hand under Lyndon Johnson and the escalation of war in general were inseparable.

From the earliest scientific concerns in 1964 to the scientists' testimony in the Senate in 1971, to Gerald Ford's formal renunciation of herbicidal warfare in 1975, the scientists tread over a deeper concern, namely, their feelings about the war in general. As private citizens, Arthur Galston and his colleagues were clearly against the war — but they were careful to separate this sentiment from their campaign to end herbicidal warfare. Still, the scientists' private attitudes galvanized their political persistence. As Galston bluntly told the author in an interview, if herbicides could have exposed German gunners on the beaches of Normandy, then he would have adamantly supported their inclusion in the Allied arsenal. But for Galston and his colleagues, World War II was a "good" war, whereas Vietnam was not. If ending ecocide could help end the war, so much the better.

But the scientists saw little reason to conflate these goals publicly. The strategy was prudent; it allowed the scientists to maintain a narrow focus and thus avoid alienating the military and political officials whose cooperation was vital to their mission. As with the environmentalist aspect of their agenda, they left the larger antiwar project to others. By the end of the decade, public demands to pull U.S. forces out of Vietnam had grown from the fringe to mainstream political discourse. And at the same time, the scientists' contention that the environmental ills of a land on the other side of the world could have planetary ramifications tracked with broader 1960s concerns about ecology and global survival. As the environmental historian Adam Rome argues, a culture living in the shadow of nuclear holocaust was conceptually primed to approach ecological issues beyond national boundaries.[3] By the end of the decade, the key environmental question was would humanity survive? not, would *Americans* survive? as Rachel Carson had asked in *Silent Spring.*

Buoyed by broader anxieties about the Vietnam War and the environmental state of the world, the scientists were nonetheless ambivalent toward the antiwar and environmental movements beyond their particular purview. The scientists' success could not have happened in the absence of either movement, and yet they stood aloof from both. Doing so allowed Arthur Galston and his colleagues to maintain an air of scientific objectivity, without which it would have been impossible to gain access to sprayed war zones in Vietnam and to enjoy a sympathetic audience before the SCFR. The operative word here is "air" because of course there was nothing objective about the campaign to end herbicidal warfare. Their agenda was the politicization of science par excellence.

It was before the Senate committee that the scientists fully articulated a new vision of international security—one that had nothing to do with the tactics and strategies that had informed American policies since the beginning of the cold war. Insofar as these policies created herbicidal warfare in Vietnam, the protesting scientists usurped authority to define the meaning of Operation Ranch Hand. Where military and political officials championed the program as an indispensable tactic to win the war, the scientists decried it as an act of ecocide—a moral calamity and a contravention of international norms. The environmental catastrophe caused by Operation Ranch Hand—and the prospect that nations great and small could replicate it anywhere on the planet—convinced the scientists that even the greatest fears of global communist encroachment could never justify its future use. And contrary to the inflated rhetoric surrounding Richard Nixon's chemical and biological weapons policies, there was no better opportunity to halt CBW proliferation than to renounce weapons that the United States actually used—not simply the ones its military had stockpiled for some future hypothetical conflict.

The disaffection caused by the Vietnam War and the consequent discrediting of U.S. containment policy afforded space to conceptualize international security in new ways.[4] Amid growing concerns about rapidly diminishing resources for an exploding global population, the specter of massive ecological destruction in war, in the scientists' view, was folly in the extreme. Herbicidal warfare created an actual catastrophe in a particular place, but it was also a hypothetical (but realistic) catastrophe-in-waiting across the globe. Their insistence that the United States pledge a formal renunciation of herbicidal warfare had no curative effect on Vietnam. Instead, it was a well-crafted and logical explanation of the ease with which environmental threats traverse political boundaries. This reality required an internationalization of the scientists' legislative victory beyond Washington.

For Arthur Galston and his colleagues, the ratification of the Geneva Protocol was a tremendous success and one long in the making. The herbicide controversy was an episode in which a platform of political lobbying and protest by a group of nongovernment actors was able to alter official U.S. policy at the highest levels — a rarity in the broad and convoluted history of antiwar protest in the Vietnam era. But the scientists' work would remain incomplete as long as they limited their actions to the domestic sphere. Although Gerald Ford's formal renunciation of first use of herbicides in war gave legal and political heft to the proposition that environmental issues had entered the realm of international security, the Geneva Protocol itself was not, of course, an instrument of international environmental law or policy. And so without further work in the global arena to create a broader mechanism of international environmental cooperation — an international environmental regime — the scientists could not be satisfied that their work was complete.

To their good fortune, such a regime was in its early stages and potentially receptive to taking on "hot button" issues such as the Vietnam War. UNEP was an organization whose development was directly linked to the international fissures caused and exacerbated by the Vietnam War. Crucially, UNEP offered the scientists an official political infrastructure that was lacking in more informal associations such as Earth Day, whose organizers invariably shared UNEP's founding vision but lacked the backing authority of the United Nations and its member states. In this new forum, the scientists believed that their campaign to end herbicidal warfare, as a matter of transnational environmental protection, could become enshrined in the mandates of international policy.

The impetus to include environmental issues under the aegis of the United Nations came from Sweden, whose representative in 1968 successfully passed a resolution "to provide a framework for comprehensive consideration within the UN of the problems of the human environment in order to focus the attention of governments and public opinion on the importance and urgency of this question."[5] Two years and several planning committees later, the Canadian industrialist Maurice Strong became secretary general of UNEP and warned frequently of the planetary threats posed by environmental degradation. In debate in the General Assembly and in plenary meetings for the upcoming environmental conference, Strong's use of the now-anachronistic phrase "human environment" offered a triple connotation: first, the term suggested the inextricable (yet poorly acknowledged) link between societies and the environs upon which they depend; second, the phrase was deliberately broad so that UNEP, in concert with UN member states, could create wide-ranging policies to mitigate any number of environmental issues whose problems transcended national boundaries; third, the term was deliberately vague because the framers of UNEP understood that the new body would inherit the classic problems of the Westphalian system, namely, how to balance the national interest of sovereign nations with the common interest of supranational governance.[6]

In one of many speeches given by Strong to drum up interest in and support for UNEP and its upcoming inaugural conference, the secretary general presented the case that the environmental problems facing humanity required a new kind of global cooperation:

> The threats to man's existence from nuclear warfare can be avoided right up until the moment someone pushes the button; but the threat to man's survival which derives from our interventions in our natural environment is of a different nature. Here each of us has his finger on the button, and this responsibility requires us to act now to avoid dangers which will not materialize until the next generation or beyond — but still within the lifetime of our own children or grandchildren — and will be beyond remedy by the time they are perceived as imminent threats. To deal with issues which involve cause and effect relationships so far removed from more immediate and pressing priorities will require a degree of enlightened political will on the part of the peoples and nations of the world that is without precedent in human history.[7]

In June 1972, Stockholm played host to the first annual United Nations Conference on the Human Environment. Sweden's central role both in getting UNEP up and running and its strained relations with the United States over Vietnam was not a coincidence. In a class by itself among nations outside the communist orbit, since the mid-1960s Sweden's leaders had repeatedly denounced the American war in Vietnam as a tragic and unnecessary catastrophe.[8] For Swedish prime minister Olof Palme, the UNEP Conference in 1972 was a logical platform to continue the critiques of the Vietnam War that he had made since joining the Swedish government nearly ten years earlier. The head of the Swedish government, Palme felt no compunction to tone down his rhetoric, although he knew full well that his comments could derail the entire conference. In his opening address, the prime minister decried the "ecocide" of Vietnam. "It is of paramount importance," he declared, "that ecological warfare cease immediately."[9]

Since the debacle of the Geneva Protocol in the Senate and the Nixon administration's newfound appreciation for the controversy and passions aroused by Agent Orange, the president sent Russell Train, the U.S. representative to UNEP, with the directive to keep all references to Vietnam off the official agenda. UNEP's promised silence concerning the environmental destruction in Vietnam was, in fact, a precondition to U.S. participation in the conference. According to one newspaper account, upon hearing Prime Minister Palme's denunciation of the American "ecocide," Train became visibly incensed, called Palme's statements a "gratuitous politicizing of our environmental discussions," and threatened that the U.S. delegation would abandon the conference.[10] The following day, the Chinese delegate added to Palme's remarks. According to a State Department telegram, the delegate objected that there was no good reason why America's policy of "poisoning the environment of Vietnam" should be kept off the official record of the conference.[11] Whether or not there was a "good reason," the United States managed to keep all references to Vietnam out of the record.[12]

Detractors of UNEP have pointed to the official exclusion of ecocide as evidence that the organizers of the Stockholm Conference were more concerned with putting on a good show than tackling the most pressing issues of the day. Russell Train's protest against the "politicizing" of environmental issues, if taken to its logical conclusion, would have rendered moot any substantive discussions of any matter on the UNEP agenda. More to the point, Article 21 of the Stockholm Declaration (the executive summary of the conference proceedings) states that "the sovereign rights of states to exploit their own resources in line with their own environmental policies ensure that activities in their control do not damage the environment of other states." As one critic observed of Article 21, "In short, the participating states agreed to cooperate, but they also wanted it to be made absolutely clear that this was not to infringe on any decision-making powers they held."[13] An even blunter assessment is that, lofty rhetoric of its secretary general aside, nothing inherent in UNEP actually suggested that environmental problems would not remain essentially national problems — even though the whole basis of UNEP was that such thinking was old-fashioned at best and dangerous at worst.

Yet the law of unintended consequences — as was the case with the Nixon administration and its miscalculation regarding the relative importance of the herbicide controversy — yielded the most interesting results to emerge from the conference. There were actually two parallel conferences occurring in Stockholm: the one under official UN auspices, and a much more rambunctious conference held in the adjoining streets and parks. Some participants cleverly titled this alternative convention "Woodstockholm."[14] The event lived up to its nickname, with thousands of people erecting tent cities and staging rock concerts and protest marches. Although the participants of the alternative conference could claim no more of a unified agenda than their bureaucratic counterparts, they shared the basic premise that the limits and strictures placed on the official record would ensure that UNEP would not create meaningful solutions to real transnational environmental problems. On the other hand, the participants of "Woodstockholm" recognized that, from a publicity perspective, the Stockholm conference was a remarkable event: the eleven-day conference attracted some twelve hundred diplomats and heads of state, several thousand experts on environmental issues and global governance, and the curiosity of the international press corps. It was a rare opportunity for environmental attention-grabbing.

Two of the key scientists who protested herbicidal warfare, Arthur Westing and E. W. Pfeiffer, attended the parallel conference, though they would have much preferred that the United States allow the Agent Orange issue to be aired in the official forum. Still, it was not an opportunity to be lost. Two days before the start of the official conference, Westing and Pfeiffer helped organize a conference on the consequences of ecocide in Vietnam and other ravages endured by the Vietnamese landscape and its people as a result of the war. The meeting, which was far more solemn than many of the festivities that would ensue, brought together legal theorists and scientists from around the world.[15] During these talks and presentations, it became apparent why the official U.S. delegation worked to keep Vietnam off the agenda: UNEP would have otherwise become an impromptu war crimes commission, based largely on the presupposition that herbicidal warfare violated the Geneva Protocol.[16] As Arthur Westing recalled, these were serious allegations of criminal conduct that drew the attention of important officials. Prime Minister Olof Palme, for example, was compelled to broach the ecocide issue in his opening address after he was briefed by Westing and Pfeiffer about their work and experiences studying the ecological destruction in Vietnam.[17]

Although it is impossible to measure precisely the effect of the scientists with regard to ecocide and international behavior, it would be difficult to dismiss their work in explaining the absence of herbicidal warfare from international conflict in the post-Vietnam era. Between the Geneva Protocol and UNEP, the scientists' efforts combined for a one-two punch. In Washington they effectively forced government policy to adhere to an international treaty based on an environmental rather than a legal argument; in Stockholm they confronted and neutralized what they saw as a craven attempt by the United States to censor all references to herbicidal warfare in Vietnam — a wartime operation whose effects were possibly the most dramatic intersection of environmental and international issues in modern times.

Still, the scientists' victory remained qualified until the creation of an international mechanism that combined the proscriptions of treaty law with the breadth of an international agreement. That is, neither the Geneva Protocol nor the Stockholm Conference were tailor-made to fulfill the scientists' basic goal: preventing the deliberate destruction of environments during war. Herbicides were cheap and readily available, but the scientists recognized that laws specifically geared to ban herbicidal warfare could merely compel the fertile minds of the "military-industrial complex" in the United States and elsewhere to develop different technological means to achieve the same ends. The first sign of a fuller solution to the scientists' efforts came in 1974, when the United States and the Soviet Union explored the possibility of jointly declaring voluntary restraints on environmental warfare.[18] At that juncture, President Ford was already prepared to renounce herbicidal warfare, and the more generic term "environmental warfare" obviously would place herbicides under the restraints of a future treaty without directly acknowledging the fact that preventing future acts of ecocide was the evident inspiration of such a treaty.

This agreement eventually morphed into the United Nations "Convention on the Prohibition of Military or Any Other Hostile Use of Environmental Modification Techniques," which was opened for signature in Geneva on May 18, 1977.[19] A great majority of the world's nations have signed this treaty. Although at least one of the protesting herbicide scientists has expressed criticism that ENMOD, as the environmental modification treaty is known, has too many loopholes to ensure stringent control and compliance verification,[20] it is difficult to argue with history: whether as a result of the Geneva Protocol, the Stockholm Conference, or a treaty specifically designed to prevent environmental destruction in times of war (or some combination of the three), no major nation has embarked on a systematic and deliberate campaign to harm environments during times of war.

The major exception to this international norm was Saddam Hussein's destruction of the marshlands of southern Iraq in the years after the first Persian Gulf War. The Baathist policy of upriver damming of the Tigris and Euphrates rivers intentionally devastated the ancient way of life of the Marsh Arabs, the majority of whom were Shia Muslims who had sought greater autonomy from Saddam after his army was routed by coalition forces in Operation Desert Storm.[21] The war against the Marsh Arabs and their ancestral lands has been recognized in the legal literature as an act of ecocide and a violation of the terms of the ENMOD treaty.[22] It is notable that in Saddam Hussein, we see that the major perpetrator of environmental warfare since the Vietnam War was also, arguably, the greatest violator of the norms of warfare in general in recent times. Equally notable is that UNEP spearheaded international efforts to bring the plight of the Marsh Arabs and their environs to the world's attention.[23] Finally, in what may be seen as an environmental component to Washington's ongoing attempt to kick the "Vietnam syndrome" in all its forms, the USAID launched a resettlement and restoration project of the marshlands only months after the U.S. invasion of Iraq in March 2003.[24] This ongoing project has accomplished substantial reflooding in the region and the return of thousands of refugees to their ancient homeland.[25]

The international community's response to the Iraqi marshland crisis stands as testament both to the conception of ecocide as formed by Arthur Galston and his colleagues and to the current normative status of environmental issues among international organizations. Standing apart from environmental degradation that occurs as a by-product of industrial processes and resource extraction, ecocide was, and remains, a tactic of war that targets humans through environmental destruction. It is an offense recognized in international law that will likely be enforced against combatants who attempt to commit ecocide in future wars. The introduction of UNEP's founding declaration in 1972 epitomizes the ecological and internationalist concerns that launched the protest against herbicidal warfare, which resulted in the subsequent international prohibitions of environmental warfare:

> Man is both creature and moulder of his environment, which gives him physical sustenance and affords him the opportunity for intellectual, moral, social and spiritual growth. In the long and tortuous evolution of the human race on this planet a stage has been reached when, through the rapid acceleration of science and technology, man has acquired the power to transform his environment in countless ways and on an unprecedented scale. Both aspects of man's environment, the natural and the man-made, are essential to his well-being and to the enjoyment of basic human rights the right to life itself.
>
> The protection and improvement of the human environment is a major issue which affects the well-being of peoples and economic development throughout the world; it is the urgent desire of the peoples of the whole world and the duty of all Governments.[26]

This sentiment was radical in 1965, cutting-edge in 1972, and arguably normative today. In the ongoing historical debate over the "lessons" of Vietnam, this present study has demonstrated how a group of nongovernment actors were able to advance a vision of international security based on interdependence and environmental threats common to all people. As one of the last "wounds" of the Vietnam War, the complex and sad legacy of Agent Orange offers a powerful lesson of political resolve. Since the termination of Operation Ranch Hand in 1971, Agent Orange has remained unique to the Vietnam War. In the mid-1960s, when the scientific protest movement was just beginning, both that accomplishment and the international norms it engendered would have seemed inconceivable.

NOTES

CHAPTER ONE. Introduction

1. The process by which herbicides kill plants is known in plant physiology as the herbicidal mode of action.

2. The question of whether the benefits of the postwar chemicalization of agriculture have outweighed the liabilities remains hotly debated. For a critique of the Green Revolution, see, for example, Sonnenfeld, "Mexico's 'Green Revolution,'" and Yapa, "What Are Improved Seeds?" A more positive (and self-serving) analysis is Ford Foundation, *Richer Harvest*. For a broader overview, see Cullather, "Miracles of Modernization."

3. Whether herbicidal applications are actually more economical than mechanical or manual weeding is a separate question.

4. The full text of the Geneva Protocol is available from the Department of State, "Text of the Geneva Protocol," at http://www.state.gov/t/isn/4784.htm.

5. The full text of the resolution is available from the Avalon Project at Yale University, http://avalon.law.yale.edu/20th_century/warpower.asp. See also http://www.fas.org/nuke/control/geneva/text/geneva1.htm.

6. See especially K. Moore, *Disrupting Science*; and Wisnioski, "Inside the System."

7. For scholarship on environmental politics and activism, see, for example, Hays, *Beauty, Health, and Permanence*; Rome, *Bulldozer in the Countryside*; Gottlieb, *Forcing the Spring*; and Sale, *Green Revolution*.
On the impact of Vietnam on cold war politics see, for example, Suri, *Power and Protest*; Woods, *J. William Fulbright*; Schulzinger, *Time for Peace*; Garthoff, *Détente and Confrontation*; Buzzanco, *Vietnam and the Transformation of American Life*; and Neu, *After Vietnam*.

8. The best challenge to move beyond these boundaries is Dorsey, "Dealing with the Dinosaur."

9. See, for example, A. Nelson, *Cold War Ecology*; R. P. Tucker and Russell, *Natural Enemy, Natural Ally*; and McNeill, "Woods and Warfare." One of the few books devoted exclusively to environmental history and international diplomacy is Dorsey, *Dawn of Conservation Diplomacy*.

10. This line of reasoning is most clearly spelled out in U.S. Military Assistance Command, Vietnam, *Herbicide Policy Review*, 35.

11. The most recent examination of the state of Agent Orange environmental remediation and compensation for U.S. veterans and Vietnamese nationals is a collaborative effort by the Ford Foundation, the New America Foundation, and the news outlet *Washington Monthly*. A transcript of a panel discussion, held in Washington, D.C., on January 6, 2010, discussing these efforts, is available at http://www.c-spanarchives.org/program/291101–1.

12. Phung Tuu Boi, interview with the author, August 23, 2007, Hanoi, Vietnam. Boi was profiled in Aschwanden, "Through the Forest."

13. Dwernychuk, "Dioxin Hot Spots in Vietnam."

14. Dr. Tuan Vo, a Vietnamese obstetrician, is one of the country's leading researchers on Agent Orange and birth defects. Interview with the author, August 4, 2007, Ho Chi Minh City, Vietnam.

15. See, for example, Schecter and Constable, "Commentary." See also Schecter et al., "Recent Dioxin Contamination."

16. Halperin, Honchar, and Fingerhut, "Dioxin," 285.

17. Clary, quoted in Grotto and Jones, "Agent Orange's Lethal Legacy." A wartime reference to the toxicity of Agent Orange as determined in laboratory tests on animals corroborates Clary's charge. See U.S. Military Assistance Command, Vietnam, "Use of Herbicides in Vietnam," folder 201–30 (3), box 2, RG 472, Records of the U.S. Forces in Southeast Asia, National Archives and Records Administration (hereafter NARA), College Park, Maryland. See also Joyce, "American Government."

18. The most accessible executive summary of the relationship between cancer and Agent Orange exposure is available from the American Cancer Society at http://tinyurl.com/3yq6urd.

The Institute of Medicine of the National Academies periodically updates its study *Veterans and Agent Orange*. While eschewing the word "conclusive," the 2004 edition identifies "sufficient evidence of an association" between Agent Orange exposure and the incidence of soft-tissue sarcoma, non-Hodgkin's lymphoma, chronic lymphocytic leukemia, and Hodgkin's disease.

19. President George H. W. Bush's directive signing the act into law is available at *The American Presidency Project*, University of California at Santa Barbara, http://www.presidency.ucsb.edu/ws/index.php?pid=19283.

20. A. L. Young, *History, Use, Disposition*, 11. Young's book combines materials on Agent Orange that he has worked on or collected over the past forty years, many of which are available online in the "Alvin L. Young Collection on Agent Orange" at the National Agricultural Library, http://www.nal.usda.gov/speccoll/findaids/agentorange/index.htm. For a more pointed argument on the "debasement" of science amid the policy of Agent Orange financial compensation without proved causation, see Gough, "Agent Orange."

21. A U.S. diplomat, interview with the author conducted off-the-record, August 23, 2007, Hanoi, Vietnam.

22. The U.S. embassy in Vietnam offers a useful primer on the milestones achieved in the U.S.-Vietnamese bilateral relationship since 1991, available at http://vietnam.usembassy.gov/chronology.html.

23. See, for example, Vinnedge, "Let's Hear It for Pollution."

24. Kennedy's reaction to *Silent Spring* and subsequent policy study is detailed by the Environmental Protection Agency, in "Rachel Carson," by Frank Graham Jr., *EPA Journal*, November/December 1978, available at http://www.epa.gov/history/topics/perspect/carson.htm.

25. Hayes et al., *Earth Day*, 2–3.

26. Complementing Cecil's emphasis on the tactical and operational aspects of Ranch Hand is the official air force history of the program, Buckingham, *Operation Ranch Hand*.

27. The law that launched federal research on the health effects of Agent Orange was H.R. 1961 (October 24, 1984). See President Ronald Reagan's statement, "Signing the Veterans' Dioxin and Radiation Exposure Compensation Standards Act," available at http://www.reagan.utexas.edu/archives/speeches/1984/102484e.htm.

28. See also Berenstein, "Comment"; and Lacey and Lacey, "Agent Orange".

29. For the legal defense position of Dow Chemical Company, see Hanes, "Agent Orange Liability." Hanes was associate general counsel for Dow.

30. For Weinstein's full decision, see Judge Jack B. Weinstein, U.S. District Court, Eastern District of New York, *In re "Agent Orange Product Liability Litigation,"* March 10, 2005, available at http://www.ffrd.org/AO/10_03_05_agentorange.pdf. A useful collection of pertinent court documents pertaining to the lawsuit and the appeals process is available from the War Legacies Project at http://www.warlegacies.org/court.htm. For an analysis of the legal basis of the lawsuit, see Zierler, "Vietnamese Plaintiffs." For a socioeconomic analysis of the impact of Agent Orange on Vietnamese in heavily sprayed areas (which provides context for the basis of the plaintiffs' lawsuit), see Palmer, "Legacy of Agent Orange."

CHAPTER TWO. An Etymology of Ecocide

1. Walzer, *Just and Unjust Wars*, 21.

2. Messing, "American Actions in Vietnam."

3. The meeting, held in Washington, was organized by the Congressional Conference on War and National Responsibility, at the initiative of U.S. representatives Abner Mikva (D-Ill.) and Robert Kastenmeier, (D-Wis.).

4. Galston et al., "Scientists' Petition to President Johnson."

5. Buckingham, *Operation Ranch Hand*, 11.

6. These figures are cited by the first independent American scientists to survey

the effects of herbicidal warfare in Vietnam. See E. W. Pfeiffer and Gordon H. Orians, "Military Use of Herbicides in Vietnam," in Neilands et al., *Harvest of Death*, 117–76, at 120–21.

7. B. Nelson, "Studies Find Danger."

8. For example, see Westmoreland (Commander of Military Assistance Command, Vietnam) to President Johnson, "Assessment for the Month of October 1967," box 234, Vietnam Country file, National Security file, Lyndon Baines Johnson Presidential Library (hereafter LBJL).

9. Excerpts of a leaked report detailing Pentagon contingency plans to conduct herbicide missions on every continent in the world appear in "Defoliation: Secret Army Study Urges Use in Future Wars."

10. U.S. Congress, House, Report to the Subcommittee on Science, Research and Development, *Technology Assessment*, 61.

11. "Defoliating the World."

12. Pearce, "Arthur Galston."

13. Arthur Galston, interview with the author, March 9, 2007, New Haven, Conn. Galston successfully demonstrated that a chemical compound called 2,3,5-triiodobenzoic acid (TIBA) sped up the flowering cycle of soy plants. Galston also found that TIBA in higher dosages was a powerful herbicide.

14. The best analysis of 1960s environmental activism is Rome, "Give Earth a Chance." Rome cites the centrality of a possible nuclear holocaust to the development of a globally oriented environmental platform.

15. Galston, interview.

16. Ibid.

17. See especially Cronon, "Uses of Environmental History"; and Richard White, "'Are You an Environmentalist or Do You Work for a Living?': Work and Nature," in Cronon, *Uncommon Ground*, 171–85.

18. The conference proceedings are reprinted in Knoll and McFadden, *War Crimes*. Galston's quote appears on pp. 71–72.

19. Hersh expanded his original investigative series into book form the following year; see Hersh, *My Lai 4*. For a contemporary survey that rooted My Lai within a larger matrix of American war crimes, see Herman, *Atrocities in Vietnam*.

20. "Viet Cong" is the derogatory moniker apparently invented by the regime of President Ngo Dinh Diem, president of the Republic of Vietnam (1955–63). American soldiers quickly adopted the term, often shortening it to VC, "Victor Charlie," or simply "Charlie."

21. Quoted in Cookman, "American Atrocity," 160. The most comprehensive and best-researched work on My Lai to date is Belknap, *Vietnam War on Trial*.

22. Recent scholarship indicates that the gap in transatlantic attitudes toward the Vietnam War was even greater than scholars had previously thought. See Ricard, "Feature

Review." For a discussion of the sharpest bilateral break in transatlantic relations over Vietnam, see Logevall, "Swedish-American Conflict over Vietnam."

23. Limqueco and Weiss, *Prevent the Crime of Silence*. Russell's quote appears on pg. 57; Sartre's quote appears on pg. 63.

24. Lederer, "Report of the Sub-committee."

25. "Resolution: Reunion internationale des scientifiques sur la guerre chimique au Viet Nam," personal manuscript collection of Egbert W. Pfeiffer, Missoula, Mont. (hereafter EWP papers).

26. Ibid. Because the terms "biocide" and "ecocide" were newly minted and designed for political impact, antiwar activists thereafter came to use them interchangeably.

27. U.S. Army Foreign Science and Technology Center, "Extract from Foreign Broadcast Information Service Daily Report," folder 11, box 197, National Security file, John F. Kennedy Presidential Library (hereafter JFKL).

28. Colonel-General Van Tiên Dung, "A Statement of the National Liberation Front of South Vietnam," 1965, Vietnam files, American Friends Service Committee Central Archives (hereafter AFSC Central Archives), Philadelphia.

29. Brigham, *Guerrilla Diplomacy*, xi.

30. *American Use of War Gases*.

31. The Committee to Denounce the War Crimes of the U.S. Imperialists and Their Henchmen in South Vietnam published *The Biggest War Criminal of Our Time* in 1967. The section on chemical warfare was reissued in 1970 in expanded form under the title *The U.S. Imperialists' Plan and Methods regarding the Chemical Warfare in South Vietnam*, box 13, Arthur W. Galston Papers (hereafter AWG Papers), Yale University Library Manuscript and Archives. The reference to Galston appears in Juridical Sciences Institute, *U.S. War Crimes in Viet Nam*, 217.

32. The earliest account of Operation Ranch Hand located by the author is Bigart, "U.S. Spray Strips Foliage." It would take three more years and more intense news coverage before scientists became aware of the issue. The article that most likely caught Galston's attention was Raymond, "Weed Killers Aid War." The story ran after Secretary of State Dean Rusk, in an early attempt to stanch criticism of the herbicide program, made a statement (quoted in the article) assuring Americans of the harmlessness of military herbicides, which were vital to winning the "mean, dirty war" in South Vietnam.

33. Robert A. Divine, "Forward," in Herring, *America's Longest War*, vii.

34. Ehrlich and Holdren, "Starvation as a Policy," 91.

35. For an explication of the events leading up to the UN Convention, see Power, *Problem from Hell*, 47–60.

36. The major study on this topic is LeBlanc, *United States and the Genocide Convention*.

37. "ABA on Genocide."

38. Ibid.

39. The question of whether natural environments have certain legal rights that can be protected in courts ("standing," in legal parlance) is addressed in Stone, "Do Trees Have Standing?"

40. The first work to place ecocide within the larger framework of America's alleged genocidal policies in Vietnam was Weissberg, *Ecocide in Indochina*. The anthology opened with Jean-Paul Sartre's essay "On Genocide" reprinted from *Ramparts*. For an analysis on the impact of ecocide on the broader chemical warfare policy of the United States, see L. Johnston, "Ecocide and the Geneva Protocol."

41. Galston, interview. See also Galston, "Herbicides."

42. Falk, "United States Policy and the Vietnam War," 82.

43. Falk, "Environmental Warfare and Ecocide," 80. Mao Zedong's analogy first reached English-speaking audiences in *Mao Tse-tung on Guerilla Warfare*.

44. Falk, "Environmental Warfare and Ecocide," 84.

45. See also Falk, "Ecocide, Genocide."

46. For contemporary and politically diverse discussions of Nuremberg and Vietnam, see D'Amato, Gould, and Woods, "War Crimes and Vietnam"; Farer et al., "Vietnam and the Nuremberg Principles"; Ferencz, "War Crimes Law"; and T. Taylor et al., "War Crimes, Just and Unjust Wars."

47. Read, "Nuremberg Statement of the Vietnam Day Committee," box 40, DG series 58, Swarthmore College Peace Research Collection (hereafter SCPC). Students for a Democratic Society (SDS) adopted a Nuremberg-style defense that same year to justify its antiwar activities. For a Nuremberg defense within the military, see Roger Priest, "A Call to Resist Illegitimate Authority," 1–3, files G–P, SCPC Alternative GI Newspaper Collection.

48. The most comprehensive overview of the Vietnamese charge in English is "Genocide — Ethnocide — Ecocide," in *Viet Nam: Destruction/War Damage*, 9–19.

49. Quoted in Griswold, "Agent Orange Story." For a photographic essay of third-generation Vietnamese children born with a variety of physical and mental defects, see Griffiths, *Agent Orange*.

50. See, for example, "Defoliation in South Viet Nam"; and Committee of Concerned Asian Scholars, *Indochina Story*, 111–22.

51. On the environmental effects of war, see especially R. P. Tucker and Edmund, *Natural Enemy, Natural Ally*. On environmentally based wartime tactics, see Brady, "Wilderness of War"; McNeill, "Woods and Warfare."

52. See, for example, Chu Thao, "Resuscitation of the Dead Earth," 53–61, in Ly Qui Chung, *Between Two Fires*, 53–61; and "Vietnam: A Chemical Hiroshima."

53. Chomsky, *American Power*, 12.

54. See, for example, Dower, *War without Mercy*; Lauren, *Power and Prejudice*; and Hunt, *Ideology and U.S. Foreign Policy*, especially pp. 46–91.

55. ARVN commanders often initiated requests for spray operations and provided lo-

gistical support during the mission. See, for example, letter dated October 19, 1965, from Robson to Vien approving crop destruction and forest defoliation targets in Phuoc Thanh, box 10, Herbicide Operations Plans, Chemical Operations Division, RG 472, NARA. See also United States-Vietnam Joint Development Group, *The Postwar Development of the Republic of Vietnam*, box 10, Confidential files 1969–74, White House Central files, Nixon Presidential Materials Project (hereafter Nixon Project), NARA.

56. See Gibson, *Perfect War*, 13–21.

57. In May 1963, Senator Barry Goldwater suggested on a television news program that in Vietnam "defoliation of the forests by low-yield atomic weapons could well be done." Quoted in Barnes, "Barry Goldwater, GOP Hero, Dies."

58. Editors' introduction, in Fadiman and White, *Ecocide — and Thoughts toward Survival*, 9.

59. Regarding American Indian cultures, see Grinde and Johansen, *Ecocide of Native America*; and Churchill, *Struggle for the Land*. Regarding equatorial rainforest destruction, see McCuen, *Ecocide and Genocide*. Regarding corporate destruction of a Pacific island, see Gillespie, "Ecocide." Regarding the debt crisis in emerging nations, see George, "Financing Ecocide." Regarding species extinction, see Broswimmer, *Ecocide*. Regarding totalitarian economies in Eurasia, see Feshbach and Friendly, *Ecocide in the USSR*.

60. Eisendrath, *Military Ecocide*; and Cutter, "Ecocide in Babylonia."

61. Diamond, *Collapse*, iv.

62. Activists carrying signs with this message can be viewed in the documentary *The Great Global Warming Swindle*, available at http://tinyurl.com/26nba9t.

63. "X" [George Kennan], "Sources of Soviet Conduct." For an eye-opening analysis of Kennan's writing style, see Costigliola, "Unceasing Pressure For Penetration." A full treatment of Kennan's alienation from national-security politics is offered in Hixson, *George F. Kennan*.

64. "Introductory Remarks by the Hon. George F. Kennan," Newark, N.J., 29 February 1968, folder 6, box 265, George F. Kennan Papers (hereafter GFK Papers), Seeley Mudd Library, Princeton University, Princeton, N.J.

65. All quotes from George Kennan, "The United States, Its Problems, Impact and Image in the World," folder 13, box 266, GFK Papers. See also Kennan, "Rebels without a Program."

66. Jervis, "Was the Cold War a Security Dilemma?" 36.

67. Kennan, "To Prevent a World Wasteland," 401–2.

68. "Inaugural Address of John F. Kennedy," January 20, 1961, available from the Avalon Project of Yale University Law School at http://avalon.law.yale.edu/20th _century/kennedy.asp.

69. Bowie and Immerman, *Waging Peace*.

70. Ghamari-Tabrizi, *Worlds of Herman Kahn*, 20.

71. Kahn, *On Thermonuclear War*, 40–95.

72. Nuclear war and the very existence of nuclear weapons were vigorously protested across the globe during the cold war. The definitive history of this phenomenon is Wittner's three-volume study *The Struggle against the Bomb*. See especially vol. 2, *Resisting the Bomb*. For a brief rebuttal of Kahn's survival estimates, see Commoner, "Feasibility of Biological Recovery."

73. For the text and negotiating history of the test ban treaty, see "Treaty Banning Nuclear Weapons Tests, in the Atmosphere, in Outer Space and Under Water," available at http://www.state.gov/www/global/arms/treaties/ltbt1.html#2. For an analysis of the negotiating history behind the treaty, see Loeb, "Limited Test Ban Treaty."

74. Trachtenberg, *Constructed Peace*.

75. The prevalence of nuclear fears among Americans in the early cold war is examined in Boyer, *By the Bomb's Early Light*. For a discussion of Carson's impact on the environmental movement, see Gottlieb, *Forcing the Spring*, 81–114.

76. A useful contemporary catalog of environmental problems is Horowitz et al., *Eco-Catastrophe*.

77. McNeill, *Something New under the Sun*, 337. On the tensions between cold war authority and 1960s protest, see Suri, *Power and Protest*.

78. For an analysis of these tensions, see Isenberg, "Historicizing Natural Environments." The critique itself is best represented in William Cronon, "The Trouble with Wilderness; or, Getting Back to the Wrong Nature," in Cronon, *Uncommon Ground*, 69–90. See also Bailey, "Earth Day Then and Now."

79. "A Fable for Our Times."

80. Allman, "How to Kill the Earth." See also Schell, "Silent Vietnam."

CHAPTER THREE. Agent Orange before Vietnam

1. Darwin, *Power of Movement in Plants*, 547–48.

2. Botanists have long considered Darwin among their ranks and despair the politicized nature of his early work. See, for example, Robbins, "Expanding Concepts," 13.

3. On the early history of plant growth research, see Kirby, *Hormone Weedkillers*, 7–11; and Roberts and Hooley, *Plant Growth Regulators*, 4–7.

4. Went and Thimann, *Phytohormones*, 111.

5. The excitement created by the nascent field of synthetic hormones is detailed in Tukey, *Plant Regulators in Agriculture*. A more recent account is Busch and Lacy, *Science, Agriculture*.

6. Skoog and Thimann, "Further Experiments."

7. Researchers at the time were also exploring the benefits of arsenical compounds in controlling agricultural pests such as the boll weevil. See Dunlap, *DDT*, 31–35.

8. A. W. A. Brown, *Ecology of Pesticides*, 7.

9. Troyer, "In the Beginning," 290.

10. Thompson, quoted in "A History of BTI," http:// tinyurl.com/2uqvqcb. See also Crocker, *Growth in Plants*; and Hagedorn, *Magnate*.

11. Peterson, "Discovery and Development of 2,4-D," 244. The original findings are discussed in Zimmerman and Hitchcock, "Aerosol Method."

12. Rasmussen, "Plant Hormones," 296–98.

13. George S. Avery Jr., quoted in Rasmussen, "Plant Hormones," 295, emphasis added.

14. Templeman and Marmory, "Effect upon the Growth of Plants."

15. Pokorny, "New Compounds."

16. John Lontz, "Plant Regulant Composition and Method," patent application filed February 20, 1942, issued June 29, 1943, Washington, D.C., U.S. Patent Office. Full text available online at United States, Patent and Trademark Office, http://patft.uspto.gov/. See also F. D. Jones, "Letter to the Editor," which advocates the primacy of Jones's and Lontz's discovery.

17. Zimmerman and Hitchcock, "Substituted Phenoxy and Benzoic Acid Growth Substances." These findings were expanded with special emphasis on the selectivity of 2,4-D by Marth and Mitchell, "2,4-dichlorophenoxyacetic Acid."

18. F. D. Jones, "New Chemical Weedkillers." Jones's work is detailed in Haynes, *American Chemical Industry*, 17–19.

19. Arthur Galston, interview with the author, March 9, 2007, New Haven, Conn.

20. Templeman, "Uses of Plant Growth Substances." Templeman's discovery became British Patent Number 573,929 filed on April 7, 1941.

21. Like Templeman, Nutman and his colleagues were restricted from publishing their discoveries until the end of the war. See Nutman, Thornton, and Quastel, "Plant Growth Substances."

22. For an "insider" account of the social and political dimensions of scientific research, see Hargreaves, *Visions and Discoveries*.

23. J. J. Craig, 2,4-D *Weed Control*.

24. The United States introduced DDT in Naples, Italy, in 1943 to combat a typhus epidemic that threatened to decimate both the local population and advancing Allied forces.

25. See especially Winston, *Nature Wars*, 59–79.

26. I analyze the tactical value of herbicidal warfare in Vietnam in chapter 5.

27. Rasmussen, "Plant Hormones," 299.

28. For an overview of the research conducted at Chicago's Department of Botany, see Mitchell and Stewart, "Comparison of Growth Responses."

29. Hamner and Tukey, "Herbicidal Action," 154. This was the first article to compare the toxic effects of the two compounds.

30. Merck recounted his experience as WBC director in "Peacetime Implications of Biological Warfare," 2:131–46.

31. The original paper by Kraus, "Plant Growth Regulators: Possible Uses," December 18, 1941, is located in folder "WBC Committee Report, Exhibit F," box 1, Chemical and Biological Warfare files, United States National Academy of Science Archives, Washington, D.C. The author obtained a copy of this report from the personal manuscript collection of Matthew S. Meselson (hereafter MSM Papers), Department of Biological Sciences, Harvard University, Cambridge, Mass.

32. For an overview of this program, see Bernstein, "America's Biological Warfare Program"; and J. B. Tucker, "Farewell to Germs."

33. The Zimmerman-Kraus exchange is recounted in Peterson, "Discovery and Development of 2,4-D," 246.

34. Galston, interview.

35. Scientists' warnings against dropping the atom bomb are discussed in Badash, "American Physicists."

36. Kraus and Mitchell, "Growth-Regulating Substances as Herbicides." An earlier discussion of this research without mention of war-related research is Marth and Mitchell, "2,4-dichlorophenoxyacetic Acid."

37. Butler, "Connections," 536.

38. Brophy, Miles, and Cochrane, *Chemical Warfare Service*, 310.

39. Rasmussen, "Plant Hormones," 304.

40. Merck, quoted in Shalett, "U.S. Was Prepared."

41. Minarik, "Crop Division Defoliation Program," 11.

42. Moon, "United States Chemical Warfare Policy," 501.

43. Roosevelt, quoted in U.S. Department of State, Current Treaties and Agreements, "Narrative on the Geneva Protocol," available at http://www.state.gov/t/isn/4784.htm.

44. "Biological warfare" is a modern umbrella term that covers "bacteriological methods warfare" as referred to in the Geneva Protocol and includes warfare involving the use of viruses and toxins.

45. See, for example, J. N. Moore, "Ratification of the Geneva Protocol"; and Bunn, "Gas and Germ Warfare."

46. I discuss issues relating to international law and chemical and biological warfare in chapter 8.

47. In Senate hearings on the Geneva Protocol, legal expert George Bunn cites William Leahy's 1950 memoir *I Was There: The Personal Story of the Chief of Staff to Presidents Roosevelt and Truman* to exemplify this sentiment. Bunn, testimony, in U.S. Congress, Senate, Committee on Foreign Relations, Hearings, *Geneva Protocol of 1925*, 72.

48. Dallek, *Franklin D. Roosevelt*, 86, 91.

49. Merck, "Peacetime Implications of Biological Warfare," 140.

50. "War against Weeds."

51. Carleton, "New TCP Kills Toughest Weeds," 95. On the connections between agricultural and military chemicals up to the Vietnam War, see Russell, *War and*

Nature. The racist caricature of the honeysuckle as a "Jap invader" was common in American discourse during the war. See Dower, *War without Mercy*, especially 77–180.

52. See, for example, Agricultural Research Service, *Leader's Guide to Agriculture's Defense*; Novaresi, *Control of Vegetation through Herbicides*; and Weed Science Society of America, *Effects of Herbicides in Vietnam*.

53. Crafts, *Chemistry and Mode of Action*, 52.

54. Ibid.

55. Kraus, "Remarks." For a more sober contemporary perspective from Britain, see Blackman, "Comparison of Certain Plant-Growth Substances."

56. McNew, "Broader Concepts," 4.

57. Rasmussen, "Plant Hormones," 308–9.

58. Figures cited in Peterson, "Discovery and Development of 2,4-D," 252.

59. Quoted in J. J. Craig, 2,4-D *Weed Control*, 1. On the expansion of the domestic lawn-care industry, see especially Jenkins, *Lawn*, 91–116, 133–58.

60. Figure cited in Hoffman, "Economics of Chemical Weed Control."

61. See, for example, Stamper, "Airplane Applications"; and Motooka et al., "Control of Hawaiian Jungle."

CHAPTER FOUR. Gadgets and Guerrillas

1. The quote paraphrases Logevall, *Choosing War*.

2. See, for example, Adas, *Dominance by Design*, 281–336; and Marr, "Technological Imperative."

3. *Public Papers of the Presidents of the United States* (hereafter *PPPUS*), 401, emphasis added.

4. Gaddis, *Strategies of Containment*, 164.

5. Bowie and Immerman, *Waging Peace*, 5, 83–148.

6. "The Inaugural Address of John F. Kennedy," January 20, 1961, available from the Avalon Project at Yale Law School at http://avalon.law.yale.edu/20th_century/kennedy .asp.

7. The missile gap controversy receives exhaustive treatment in Preble, *John F. Kennedy and the Missile Gap*.

8. Bowie and Immerman, *Waging Peace*.

9. See, for example, Immerman, *CIA in Guatemala*.

10. Taylor, *Uncertain Trumpet*, 4.

11. The standard study of credibility and nuclear deterrence is George and Smoke, *Deterrence in American Foreign Policy*.

12. Taylor, *Uncertain Trumpet*, 5.

13. Ibid., 136.

14. Stubbs, quoted in Kelly, "Gas Warfare in International Law," 42. See also U.S. Army, *U.S. Army Activity*, 1:4-1 to 6-1.

15. Khrushchev, quoted in McNamara, Blight, and Brigham, *Argument without End*, 28. The full text is available in Taylor, "Guerilla Warfare," 44.

16. "Military and Related Aspects of Basic National Security Policy," 33, folder January 1961–May 1961, box 374, National Security file, JFKL, emphasis added.

17. Duiker, *U.S. Containment Policy*, 251.

18. Figures cited in Baldwin, "Flexibility Aim in Arms Buildup."

19. Herring, *America's Longest War*, 76.

20. See especially Maechling, "Camelot, Robert Kennedy, and Counterinsurgency."

21. Freedman, *Kennedy's Wars*, 287.

22. See especially Walt W. Rostow, "Guerilla Warfare in Undeveloped Areas," in Greene, *Guerilla and How to Fight Him*, 54–61. For a historical perspective on insurgencies, see Beckett, *Modern Insurgencies and Counterinsurgencies*; and Chaliand, *Guerrilla Strategies*.

23. The damaging effects of Kennedy's Cuba policies are outlined in Jeffreys-Jones, *CIA and American Democracy*, 118–39. On the connections between Kennedy's anti-Castro policies and the October crisis, see Zubok and Pleshakov, *Inside the Kremlin's Cold War*, 258–74.

24. "Memorandum from Robert W. Komer of the National Security Council Staff to the President's Deputy Special Assistant for National Security Affairs (Rostow)," July 20, 1961, document 100, in U.S. Department of State, *Foreign Relations of the United States* (hereafter *FRUS*), vol. 1, *Vietnam, 1961*, available at http://www.state.gov/www/about_state/history/vol_i_1961/j.html.

25. Bundy, quoted in McNamara, Blight, and Brigham, *Argument without End*, 28.

26. Kennedy, "Address before the American Society of Newspaper Editors," June 1, 1956, in *PPPUS*, 306.

27. "Program of the National Liberation Front of South Vietnam," December 20, 1960, available at http://vietnam.vassar.edu/docnlf.html. For a discussion of the "domino theory," see Berman, *Planning a Tragedy*, 8–11.

28. "National Security Action Memorandum 52," May 11, 1961, Meetings and Memoranda series, National Security file, JFKL.

29. Walt W. Rostow, memorandum to President Kennedy, March 29, 1961, quoted in Herring, *America's Longest War*, 80.

30. Country Team Staff Committee, "Basic Counterinsurgency Plan for Viet-Nam," January 4, 1961, document 1, in *FRUS*, vol. 1, *Vietnam, 1961*, available at http://www.state.gov/www/about_state/history/vol_i_1961/a.html.

31. Quoted in Freedman, *Kennedy's Wars*, 287.

32. Brig. Gen. Edward G. Lansdale, memorandum, "Vietnam," January 17, 1961, cited in Cable, *Conflict of Myths*, 187–88. Lansdale's characterization of the independent

character of the NLF has since been supported by Brigham, *Guerrilla Diplomacy*. For a broader discussion of Lansdale, see Curry, *Edward Lansdale*.

33. Schwab, *Defending the Free World*, 17–18.

34. Johnson, quoted in Warner, "Review Article," 695.

35. See Ney, "Guerrilla Warfare and Modern Strategy."

36. M. Taylor, "Guerrilla Warfare," 43.

37. Huntington, "Introduction," in Franklin, *Modern Guerrilla Warfare*, xvi.

38. Jordan, "Objectives and Methods," 57.

39. LeMay, "Counterinsurgency and the Challenge."

40. Lt. Gen. Lionel McGarr, "Tactics and Techniques of Counter-Insurgent Operations," September 1961, box 204, National Security file, JFKL.

41. See, for example, Cross, *Conflict in the Shadows*.

42. The quote and its history preceding the Vietnam War are cited in Webber and Feinsilber, *Merriam-Webster's Dictionary of Allusions*, 260.

43. Marr, "Rise and Fall of 'Counterinsurgency,'" 207.

44. Buckingham, *Operation Ranch Hand*, 9–10.

45. "Program of Action to Prevent Communist Domination in South Vietnam" is reprinted in part in the *Pentagon Papers*, 2:35–37.

46. Lansdale, quoted in Buckingham, *Operation Ranch Hand*, 11. See also Edward Lansdale, memorandum for General Taylor, undated "Summary of Recommendations," folder 7, boxes 202–3, National Security file, JFKL.

47. Brown, quoted in Cecil, *Herbicidal Warfare*, 25.

48. Buckingham, *Operation Ranch Hand*, 49.

49. A report on the early use of this equipment during herbicide missions is available in J. W. Brown, *Vegetational Spray Tests*, 23–26.

50. The first public acknowledgment of planned forest-defoliation operations in South Vietnam appeared in Raymond, "Army Seeks Way." The first public denial of herbicidal crop destruction is "Pentagon Denies Charge Defoliation Kills Crops."

51. White, quoted in Schlesinger, *Thousand Days*, 544.

52. Herring, *America's Longest War*, 80.

53. Cecil, *Herbicidal Warfare*, 25.

54. "Letter from the President's Military Representative (Taylor) to the President," November 3, 1961, document 210, in *FRUS*, vol. 1, *Vietnam, 1961*, available at http://www.state.gov/www/about_state/history/vol_i_1961/u.html.

55. Memorandum and figures cited in Rostow, "Summaries of Suggested Courses of Action," no. 19, folder 2, box 202–3, National Security file, JFKL.

56. Ibid.

57. The details of the amended program are available in "Project 'Beef-Up': Status Report of the Military Actions Resulting from the NSC Meeting, 11 November 1961," folder 11, box 195, National Security file, JFKL.

58. JCS memorandum to Robert S. McNamara, November 3, 1961, cited in Buckingham, *Operation Ranch Hand*, 16.

59. See chapter 8 for a detailed discussion of the Geneva Protocol, international efforts to ban chemical and biological warfare, and the negotiating history related to herbicidal warfare.

60. For a discussion of international communist reactions, see especially "Memorandum from the Secretary of Defense (McNamara) to President Kennedy," February 2, 1962, document 41, in *FRUS*, vol. 2, *Vietnam, 1962*, available at http://www.state.gov/www/about_state/history/vol_ii_1961–63/c.html.

61. Buckingham, *Operation Ranch Hand*, 18.

62. Dean Rusk, memorandum for the president, "Defoliant Operations in Viet-Nam," November 24, 1961, folder 10, Vietnam Security, President's Office files, JFKL. On the "lessons learned" from the British experience in Malaya, see Komer, *Malayan Emergency in Retrospect*. For a view of the Kennedy administration's stance on biological and chemical warfare issues, see McRae, "National Policy on Use of Chemical and Biological Warfare Agents," December 5, 1961, Biological/Chemical Warfare folder, box 374, National Security file, JFKL. See also U.S. Army, *Law of Land Warfare*; and O'Brien, "Biological-Chemical Warfare," 1–63.

63. Buckingham, *Operation Ranch Hand*, 16.

64. "National Security Action Memorandum 111," November 23, 1961, Meetings and Memoranda series, National Security file, JFKL.

65. These debates emphasize either continuity or breakages in policy from one presidential administration to the next. For the former, see Gelb, *Irony of Vietnam*, 69–95; for the latter, see Buzzanco, *Masters of War*, 81–113.

66. Figures cited in Stellman et al., "Extent and Patterns," 684.

CHAPTER FIVE. Herbicidal Warfare

1. See, for example, Frost, Hopkins, and Rosenthal, "Chemical Warfare," 3.

2. Walt Rostow, memorandum to the president, November 21, 1961, folder 19, box 202–3, National Security file, JFKL.

3. Michael Walzer, *Just and Unjust Wars*, 21.

4. Hilsman, *To Move a Nation*, 434. His recollection of opposing defoliation is corroborated in Hilsman's letter to W. Averell Harriman, August 24, 1962, cited in Maj. William A. Buckingham Jr., "Operation Ranch Hand: Herbicides in Southeast Asia," available at http://tinyurl.com/6x39pb.

5. Dean Rusk, memorandum for the president, "Defoliant Operations in Viet-Nam," November 24, 1961, folder 10, Vietnam Security, President's Office files, JFKL.

6. Harrigan, "Case for Gas Warfare," 12.

7. On the concept of the "humane" alternative offered by chemical warfare, as

promoted in contemporary military circles, see Rothschild, *Tomorrow's Weapons*; "Congressional Committee Hearing on CBR [Chemical, Biological, Radiological]," *Armed Forces Chemical Journal* (June 22, 1959): 18–19; and Hubbell, "Let's Face the Truth."

8. Buckingham, *Operation Ranch Hand*, 26.

9. "JCS Pass to Task Force VN Wash.," December 1961, 39, folder 9, box 195, National Security file, JFKL.

10. For a comprehensive history of the ICC, see Thakur, *Peacekeeping in Vietnam*.

11. Roswell Gilpatric, memo to the Secretary of Defense et al., "Public Affairs and Security Aspects of Operations in Vietnam," January 4, 1962, quoted in Buckingham, *Operation Ranch Hand*, 29.

12. Quoted in Buckingham, *Operation Ranch Hand*, 28.

13. James Brown, "Memorandum for Record, Subject: Meeting with Mr. William Godel on 4 December 1961," cited in Cecil, *Herbicidal Warfare*, 29.

14. "Defoliant Operations in Viet Nam," November 30, 1961, NSAM 1115, National Security Action Memoranda series, Meetings and Memoranda series, National Security file, JFKL.

15. "Project 'Beef-Up': Status Report of the Military Actions Resulting from the NSC Meeting, 11 November 1961," folder 11, box 195, National Security file, JFKL.

16. United States, Congress, House, Committee on Science and Astronautics, *Technology Assessment*, 15–16.

17. Robert McNamara, memorandum to the president, "Defoliant Operations in Vietnam," February 2, 1962, 1, folder 2, box 195, National Security file, JFKL.

18. Anonymous contributor, "Ranch Hand Vietnam: Southeast Asia 1961–1971," available at http://www.ranchhandvietnam.org.

19. McConnell, "Mission: Ranch Hand."

20. Bigart, "U.S. Spray Strips Foliage."

21. Original leaflet available in box 2, RG 472, NARA. Special thanks to the staff at Vietnam Service Inc. of South Philadelphia for their translation assistance.

22. Olenchuk et al., *Evaluation of Herbicide Operations*, 5; and Buckingham, *Operation Ranch Hand*, 34.

23. See, for example, "JCS Pass to Task Force VN-Wash.," folder 9, box 195, National Security file, JFKL.

24. U.S. Air Force, *Project Checo Report*, 2.

25. Buckingham, *Operation Ranch Hand*, 37.

26. "Project 'Beef-Up,'" 6, folder 4, box 195, National Security file, JFKL.

27. The peasants' understanding of the defoliation program remained problematic throughout the war. See, for example, "Résumé of Viet Cong and South Vietnamese Reaction to the Use of Chemicals by the United States and RVN Forces," March 3, 1966, folder III-1966, box 9, RG 472, NARA.

28. Brown's report excerpted in Michael V. Forrestal, "Memorandum for the President: Defoliation in Vietnam," April 16, 1962, folder 2, box 196, National Security file, JFKL.

29. See especially Verwey, *Riot Control Agents*, 102–4.

30. Robert McNamara memorandum to President Kennedy, "Defoliant Operations in Vietnam," February 2, 1962, 3, folder 2, box 195, National Security file, JFKL.

31. Olenchuk et al., *Evaluation of Herbicide Operations*, 5.

32. Boyne, *Beyond the Wild Blue*, 149.

33. James Brown, quoted in Cecil, *Herbicidal Warfare*, 33. See also correspondence from Col. John Larkin to Paul W. Myers, March 14, 1981, available from the Virtual Vietnam Archive of Texas Tech University, item no. 2520314003 at http://www.vietnam .ttu.edu/virtualarchive/.

34. Col. A. L. Hilpert, "Final Report of the Operational Evaluation of Operation Pink Rose," May 5, 1967, folder 2, box 20, RG 472, NARA; and Baker, "Fire Plans Memorandum," folder 11-1966, box 6, RG 472, NARA.

35. Nuttonson, *Physical Environment*, 118; and G. N. Brown et al., *Forests of Free Viet-Nam*, 8–9.

36. Brig. Gen. Fred J. Delmore et al., "Review and Evaluation of ARPA/OSD 'Defoliation' Program," cited in Buckingham, *Operation Ranch Hand*, 52.

37. Olenchuk et al., *Evaluation of Herbicide Operations*, 8.

38. See, for example, U.S. Embassy (Phnom Penh) to Secretary of State, "Priority Memorandum," May 18, 1963, folder 2, box 197, National Security file, JFKL.

39. U.S. Air Force, *Project Checo Report*, 2.

40. Prados, *Blood Trail*, 234.

41. Robert McNamara, memorandum to the president, "Defoliant/Herbicide Program in South Vietnam," November 16, 1962, folder 12, box 195, National Security file, JFKL.

42. Olenchuk et al., *Evaluation of Herbicide Operations*, 24.

43. Social-scientific studies of military effectiveness, especially those pioneered by the RAND Corporation, would not become a mainstay of war planning until the full "Americanization" of the war in the spring of 1965. See, for example, Goure, "Some Impressions."

44. On the Mansfield trip, see "Memorandum of Conversation," document 323, *FRUS*, vol. 2, *Vietnam, 1962*, available at http://www.state.gov/www/about_state/history/ vol_ii_1961–63/ze.html.

45. Kennedy, quoted in *Pentagon Papers*, available at http://www.mtholyoke.edu/ acad/intrel/pentagon2/pent11.htm. The *Papers* do not name the presenters, Maj. Gen. Victor Krulak and Joseph Mendenhall, a foreign service officer. Their mission and subsequent report to the administration is recounted in H. Jones, *Death of a Generation*, 353–59.

46. Quoted in Westmoreland, "Gen. Westmoreland and the Army of the Future,"

NACLA Report on the Americas (November 1969), available at http://nacla.org/archives.

47. Gibson, *Perfect War*.

48. McNeill, "Woods and Warfare." See also Fisher, "Environment and Military Strategy."

49. Quoted in Cable, U.S. Embassy to Secretary of State, "rvn Briefing Fact Sheet," March 20, 1963, folder 11, box 197, National Security file, jfkl.

50. Nighswonger, *Rural Pacification in Vietnam*, 21.

51. Olenchuk et al., *Evaluation of Herbicide Operations*, 25.

52. Buckingham, *Operation Ranch Hand*, 92.

53. Cecil, *Herbicidal Warfare*, 50.

54. U.S. Army, *Tactical Employment of Herbicides*, section 2, 2–3.

55. Military Assistance Command, Vietnam, "Evaluation of Herbicide Operations in the Republic of Vietnam as of 30 April 1966," available at Maxwell afb Library, Maxwell afb, Ala.

56. Herring, *America's Longest War*, 107.

57. As early as April 1963, officials in Washington began to question Diem's capacity to respond to shifting nlf tactics. See, for example, Director of Central Intelligence, "National Intelligence Estimate 53–63."

58. Jacobs, *Cold War Mandarin*, 180.

59. The best expression of this equivocal analysis is found in a memo regarding Secretary of Defense Robert McNamara's report on the situation in South Vietnam delivered to the president in March 1964: "The simple question raised in the McNamara report is whether, with ample U.S. support of counterinsurgency efforts in South Vietnam, the recent trend toward Viet Cong victory can be reversed, and substantial, sustained progress made toward stabilization. I believe the odds are 6 to 5 against this favorable trend setting in within the next 3 to 4 months, as concluded by McNamara, so long as North Vietnamese political, military and logistic support are freely available to the Viet Cong." Memorandum from Ray Cline to the Director of Central Intelligence McCone, document 80, *FRUS*, vol. 2, *Vietnam, 1964*, available at http://www.state.gov/www/about_state/history/vol_i/70_107.html.

60. Schwab, *Defending the Free World*, 42.

61. Quoted in Littauer and Uphoff, *Air War in Indochina*, 50.

62. Gaddis, *Strategies of Containment*, 247.

63. Logevall, *Choosing War*, xvii.

64. Weigley, *American Way of War*, especially 456–69.

65. Duiker, *U.S. Containment Policy*, 307.

66. Ball, quoted in Barrett, "Mythology surrounding Lyndon Johnson," 640. See also Barrett, *Uncertain Warriors*.

67. For a vivid account of U.S. soldiers attempting to fight a virtually undetectable enemy, see Henderson, *Jungle Rules*, 95–99.

68. Rep. Roman Pucinksi (D-Ill.), *Congressional Record* 111 (April 1, 1965): 6777.

69. See, for example, John Moran to Chief of Staff, "Evaluation of the Defoliation Program," October 13 1968, box 14, RG 472, NARA.

70. Buckingham, *Operation Ranch Hand*, 130.

71. Alvin L. Young, "Use of Herbicides in South Vietnam," item 0527, p. 13, available at http://www.nal.usda.gov/speccoll/findaids/agentorange/.

72. Memorandum, John A. Calhoun to U.S. Ambassador, "Helicopter Defoliation Missions," March 13, 1968, folder III-1968, box 9, RG 472, NARA.

73. Military Assistance Command, Vietnam, *Evaluation of Herbicide Operations*, 11–12.

74. Memorandum, Donald Gray to Colonel Sayre, "Pacification Aspects of Boi Loi Forest Defoliation, February 17, 1966, 1, folder III-1965, box 5, RG 472, NARA. Similar reports are available in folder III-1967, box 7, of this collection.

75. Huntington, "Bases of Accommodation," 652–53.

76. See, for example, Walt Rostow, "Guerilla Warfare in the Undeveloped Areas," reprinted in U.S. Department of State, *Bulletin*, August 7, 1961, 233–38.

77. Memorandum, Joseph Califano to the president, October 11, 1968, folder Executive MA5/Presidential Unit Citation 10/1/68, box 15, subject file MA, White House Central Files, LBJL; and "Memorandum for the record of conversation between President Johnson and Prime Minister Pearson," May 28, 1964, document 182, *FRUS, 1964–1968*, vol. 1, *Vietnam, 1964*, available at http://www.state.gov/www/about_state/history/vol_i/181_225.html.

78. Johnson, quoted in Dudney, "Guns of August 1964," 2.

CHAPTER SIX. Science, Ethics, and Dissent

1. "FAS Statement."

2. Johnson, quoted in Cotton and Laura, *Empathetic Education*, 23.

3. The text and negotiating history of the Treaty Banning Nuclear Weapon Tests is available at U.S. Department of State, http://www.state.gov/www/global/arms/treaties/ltbt1.html#2. The standard monograph on this episode is Seaborg, *Kennedy, Khrushchev, and the Test Ban*.

4. See, for example, Montague, "Barry Commoner." On Barry Commoner's involvement in the herbicide controversy, see Commoner et al., "Letter to the Editor of *Bioscience*," E-16, Vietnam files, American Association for the Advancement of Science Archives (hereafter AAAS Archives).

5. Clark, "Occurrence of Unusually High-Level Radioactive Fallout."

6. In 1956 Eisenhower remarked, "The continuance of the present rate of H-Bomb

testing by the most sober and responsible judgment does not imperil the health of humanity." Quoted in Egan, *Barry Commoner and the Science of Survival*, 53.

7. Teller, "Alternatives for Security," 204.

8. Commoner, "Fallout Problem," 1024.

9. For a statistical analysis of the CNI findings, see Reiss, "Strontium-90 Absorption by Deciduous Teeth." For a discussion of the methodology of the CNI survey, see Egan, *Barry Commoner*, 66–72.

10. Golley, *History of the Ecosystem Concept*, 205. For a contemporary examination, see Murray Bookchin, *Ecology and Revolutionary Thought* (pamphlet), available at Contemporary Culture Archives (hereafter CCA), Paley Library, Temple University, Philadelphia.

11. Commoner, *Science and Survival*, 102–3.

12. Commoner, "Toxicological Time Bomb."

13. See Bocking, *Ecologists and Environmental Politics*.

14. Goodell, *Visible Scientists*, 39–69.

15. Kuznick, *Beyond the Laboratory*, 2. Special thanks to Professor Kuznick of American University for sharing his draft paper "Creating a 'Science of Survival': Early Years through the End of 1965," November 2003.

16. Bernal, *Social Function of Science*, 1–2.

17. Ibid., 165.

18. Rosebury, "Peace or Extinction," 54.

19. Vogt, *Road to Survival*, 278. George Kennan's environmental critique and framework is outlined in his "To Prevent a World Wasteland."

20. Bush, *Modern Arms and Free Men*, 3.

21. See, for example, Stoll, *U.S. Environmentalism since 1945*, 76–82; and Gottlieb, *Forcing the Spring*, 81–86.

22. Carson, *Silent Spring*, 2–3.

23. The social critique inherent in Carson's ecological thought is analyzed in Kroll, "Rachel Carson's *Silent Spring*."

24. McCay, *Rachel Carson*, 74.

25. See especially "Desolate Year."

26. On the reaction to *Silent Spring*, see Dunlap, *DDT*, 98–125; and Lear, *Rachel Carson*, 428–56.

27. For example, Carson could have come across Raymond, "Army Seeks Way to Strip Jungles," or Bigart, "U.S. Spray Strips Foliage Hiding Vietnam Reds."

28. For an explicit comparison of Vietnam to Carson's American dystopia, see Baghat, "Vietnam: Where No Birds Sing."

29. Carson, *Silent Spring*, 7.

30. Interviews with the author, Arthur Westing, March 4, 2007, Putney, Vt., and Arthur Galston, March 9, 2007, New Haven, Conn.

31. See chapter 4 for a discussion of Kennedy's concern vis-à-vis international communist propaganda.

32. Burchett's 1963 book *The Furtive War* describes guerrilla tactics and arcane counterinsurgency methods to combat them.

33. Burchett, "War against the Trees," 26.

34. Dower, *War without Mercy*.

35. Kastenmeier, "Pentagon Booby-Trap." See also *Congressional Record* 109 (March 4, 1963): 11187. Senator Mike Mansfield voiced his concerns about the herbicide operations and included critical reports of herbicidal warfare written by Richard Dudman of the *Washington Evening Star*.

36. Robert Kastenmeier to President Kennedy, March 7, 1963, file unit ND19/CO 312 Vietnam (General), box 636, White House Central Files, JFKL.

37. William Bundy to Robert Kastenmeier, file unit ND19/CO 312 Vietnam (General), box 636, White House Central Files, JFKL. See also Dudman, "Kennedy Would Side-Step Issue."

38. "One Man's Meat," 5.

39. "FAS Statement," 46.

40. Ibid., 47. The notion of Vietnam as a CBW "laboratory" is most fully advanced in Lewallen, *Ecology of Devastation*, 180–84.

41. Crumpton and Teich, "Role of AAAS."

42. "Science and Human Welfare."

43. For broader discussions of these issues, see M. Brown, *Social Responsibility of the Scientist*; and Kleinman, *Science, Technology, and Democracy*.

44. Comprehensive list of "Articles, Editorials and Letters in *Science*," January 20, 1961–February 28, 1964, folder 3, Human Welfare files, AAAS Archives.

45. Wolfle, *Renewing a Scientific Society*, 247.

46. DeBenedetti, with Chatfield, *American Ordeal*, 109.

47. Resolution, "Chronological Summary of AAAS Actions Related to Proposals Concerning War in Vietnam," 1, F-16, Vietnam files, AAAS Archives.

48. The standard study of "limited nuclear war" is Kissinger, *Nuclear Weapons and Foreign Policy*.

49. Jean Pfeiffer (E. W. Pfeiffer's widow), interview with the author, May 10, 2007, Missoula, Mont.

50. Resolution, "Chronological Summary of AAAS Actions related to Proposals concerning War in Vietnam," 1, F-16, Vietnam files, AAAS Archives.

51. For a review of Pfeiffer's politics, see especially Pearson, "E. W. Pfeiffer."

52. Don Price to E. W. Pfeiffer, January 3, 1967, EWP papers.

53. "Minutes of the Meeting of the Committee on Council Affairs," December 27, 1966, October–December 1966, BCM files, AAAS Archives.

54. Don Price to Robert McNamara, September 13, 1967, EWP papers.

55. For an overview of the academy's scope of duties, see "NAS Constitution," available at http://www.nasonline.org/site/PageServer?pagename=ABOUT_constitution.

56. Peterson, "Discovery and Development of 2,4-D," 246–47.

57. Boffey, *Brain Bank of America*, 147.

58. "Scientists Decry 'Chemical Warfare.'" See also "Scientists Protest Crop Destruction"; and "Statement on the Use of Chemical Agents."

59. "CBW Materials," March 23–24, 1965, 1, Chemical and Biological Weapons folder, box 212, Vietnam Country file, National Security file, LBJL.

60. Ibid., 10. Califano was a close advisor to LBJ on a range of domestic issues. His account of the Johnson presidency is *The Triumph and Tragedy of Lyndon Johnson*.

61. "Letter from Galston et al. to President Lyndon Johnson," September 6, 1966, reprinted in *BioScience* 17 (January 1967): 10.

62. Galston, interview.

63. "Letter from Galston et al. to President Lyndon Johnson."

64. Ibid.

65. "Letter from Dixon Donnelly to Arthur Galston," reprinted in *BioScience* 17 (January 1967): 10. For an identical explanation from a different source, see the letter from R. G. Cleveland to Dael Wolfle, August 14, 1966, F-16, Vietnam files, AAAS Archives.

66. For an early yet comprehensive overview of proposed scientific contributions in Vietnam, see White, "Lower Mekong," 6–10.

67. For neo-Malthusian scarcity literature, see especially Ehrlich, *Population Bomb*; and Meadows et al., *Limits to Growth*. On the impact of the NASA photograph of the "blue marble" in the sky, see Jeff Sanders, "Environmentalism," in Farber and Bailey, *Columbia Guide*, 273–80.

68. For a comprehensive review of the Johnson administration's environmental policies, see U.S. President's Science Advisory Committee, *Restoring the Quality of Our Environment*.

69. The "nuclear option" was not totally unthinkable in connection with U.S. policy in Vietnam; presidential administrations from Eisenhower to Nixon considered using tactical or low-yield nuclear weapons against the communists who ruled North Vietnam. National Security Archive Electronic Briefing Book no. 195, "Nixon White House Considered Nuclear Options against North Vietnam, Declassified Documents Reveal," available at http://www.gwu.edu/~nsarchiv/NSAEBB/NSAEBB195/index.htm.

70. Since the beginning of large-scale military drafting for the Vietnam War, college-aged resisters cited CBW in Vietnam as a primary reason to protest the war. See, for example, Committee for Nonviolent Action et al., "Declaration of Conscience," reprinted in Gettleman et al., *Vietnam and America*, 305–6.

71. "Topic: Washington Scene — AAAS and Ethics," June 24, 1968, folder 4, Council Minutes 1968, AAAS Archives.

72. "Use of CB Weapons."

73. U.S. Congress, House, Report to the Subcommittee on Science, Research and Development, *Technology Assessment*, 35.

74. Boffey, *Brain Bank of America*, 149.

75. John S. Foster, quoted in Arthur W. Galston, "Reaction of the United States Scientific Community to the Use of Herbicides in Vietnam," February 28, 1968, unpublished draft, box 17, AWG Papers.

76. Carson's tendency toward ecological hyperbole has remained to this day key ammunition for her critics. See, for example, Tierney, "Fateful Voice of a Generation."

77. Westing, interview.

78. "Bright '68 for Ag Chemicals," 32.

79. See Nicosia, *Home to War*, 482–83; and "Agent Orange and the Pentagon."

80. Galston, "Changing the Environment," 123.

81. Commoner, quoted in Minutes, "Scientists' Committee on Chemical Warfare in Vietnam," EWP papers.

82. John S. Foster to Don Price, September 29, 1967, F-12, Vietnam files, AAAS Archives.

83. Llewelyn Williams, "Forests of Southeast Asia, Puerto Rico and Texas," quoted in House et al., "Assessment of Ecological Effects," 130.

84. Ibid., 145.

85. The NAS review is excerpted in National Academy of Sciences, *News Report* 18 (March 1969): 3.

86. Frederic Seitz to John S. Foster, January 31, 1969, quoted in Boffey, *Brain Bank of America*, 149.

87. See, for example, U.S. Congress, House, Report, *Technology Assessment*, 44–46; and Novick, "Vietnam Herbicide Experiment," 20–21. Fred Tschirley, a scientist with the USDA, offers a more sympathetic view in "Review."

88. "On the Use of Herbicides," 253–54.

89. For a fuller treatment of scientific skepticism of government policy during the Vietnam War, see Robert J. Lifton, "The Circle of Deception," tab L, Vietnam files, AFSC Central Archives.

90. E. W. Pfeiffer to Dael Wolfle, November 26, 1968, EWP papers.

91. Agenda minutes, "Meeting of the Committee of Council Affairs," December 27, 1968, 1–2, tab K, 1960–69, Bureau Council Minutes files, AAAS Archives.

92. Wittner, *Rebels against War*, 301.

93. Zacharias, "Absolute Weapons . . . More Deadly than the Atom," box 4, Document Group 58, SCPC, emphasis added. The quote also appears in "International: Alphabet of Destruction."

94. The amount of literature and committee action concentrating on CBW-related issues rose sharply in the late 1960s, largely as a result of American actions in Vietnam.

For literature, see Barnaby et al., *Supreme Folly*; Rose, *CBW*; Langer, "Chemical and Biological Warfare (I)"; Harvey, *Vietnam*. For committees, see Union of Concerned Scientists, "CBW Pamphlet," box 40, RG 58, SCPC; "CBR Warfare," 1969 Files, Committee for World Development and World Disarmament, AWG Papers; "Proceedings," Edinburgh University Teach-In on Chemical and Biological Warfare, box 7, AWG Papers.

95. Barbara Tischler, "The Antiwar Movement," in Young and Buzzanco, *Companion to the Vietnam War*, 391.

96. For works that specifically examine antiwar protest on college campuses, see Heineman, *Campus Wars*; and Degroot, *Student Protest*. For contemporary analyses, see Schuman, "Two Sources of Antiwar Sentiment"; and U.S. Congress, House, Ad Hoc Committee, *Student Views*, 1970.

97. For extremist literature on this subject, see, for example, *Science for the People*, April 23, 1971, available at CCA, Paley Library, Temple University, Philadelphia.

98. "New Bag on Campus."

99. Thomas Pettigrew Jr., in U.S. Congress, House, *Student Views*, 37.

100. Sierra Club, "Conservation Policies."

101. See, for example, Wells, *War Within*, which argues that antiwar protestors failed to end the war. Jeffreys-Jones, *Peace Now!* argues the opposite point. A more balanced view is Small, *Johnson, Nixon, and the Doves*.

102. See, for example, Lappé, "Chemical and Biological Warfare: The Science of Public Death" (Publication for Science Students for Social Responsibility), box 40, RG 58, SCPC.

103. Geiger, "Science, Universities and National Defense," 45. See also Chomsky et al., *Cold War and the University*.

104. See, for example, Price, "Some Aspects of Air Force-University Relations."

105. Kolko analyzed his own experiences at Penn and military-university collaboration generally in "War on Campus."

106. This episode is examined in detail in Jonathan Goldstein, "Agent Orange on Campus: The Summit-Spicerack Controversy at the University of Pennsylvania, 1965–1967," in Tischler, *Sights on the Sixties*, 43–61. See also Stern, "War Catalog."

107. The iconic image of a naked young girl and other Vietnamese villagers fleeing a napalm attack is available at http://tinyurl.com/3c3rhd. A biography that examines the life of the girl, Kim Phuc, and the worldwide impact of the photograph, is Chong, *Girl in the Picture*.

108. Zinn, *Dow Shalt Not Kill*, available at CCA, Paley Library, Temple University, Philadelphia.

109. For an overview of Dow protest, see Eden, "Historical Introduction." For opposing viewpoints on Dow's moral association with universities, see Ford, "Right to Recruit"; and Rowley, "Blood and Fire."

110. Doan, quoted in "Ire against Fire." See also Dow Chemical Company, "Let's Stick with the Facts,"1969, 1–6, press packet, Dow Foundation Archival Records, Midland, Mich.; and Whitehead, *Dow Story*, 263–69.

111. See, for example, Sigal, *Fighting to a Finish*. For a broader discussion of how wars end, see Craig and George, *Force and Statecraft*, 229–44.

CHAPTER SEVEN. Surveying a Catastrophe

1. Figure cited and quoted in G. N. Brown et al., *Forests of Free Viet-Nam*, 45. For an overview of the Japanese quest for natural resources during the World War II, see Marshall, *To Have and Have Not*. For an earlier French perspective on the military value of forests, see Demorlaine, "L'importance stratégique des forêts."

2. Sterling, Hurley, and Minh, *Vietnam*, 261–63.

3. Turner, *Ecology of Trees*, 6.

4. Thái, *Natural Environment*, 18 and 63–67.

5. Nuttonson, *Physical Environment*, 118.

6. Figures cited in Vietnam, Embassy to the United States, "Flora and Fauna of Vietnam," available at http://tinyurl.com/3ytvgxq.

7. Expressed as a ratio of species to land area, the biodiversity of Vietnam is extremely high. By contrast, China boasts approximately triple the number of Vietnam's species but is nearly thirty times the size of Vietnam. Figures cited in China, "Facts and Figures — Fauna and Flora Resources," available at http://www.china.org.cn/english/features/china/203701.htm.

8. Sterling et al., *Vietnam*, 24.

9. For a contemporary and at times rhapsodic discussion of Vietnamese culture and land use, see especially Fitzgerald, *Fire in the Lake*, 10 and 142–45.

10. Galston, quoted in Knoll and McFadden, *War Crimes*, 71.

11. Minarik report, cited in "Army Scientist Defends Defoliant Use," 17.

12. "Herbicide Hassle."

13. Foster, quoted in "Herbicide Controversy May Flare Anew," 28. See also "Defoliants: Use Still Controversial."

14. Harold J. Coolidge to Dael Wolfle, May 23, 1968, F-16, Vietnam files, AAAS Archives, emphasis added.

15. O'Toole, "Pentagon Defends Use of Herbicide."

16. "Herbicide Controversy May Flare Anew." See also "Defoliants: Use Still Controversial."

17. Schwab, *Clash of Cultures*, 123–42. The classic study on the topic is Huntington, *Soldier and the State*, especially 345–455.

18. Barry Flamm, "A Partial Evaluation of Herbicidal Effects," April 10, 1968, folder 1, box 20, RG 472, NARA.

19. The parameters of MACV studies remained virtually unchanged throughout the

war. For a contemporary analysis, see the declassified portion of MACVJ2, "Herbicide Program Seminar," January 28, 1968, available from Texas Tech Virtual Vietnam Archive, item no. 2520308001, at http://www.vietnam.ttu.edu/virtualarchive/.

20. See, for example, Russo, *Statistical Analysis*.

21. See, for example, transcript, "The Chemical War against Plants and People," WTIC (Yale University Radio) interview with Arthur Galston, February 4, 1968, box 17, AWG Papers.

22. Commoner et al., "Defoliation Controversy," 1097.

23. Commoner was referencing the standard justification for dropping the atomic bomb against Japan.

24. Tschirley, "Review."

25. The ambiguous character of Tschirley's report was reflected in two newspaper accounts: Robinson, "Study Finds Defoliants Change Vietnam Ecology"; and Lescaze, "U.S. Study Finds Defoliant Harmless."

26. Tschirley, "Defoliation in Vietnam," 786 (quotation).

27. Charles Bohlen to Dael Wolfle, September 3, 1968, F-16, Vietnam files, AAAS Archives.

28. Rodney Nichols to Dael Wolfle, November 7, 1968; and Donald Macarthur to Dael Wolfle, October 2, 1968, both in F-16, Vietnam files, AAAS Archives.

29. Figures cited in Galston, "Military Uses of Herbicides in Vietnam," 10.

30. Jean Pfeiffer, interview with the author, May 10, 2007, Missoula, Mont. This official was identified in as Mr. A. E. Hayward, in the Office of the Director of Defense Research and Engineering, Department of Defense, in a letter from W. C. Shaw, chairman of the Weed Science Society of America to Dael Wolfle, executive director of the AAAS, December 11, 1969, F-13, Vietnam files, AAAS Archives.

31. For a general overview of the difficulties facing epidemiologists attempting to establish correlation, see Kleinbaum, Kupper, and Morgenstern, *Epidemiologic Research*, 1–15.

32. U.S. officials confirmed drift on rubber plantations. See, for example, "United States Experts Report on Defoliation in Cambodia," in U.S. Department of State, *Bulletin*, December 29, 1969, 635.

33. Pfeiffer and Orians, "Mission to Vietnam," pts. 1 and 2.

34. W. Sullivan, "Zoologist, Back from Vietnam."

35. Pfeiffer, letter to the editor.

36. DeBenedetti, with Chatfield, *American Ordeal*, 253. The quoted characterization is from Lynn, "Charles Goodell."

37. Appropriately, *Science* hosted the controversy in its letters section. See, for example, Komer (former member of the NSC), letter to the editor; Sachs, "Vietnam: AAAS Herbicide Study" (This letter quotes Westing's remark to Fort Detrick personnel: "I am the enemy."); and Chamlin, "Defoliation Saves Lives."

38. Haseltine, Carter, and Long, "Human Suffering in Vietnam," 6. Human health

concerns relating to the Vietnam War extended far beyond the herbicide controversy. See, for example, Collins et al., *Medical Problems of South Vietnam*; Clayton, "Health in Vietnam"; Alland, "War and Disease"; and Leo, "Threat of Plague."

39. For Pfeiffer's response to Haseltine, see Pfeiffer, "United States Goals in Vietnam."

40. Legator's biography is available at http://www.ems-us.org/Content/Membership/mlegator.asp.

41. William A. Haseltine, interview with the author, April 20, 2007, Washington, D.C.

42. NARMIC Project Overview and related materials available in (two boxes) NARMIC files, AFSC Central Archives. See also Klare et al., *Weapons for Counterinsurgency*.

43. Haseltine, interview.

44. The most comprehensive analysis of the Bionetics report is Epstein, "Family Likeness." Epstein was chief of the Laboratories of Environmental Toxicology, Children's Cancer Research Inc., Boston, Mass.

45. Haseltine, Cook, and Galston, "Deliberate Destruction of the Environment." See also Primack and Hippel, *Advice and Dissent*; and Whiteside, "Reporter at Large."

46. Quoted in "Defoliants, Deformities," 15.

47. Flint, "Dow Aides Deny Herbicide Risk."

48. Dow Chemical maintains this position today. See http://www.dow.com/commitments/debates/agentorange/index.htm. In litigation against the chemical producers of Agent Orange begun in 1979, Vietnam Veterans plaintiffs (and later, Vietnamese nationals) argued the corporate defendants could have prevented the incidence of dioxin in their herbicide products, thereby reducing the risk associated with human exposure to a known toxin. See Schuck, *Agent Orange on Trial*, 99–100.

49. Phuoc et al., *Congenital Malformations*, 7.

50. These famous discoveries are detailed in Holmes, *Meselson, Stahl and the Replication of DNA*.

51. Matthew Meselson, interview with the author, March 6, 2007, Cambridge, Mass.

52. Quoted in Primack and Hippel, *Advice and Dissent*, 77. For Nelson's story, see B. Nelson, "Studies Find Danger in Defoliation Herbicides." Nelson included DuBridge's plan for restricting 2,4,5-T. For a full response, see U.S. Department of Health, Education, and Welfare, *Report of the Secretary's Commission*.

53. DuBridge, quoted in "Herbicides: Order on 2,4,5-T."

54. W. C. Shaw to John Ringle, December 16, 1969, F-13, Vietnam files, AAAS Archives. A similar perspective from another USDA official is a letter from Philip Kearney to Matthew Meselson and Arthur Westing, March 25, 1970, box 7, AWG Papers. For the Pentagon's similar response, see Anderson, "Defoliants May Cause Deformities."

55. See, for example, Lamade, "Fact, Not Sensationalism."

56. Joint Statement, Departments of Agriculture, Interior, and Health, Education, and Welfare, "Home Use of 2,4,5-T Suspended," available at http://www.nal.usda.gov/speccoll/findaids/agentorange/.

57. Quoted in Gruchow, "Curbs on 2,4,5-T Imposed."

58. Testimony, Lee DuBridge, in U.S. Congress, Senate, *Effects of 2,4,5-T and Related Herbicides*, 57–58.

59. J. Johnson, "Safety in the Development of Herbicides."

60. Many scientists in government and academia questioned the validity of extrapolating intense exposure of lab mice to 2,4,5-T to less direct exposure of humans to the compound. See, for example, Newton and Norris, "Herbicide Usage."

61. "Scientists' Committee on CBW, "2,4,5-T Resolution," N–D 1969, 1969–1970, Bureau Council Minutes, AAAS Archives.

62. Walter Orr Roberts to Ellsworth Bunker, January 2, 1969, F-16, Vietnam files, AAAS Archives.

63. Memorandum, Walter Orr Roberts to AAAS Board, "More about Vietnam Herbicides," January 19, 1969, F-16, Vietnam files, AAAS Archives.

64. "AAAS Minutes of the Meeting of the Board of Directors," 2, N–D, 1969–1970, Bureau Council Minutes, AAAS Archives.

65. Matthew Meselson to Dael Wolfle, January 29, 1970, F-13, Vietnam files, AAAS Archives.

66. Matthew Meselson to J. H. Davidson, Agricultural Department, Dow Chemical, January 27, 1970, MSM Papers.

67. R. L. Johnson to Bentley Glass, March 12, 1970, MSM Papers.

68. See, for example, Herman Pollock to Athelstan Spilhaus, AAAS president, July 24, 1970; and Athelstan Spilhaus to Secretary of Defense Melvin Laird, July 25, 1970, both in F-13, Vietnam files, AAAS Archives.

69. Draft notes, Herbicide Assessment Commission, Woods Hole Conference (June 15–19, 1970), F-13, Vietnam files, AAAS Archives. The abbreviated report appeared as "Herbicides in Vietnam: AAAS Study Finds Widespread Devastation."

70. McArthur, "U.S. Reduces Defoliation."

71. The earliest official considerations regarding the termination of Operation Ranch Hand surfaced in August 1969, although the government refused to offer details. See Woodruff, "U.S. Is Expected to End Task of Viet Defoliation."

72. See Canatsey, "Bigger Bite for Bulldozers."

73. Robert Cook, interview with the author, March 6, 2007, Cambridge, Mass.

74. Arthur Westing, personal diary of the HAC mission, 17. Copy in the author's possession, original with Westing in Putney, Vt.

75. Robert Cook, personal diary of the HAC mission, 8. Copy in the author's possession, original with Cook in Cambridge, Mass.

76. Cook diary, August 13, 1970, 29.

77. Herbicide Assessment Commission, Report, 30–32, F-14, Vietnam files, AAAS Archives.

78. Meselson, quoted in "Pentagon Seen Blocking Study of Defoliation."

79. On the effects of crop destruction on civilian populations, see Mayer, "Starvation as a Weapon."

80. Packet of letters enclosed in letter, Matthew Meselson to William Bevan, December 4, 1970, MSM Papers.

81. "Herbicides in Vietnam: AAAS Study Finds Widespread Devastation," 43.

82. Arthur Westing, "The Effects of Large-Scale Use of Herbicides and Defoliants," from the proceedings recorded on four cassette tapes, located in the AAAS Archives and transcribed by the author.

83. McElheny, "Herbicides in Vietnam."

84. Hodgkin, "Rains of Destruction in Vietnam."

85. Lewis, "Poison Is Good for You." Lewis took interest in the matter after Pentagon officials disputed the HAC's negative characterization of Operation Ranch Hand. See "Pentagon Disputes Defoliation Study"; and Schmidt, "Pentagon Disputes Study of Spraying Devastation."

86. "U.S. Added Herbicidal Rape."

87. Stanford Biology Study Group, *The Destruction of Indochina: A Legacy of Our Presence* (1970), CCA, Temple University, Philadelphia.

88. Westing's many works include Westing, "America in Vietnam"; Westing, "Ecological Effects of Military Defoliation"; Westing, "Forestry and the War"; Westing, "Leveling the Jungle"; and Haseltine and Westing, "Wasteland."

89. Westing, *Ecological Consequences*; and Westing, *Herbicides in War*.

90. The firm's name is Westing Associates in Environment, Security and Education, Putney, Vt.

91. Pfeiffer, interview.

92. Pfeiffer's contributions include Neilands et al. *Harvest of Death*; Pfeiffer, "Degreening Vietnam"; Pfeiffer, "Operation Ranch Hand"; Pfeiffer, "Post-War Vietnam"; and Pfeiffer, "Some Effects of Environmental Warfare."

93. Meselson and Constable, "Ecological Impact." For an account of Meselson's activities since the herbicide controversy, see "Interview with Matthew Meselson."

94. See, for example, Dwernychuk et al., "Dioxin Reservoirs in Southern Viet Nam"; and Schecter et al., "Recent Dioxin Contamination."

95. John Constable, interview with the author, June 12, 2007, Cambridge, Mass.

96. Galston, "Plants, People, and Politics," 405. On the phenomenon of youth disaffection and consequent postmodern nihilism in the post-Vietnam era, see especially Suri, *Power and Protest*, 259–60, 262. See also Galston, "Science and Social Responsibility"; Galston, Lecture at the Agent Orange Victims International National Convention,

October 23, 1982, Stamford, Conn., available at Texas Tech Virtual Vietnam Archive, item no. 6170101014, http://www.vietnam.ttu.edu/virtualarchive/.

97. Galston, "Vietnamese Journey"; "Statement of Policy," June 2, 1975, box 15, AWG Papers; Galston, with Savage, *Daily Life in People's China*. On Galston's broader work on society and plant biology, see Galston, "Plant Biology"; and Galston, *Green Wisdom*.

98. Arthur Galston, interview with the author, March 9, 2007, New Haven, Conn. A tribute to Galston's contributions to the Interdisciplinary Center for Bioethics is available at http://www.yale.edu/bioethics/InMemoriam.htm.

99. Race, Review of *Harvest of Death*.

CHAPTER EIGHT. Against Protocol

1. U.S. President, *U.S. Foreign Policy for the 1970s*, 2.

2. The most authoritative accounts of the Nixon/Kissinger détente strategy with regard to Vietnam are Garthoff, *Détente and Confrontation*, 248–56; and Gaddis, *Strategies of Containment*, 274–308. For an analysis that focuses specifically on Vietnam, see especially Kimball, *Vietnam War Files*, 8–28. In his memoirs, Nixon describes the entire détente framework as hinging on ending the Vietnam War. It was "the key to everything," he recalled; Nixon, *RN*, 16.

3. Federal Civil Defense Administration, "General Concepts of Chemical Warfare"; and J. B. Tucker, "Farewell to Germs," 110. For an earlier perspective, see U.S. War Department, Military Intelligence Division, "Intelligence Review."

4. For a comprehensive overview of Nixon's disarmament initiatives, see "Ninth Annual Report of ACDA Transmitted to the Congress," reprinted in U.S. Department of State, *Bulletin*, May 4, 1970, 585–92.

5. U.S. President, "Statement on Chemical and Biological Defense Policies and Programs." The full text is available from *The American Presidency Project*, University of California, Santa Barbara, http://www.presidency.ucsb.edu/ws/?pid=2343.

6. Nixon's speeches almost always displayed a flair for the dramatic. As William Bundy observes of Nixon's style, "The model of Charles de Gaulle was always with him: saying little until the timing was right and then speaking with the greatest possible force"; Bundy, *Tangled Web*, 517.

7. Memorandum from Henry Kissinger to Richard Nixon, December 9, 1969, folder 6, box 310, NSC files, Nixon Project, NARA.

8. See, for example, letter from Edward F. Snyder to Richard Nixon, November 26, 1969, folder 6, box 310, NSC files, Nixon Project, NARA. For a historical defense of the legality of herbicidal warfare, see Lewy, *America in Vietnam*, 257–66.

9. Matthew Meselson, testimony, U.S. Senate, Committee on Foreign Relations, *Chemical and Biological Warfare*, 24.

10. This line of reasoning gained traction in Congress before the Geneva Protocol affair. See, for example, Congressman John Dellenback, *Congressional Record* 115 (November 3, 1969): 32737.

11. Rothschild, *Tomorrow's Weapons.* The review is Meselson, "Book Review." Another invocation of Rothschild's ideas is Celick, "Humane Warfare for International Peacekeeping." For intellectual antecedents to Rothschild's analysis, see Federal Civil Defense Administration, "General Concepts of Chemical Warfare"; and U.S. War Department, "Intelligence Review."

12. J. W. Fulbright to Richard Nixon, February 19, 1970, CBW file folder 2, box 311, National Security file, Nixon Project, NARA.

13. "United States Criticizes Vote."

14. See, for example, Meselson, "Chemical and Biological Weapons"; and "FAS Statement."

15. See, for example, Edward Kennedy to Arthur Westing, June 12, 1970, MSM Papers.

16. Fry, *Debating Vietnam*, 151.

17. As a nonparty to the Geneva Protocol, the United States was technically invulnerable to charges that it had violated international law. Official statements had indicated that the United States considered itself an adherent to the Geneva Protocol since its creation in 1925 (and throughout the Vietnam War) as a matter of customary (meaning normative) international law. See "customary international law" in *Black's Law Dictionary*, 8th ed., 835.

18. CIA, Directorate of Intelligence, *Intelligence Report*, folder 7, box 310, NSC files, Nixon Project, NARA.

19. See, for example, Petrov, "Important Aspect of Disarmament"; Bach, "Law"; Nechayuk, "Weapons of 'Civilised Barbarians'"; "Nixon Administration's Escalations"; Grümmer, *Accusation from the Jungle.*

20. For background information on U.S. military participation in chemical warfare prior to Vietnam, see Heller, *Chemical Warfare in World War I*; and Kleber and Birdsell, *Chemical Warfare Service.*

21. The full text and negotiating history of the Washington Conference appears in Goldblat, *Problem of Chemical and Biological Warfare*, 4:46–49.

22. The successful lobbying campaign in the Senate is recounted in D. P. Jones, "American Chemists." See also U.S. Senate, Report, *Chemical-Biological-Radiological Warfare*, 3–10. For a contemporary legal analysis, see Hudson, "Geneva Protocol."

23. UN Resolution 2162 (XXI), *Official Records of the General Assembly, Twenty-fourth Session*, 10–11.

24. UN Resolution 2603 (XXIV) in *Official Records of the General Assembly, Twenty-first Session*, 16–17. The majority opinion of this resolution was reaffirmed by Secretary General U. Thant in United Nations Report E. 69 I. 24, published as

Chemical and Bacteriological (Biological) Weapons and the Effects of their Possible Use, xxvi.

25. Genocide became a crime of international law under UN Resolution 96 (I) of December 11, 1946. The term was fully defined by international agreement at the Convention on the Prevention and Punishment of the Crime of Genocide (known as the "Genocide Convention") of December 1948. The full text of the convention is available at http://www.yale.edu/lawweb/avalon/un/genocide.htm.

26. Falk, "Environmental Warfare and Ecocide," 84. In response to Operation Ranch Hand, Falk proposed the "Convention on the Crime of Ecocide" in 1973, which combined the norms established at the Genocide Convention with the Declaration of the 1972 Conference on the Human Environment of the United Nations General Assembly.

27. See R. D. Johnson, *Congress and the Cold War,* 69–104, on the key role played by the "liberal new internationalists" in the formulation of U.S. cold war policy in the Vietnam era.

28. Senator Stephen Young, *Congressional Record* 116 (June 17, 1970): 20079.

29. The resolution is reprinted in Bevan, "AAAS Council Meeting 1970."

30. U.S. Department of State, *Bulletin,* January 18, 1971, 77. The similarity in wording was probably not accidental. On December 15, Matthew Meselson had met with Henry Kissinger at the White House to brief him on the pending AAAS announcement. Memorandum, Michael Guhin to Dr. Kissinger, National Security Council, "Memcon of Meeting with Matt Meselson and Information as Requested," available from the Digital National Security Archive, http://nsarchive.chadwyck.com/marketing/index.jsp, hereafter DNSA.

31. The details of the report appear in "Defoliation: Secret Army Study Urges Use in Future Wars." Congressman and future defense secretary Les Aspin called such plans "a flight of fancy right out of Dr. Strangelove, a real nightmare of computer lunacy"; *Congressional Record* 118 (August 18, 1972): 29243.

32. In this context "civilians" include representatives from the major chemical manufacturers of herbicides, including Dow and Monsanto.

33. A detailed analysis on the congressional stance toward environmental issues generally and the herbicides specifically is U.S. Congress, Senate, *Effects of 2,4,5-T and Related Herbicides.*

34. Memorandum from Melvin Laird to Henry Kissinger, "U.S. National Policy on Chemical and Biological Warfare Activities," April 30, 1969, available at DNSA.

35. "Convention on the Prohibition of the Development, Production and Stockpiling of Bacteriological (Biological) and Toxin Weapons and on Their Destruction," signed at London, Moscow, and Washington, D.C., April 10, 1972. Full text available at http://www .opbw.org/convention/conv.html.

36. Congressman Robert Kastenmeier, testimony, U.S. Congress, Senate, *Chemical and Biological Warfare,* 136.

37. See, for example, SR 154, proposed by Senator Hubert Humphrey, *Congressional Record* 117 (July 23, 1971): 26931.

38. In a December 1969 memorandum, the White House science advisor Lee DuBridge warned Henry Kissinger that the November 25 announcement had "touched off another round of sharp criticism" of the use of chemicals in Vietnam. DuBridge counseled that the administration should demonstrate flexibility by indicating its willingness to conduct a review of the chemical agents "after termination of hostilities in Vietnam." Lee A. DuBridge to Henry A. Kissinger, December 22, 1969, available at DNSA.

39. The first official denial that U.S. military policy was in violation of the Geneva Protocol was offered by Secretary of State Dean Rusk during a news conference in 1965, where he affirmed, "We are not embarking on gas warfare in Vietnam." Excerpts of the conference were reprinted in *New York Times*, March 25, 1965.

40. Condensed and paraphrased by the author. Department of State, Memorandum for the President, "Submission of 1925 Geneva Protocol to the Senate," February 2, 1970, available at DNSA.

41. General Assembly Resolution 2603 of December 16, 1969, had demonstrated that a great majority of nations viewed the Geneva Protocol inclusively, to include all wartime use of chemicals.

42. U.S. National Security Council, "National Security Decision Memorandum 78: Authorization for Use of Riot Control Agents and Herbicides in War," August 11, 1970, available at DNSA.

43. The president's "talking points" with Fulbright and others, as laid out by Henry Kissinger, are in "Game Plan for the Geneva Protocol," folder 4, box 311, CBW file folder 2–3, NSC files, Nixon Project, NARA.

44. Nixon's message to the Senate and Rogers's accompanying report are reprinted in U.S. Department of State, *Bulletin* 63, September 7, 1970.

45. Among the witnesses was McGeorge Bundy, who had left government service to become president of the Ford Foundation. Bundy opposed the White House view "in the interest of the future safety of mankind" and, remarkably, was not pressed to explain why his change of heart had not occurred earlier in his career. For a scathing critique of the tendency of Kennedy- and Johnson-era national security officials to distance themselves from Vietnam during the Nixon years, see Robert Kagan's review of *A Tangled Web*, by William Bundy (brother of McGeorge and a major player in his own right on Vietnam for the Kennedy and Johnson administrations); Kagan, "Disestablishment."

46. U.S. Congress, Senate, *Geneva Protocol of 1925*, 435.

47. Ibid., 297.

48. Ibid., 234–35.

49. Ibid., 325–26.

50. J. William Fulbright to Richard Nixon, April 15, 1971, folder 21, box 32, series 71,

J. William Fulbright Papers, University of Arkansas Libraries, Fayetteville. Thanks to Vera Ekechukwu, Fulbright Papers archivist, for locating this letter.

51. SR 154 and 158 are reprinted in U.S. Congress, Senate, *Geneva Protocol of 1925*, 436–39.

52. National Security Council, Memorandum to Secretaries of State and Defense, Chairman of Central Intelligence, Acting Director of ACDA and Director of Office of Science and Technology, "The Geneva Protocol of 1925," September 8, 1971, available at DNSA.

53. By 1970 the directors of the NAS had found that the herbicide issue had become too controversial and well known to ignore, and they promptly consented to lead an exhaustive research project in Vietnam. The four-year study produced a massive, two-part report. See National Academy of Sciences, *Effects of Herbicides in South Vietnam*. See also Finney, "Vietnam Defoliation Study." The AAAS Herbicide Assessment Commission noted the fundamental similarities in the NAS and AAAS evaluations; see Constable et al., "Letter."

54. National Security Council, memorandum, "Interdisciplinary Political-Military Group's Final Report of the Geneva Protocol of 1925," September 8, 1971, available at DNSA.

55. Fulbright, introductory note, U.S. Congress, Senate, *Geneva Protocol of 1925*, iii–iv.

56. Department of State, Memorandum for Maj. Gen. Brent Scowcroft, "Ad Hoc Group Report on U.S. Policy toward the 1925 Geneva Protocol," April 25, 1974, available at DNSA.

57. The full list of reservations can be found in United States, President, Executive Order no. 11,850, *Renunciation of Certain Uses in War of Chemical Herbicides and Riot Control Agents*, April 5, 1975. The full text is available at *The American Presidency Project*, University of California, Santa Barbara, http://www.presidency.ucsb.edu/ws/?pid=59189. The legal analysis clearing Ford's executive order was prepared by Antonin Scalia, then assistant attorney general, Office of Legal Counsel. See Antonin Scalia to Gerald R. Ford, January 22, 1975, Executive Order — Geneva Protocol of 1925, Ratification folder, box 5, Domestic Council Collection, Gerald R. Ford Presidential Library (hereafter GRFL), Ann Arbor, Mich.

58. See, for example, Frost, Hopkins, and Rosenthal, *Chemical Warfare*.

59. Statement reprinted in U.S. Arms Control and Disarmament Agency, *Arms Control and Disarmament Agreements*.

60. For a review of the environmental issues surrounding herbicide storage at Johnston Atoll, see A. L. Young, *History, Use, Disposition*, 272–74.

61. Of the 133 nations that have ratified the Geneva Protocol, 92 have issued formal reservations against a ban on the retaliatory use of chemical and biological weapons. For a complete list of all member states and explanatory notes, see International Committee

of the Red Cross, "International Humanitarian Law — Treaties and Documents by Date," http://www.icrc.org/ihl.nsf/WebSign?ReadForm&id=280&ps=P.

62. J. N. Moore, "Ratification of the Geneva Protocol." The legal analysis offered by the general counsel of the Department of Defense explicitly stated that herbicidal warfare violated no international law by which the United States was bound. Letter from J. Fred Buzhardt to J. W. Fulbright, April 5, 1971, reprinted in U.S. Congress, Senate, *Geneva Protocol of 1925*, 315–17.

CHAPTER NINE. Conclusion

1. Tomes, *Apocalypse Then*, 167–203.

2. Hatfield, "Introduction," in 6. Members of Congress for Peace through Law, *Economics of Defense*, 6.

3. Rome, "Give Earth a Chance," 542.

4. The relationship between environmental issues and global security are examined in depth by Myers, *Ultimate Security*. See also Gleick, "Environment and Security," 17–21.

5. UN General Assembly Resolution 2398 (XXIII), December 3, 1968. United Nations, *Yearbook*, 22:474. The resolution passed by unanimous vote. For an analysis of the behind-the-scenes diplomacy for this resolution, see Kay and Skolnikoff, "International Institutions and the Environmental Crisis," 469–71.

6. Sullivan, "Stockholm Conference," 267.

7. Strong, address at the National Foreign Trade Convention, Waldorf-Astoria, New York, November 17, 1971, folder 28, box 28, Maurice Strong Papers (hereafter Strong Papers), Harvard University, Cambridge, Mass.

8. Logevall, "Swedish-American Conflict over Vietnam."

9. Palme, quoted in Björk, "Emergence of Popular Participation," 16.

10. Calamai, "U.S. Furious at Ecology Attack."

11. United States, Department of State, Telegram from Washington, D.C., to American Embassy Stockholm, June 13, 1972, folder 404, box 41, Strong Papers.

12. The full record is titled "Report of the United Nations Conference on the Human Environment, Stockholm, 5–16, June 1972," A/Conf.48/14/Rev.1, Political and Security Matters Historical Collection, United Nations Archives, New York.

13. Broadhead, *International Environmental Politics*, 34.

14. Ungeheur, "Woodstockholm," 55.

15. "Effects of Modern Weapons."

16. See especially Richard A. Falk, "Adapting a World Order to the Global Ecosystem," in Harte and Socolow, *Patient Earth*, 245–57.

17. Arthur Westing, interview with the author, March 4, 2007, Putney, Vt.

18. National Security Decision Memorandum 277: "International Restraints on Environmental Warfare," box 1, National Security and Decision Memoranda, GRFL.

19. Full text of ENMOD is available at http://www.icrc.org/ihl.nsf/FULL/460 ?OpenDocument. For an analysis of the diplomacy behind ENMOD, see Juda, "Negotiating a Treaty"; and Fischer, "Environnement." For the congressional hearings on the topic, see U.S. Congress, Senate, *Prohibiting Hostile Use*.

20. Westing, "Environmental Warfare," a paper adapted from a presentation delivered at the Woodrow Wilson Center, May 7, 1996.

21. The best overview of Saddam's war on the Marsh Arabs is Human Rights Watch, "Iraqi Government Assault on the Marsh Arabs."

22. Schwabach, "Ecocide and Genocide in Iraq."

23. United Nations Environment Programme, *Mesopotamian Marshlands*.

24. U.S. Agency for International Development, "Strategies for Assisting the Marsh Arabs."

25. See, for example, Matthews, "Hope, Economic Transformation."

26. Declaration of the United Nations Conference on the Human Environment, June 16, 1972, available at http://tinyurl.com/q3530r.

BIBLIOGRAPHY

MANUSCRIPT COLLECTIONS

American Association for the Advancement of Science Archives, Washington, D.C.
Vietnam Files, 1964–73.

American Friends Service Committee Central Archives, Philadelphia, Pa. Vietnam
Files, National Association for Research on the Military-Industrial Complex (NAR-
MIC) Files.

Contemporary Culture Archive, Paley Library, Temple University, Philadelphia, Pa.
Various pamphlets.

Department of Biological Sciences, Harvard University, Cambridge, Mass. Matthew S.
Meselson Papers.

Dow Foundation Archival Records, Midland, Mich. Press Packet 1–6 (1969).

Environmental Science and Public Policy Archives, Harvard College Library, Harvard
University, Cambridge, Mass. Maurice Strong Papers.

Ford, Gerald R., Presidential Library, Ann Arbor, Mich.
   Domestic Council File
   Melvin Laird Papers, 1974–75
   National Security and Decision Memoranda Files

Johnson, Lyndon Baines, Presidential Library, Austin, Tex. National Security File,
Vietnam Country File, 1965.

Kennedy, John F., Presidential Library, Boston, Mass.
   National Security Files, 1961–63
   President's Office Files, Vietnam Security
   White House Central Subject Files, 1963

National Archives II, College Park, Md.
   Record Group 472: Records of United States Forces in Southeast Asia, 1950–75
   Nixon Presidential Materials Files
      White House Central Files, Confidential Files, 1969–74
      National Security Council Files, 1969
      National Security Files, 1969–70

Pfeiffer, Dr. Egbert W., personal papers, Missoula, Mont.

Seeley Mudd Library, Princeton University, Princeton, N.J. Kennan, George F., Papers, subseries 1B: Drafts and reproductions of articles, speeches, and lectures, published in full or in part, 1938–69.

Swarthmore College Peace Research Collection, Swarthmore, Pa.

    Alternative GI Newspaper Collection

    Document Group 58: Committee for a SANE Nuclear Policy

United Nations Archives, New York, N.Y. Political and Security Matters Historical Collection.

University of Arkansas Libraries, Fayetteville, Ark. J. William Fulbright Papers, series 71.

Yale University Library Manuscript and Archives, Yale University, New Haven, Conn. Arthur W. Galston Papers. Twenty-six boxes, organized chronologically and topically.

UNITED STATES GOVERNMENT DOCUMENTS

Agricultural Research Service. *A Leader's Guide to Agriculture's Defense against Biological Warfare and Other Outbreaks*. Washington, D.C.: GPO/ United States Department of Agriculture, 1961.

Brophy, I. P., W. D. Miles, and R. C. Cochrane. *The Chemical Warfare Service: From Laboratory to Field*. Washington, D.C.: GPO/Department of the Army, 1959.

Brown, George N., et al. *The Forests of Free Viet-Nam: A Preliminary Study for Organization, Protection, Policy and Production*. Saigon: USOM, 1957.

Brown, J. W. *Vegetational Spray Tests in South Vietnam*. Fort Detrick, Md.: U.S. Army Chemical Corps, 1962.

Buckingham, William S., Jr. *Operation Ranch Hand: The Air Force and Herbicides in Southeast Asia, 1961–1971*. Washington, D.C.: Office of Air Force History, 1982.

Congressional Record. Washington, D.C.: GPO, 1963, 1965, 1969–72.

Director of Central Intelligence. "National Intelligence Estimate 53–63: Prospects in South Vietnam" (17 April 1963). In National Intelligence Council, *Estimative Products on Vietnam, 1948–1975*, 185–98. Washington, D.C.: GPO, 2005.

Dudney, Robert S. "The Guns of August 1964." *Air Force Magazine* 87 (August 2004): 4.

Federal Civil Defense Administration. "General Concepts of Chemical Warfare." In *Civil Defense Technical Bulletin*, 1–3. Washington, D.C.: GPO, 1956.

Fisher, Richard W. "The Environment and Military Strategy." *Air and Space Power Journal*, June 2003. Available at http://www.airpower.maxwell.af.mil/airchronicles/cc/fisher.html.

Frost, J., R. Hopkins, and M. Rosenthal. "Chemical Warfare: A New Military Reality." In *Association of the United States Army*, 3. Washington, D.C.: GPO, 1976.

Heller, Maj. Charles E. *Chemical Warfare in World War I: The American Experience.* Washington, D.C.: GPO, 1984.

House, W. B., L. H. Goodson, H. M. Gadberry, and K. W. Dockter. "Assessment of Ecological Effects of Extensive or Repeated Use of Herbicides." Midwest Research Institute Project no. 3103-B, sponsored by the Advanced Research Projects Agency, Department of Defense Kansas City, 1967.

Kleber, Brooks E., and Dale Birdsell. *Chemical Warfare Service: Chemicals in Combat.* Center for Military History, United States Army. Washington, D.C.: GPO, 2003.

McConnell, Lt. Col. Arthur F., Jr. "Mission: Ranch Hand." *Air University Review* (January–February 1970): 89.

Minarik, C. E. "Crop Division Defoliation Program." In *Proceedings of the Third Defoliation Conference, August 10–11, 1965,* 11. Fort Detrick, Md.: U.S. Army Biological Laboratories, 1964.

Novaresi, Sidney. *Control of Vegetation through Herbicides.* Air War College Professional Study 3927. Maxwell AFB, Ala.: Air War College, 1970.

Nuttonson, M. Y. *The Physical Environment and Agriculture of Vietnam, Laos and Cambodia.* Washington, D.C.: American Institute of Crop Ecology, 1963.

Olenchuk, P. G., Robert T. Burke, Oran K. Henderson, and Wayne E. Davis. *Evaluation of Herbicide Operations in the Republic of Vietnam, September 1962–September 1963.* Alexandria, Va.: Defense Technical Information Center, 1963.

Phuoc, Tran Huu, et al. Office of the Command Surgeon, MACV and Ministry of Health, RVN. *Congenital Malformations, Hydatidiform Moles and Stillbirths in the Republic of Vietnam, 1960–1969.* Washington, D.C.: GPO, 1970.

Price, William J. "Some Aspects of Air Force-University Relations." *Air University Review* 11 (January–February 1970): 57–64.

Public Papers of the Presidents of the United States: John F. Kennedy, 1961. Washington, D.C.: GPO, 1962.

Reagan, Ronald. "Statement on Signing the Veterans' Dioxin and Radiation Exposure Compensation Standards Act." Available at http://www.reagan.utexas.edu/archives/speeches/1984/102484e.htm.

U.S. Agency for International Development. "Strategies for Assisting the Marsh Arabs and Restoring the Marshlands of Southern Iraq," October 8, 2003. Available at http://pdf.usaid.gov/pdf_docs/PNADD293.pdf.

U.S. Air Force. *Project Checo Report: Herbicide Operations in Southeast Asia, July 1961–June 1967.* Maxwell AFB, Ala.: GPO, 1968.

U.S. Arms Control and Disarmament Agency. *Arms Control and Disarmament Agreements: Texts and History of Negotiations* (1977). Washington, D.C.: GPO, 1978.

U.S. Army. *The Law of Land Warfare: Field Manual No. 27–10.* Washington, D.C.: GPO, 1956.

———. *Tactical Employment of Herbicides.* Washington, D.C.: GPO, 1971.

———. *U.S. Army Activity in the U.S. Biological Warfare Programs*. Vol. 1. Washington, D.C.: GPO, 1977.

U.S. Congress. House. Ad Hoc Committee. *Student Views toward United States Policy in Southeast Asia*. 91st Cong. 2nd Sess. Washington, D.C.: GPO, 1970.

———. House. Report to the Subcommittee on Science, Research and Development of the Committee on Science and Astronautics. *A Technology Assessment of the Vietnam Defoliant Matter: A Case History*. 91st Cong. 1st Sess. Washington, D.C.: GPO, 1969.

———. Senate. Commerce Committee, Hearings. *Effects of 2,4,5-T and Related Herbicides on Man and the Environment*. 91st Cong., 2nd Sess. Washington, D.C.: GPO, 1970.

———. Senate. Committee on Foreign Relations, Hearings. *Chemical and Biological Warfare*. 91st Cong., 1st Sess., April 30, 1969. Washington, D.C.: GPO, 1970.

———. Senate. Committee on Foreign Relations, Hearings. *The Geneva Protocol of 1925*. 91st Cong., 2nd Sess. Washington, D.C.: GPO, 1971.

———. Senate. Committee on Foreign Relations, Hearings. *Prohibiting Hostile Use of Environmental Modification Techniques*. 94th Cong., 1st Sess. Washington, D.C.: GPO, 1976.

———. Senate. Subcommittee on Disarmament of the Committee on Foreign Relations, Report. *Chemical-Biological-Radiological Warfare and Its Disarmament Aspects*. Washington, D.C.: GPO, 1960.

U.S. Department of Health, Education, and Welfare. *Report of the Secretary's Commission on Pesticides and Their Relationship to Environmental Health*. Washington, D.C.: GPO, 1969.

U.S. Department of State. *Department of State Bulletin*. Washington, D.C.: GPO, 1961, 1969, 1970, 1971.

———. *Foreign Relations of the United States, 1961–1963*. Vol. 1, *Vietnam, 1961*. Washington, D.C.: GPO, 1988.

———. *Foreign Relations of the United States, 1961–1963*. Vol. 2, *Vietnam, 1962*. Washington, D.C.: GPO, 1990.

———. *Foreign Relations of the United States, 1964–1968*. Vol. 1, *Vietnam, 1964*. Washington, D.C.: GPO, 1992.

U.S. Military Assistance Command, Vietnam. *Evaluation of Herbicide Operations in the Republic of Vietnam as of 30 April 1966*. APOSan Francisco: GPO, 1966.

———. *The Herbicide Policy Review*. Report no. AD-779 794. August 20, 1968.

U.S. President. *U.S. Foreign Policy for the 1970s: A New Strategy for Peace*. Report to the Congress, February 18, 1970. Washington, D.C.: GPO, 1970.

U.S. President's Science Advisory Committee. *Restoring the Quality of Our Environment*. Washington, D.C.: The White House, 1965.

U.S. War Department. "Intelligence Review: Future Trends of Chemical Warfare Developments." *Military Intelligence* 45 (December 19, 1946): 56–62.

INTERVIEWS

Phung Tuu Boi, Hanoi, Vietnam, August 23, 2007.

John Constable, Cambridge, Mass., June 12, 2007.

Robert Cook, Cambridge, Mass., March 6, 2007.

Arthur Galston, New Haven, Conn., March 9, 2007.

William A. Haseltine, Washington, D.C., April 20, 2007.

Fred Ikle, Washington D.C., August 12, 2007.

Matthew Meselson, Cambridge, Mass., March 6, 2007.

Jean Pfeiffer (E. W. Pfeiffer's widow), Missoula, Mont., May 10, 2007.

Arthur Westing, Putney, Vt., March 4, 2007.

United States diplomat (anonymous), stationed at the U.S. Embassy, Hanoi, August 23, 2007.

Tuan Vo, MD, Ho Chi Minh City, Vietnam, August 4, 2007.

BOOKS

Primary Sources

American Use of War Gases and World Public Opinion. Hanoi: Foreign Languages Publishing House, 1966.

Barnaby, Frank, et al. *The Supreme Folly: Chemical and Biological Weapons*. London: NLCS, 1969.

Bernal, J. D. *The Social Function of Science*. New York: Macmillan, 1939.

Broswimmer, Franz J. *Ecocide: A Short History of the Mass Extinction of Species*. London: Pluto Press, 2002.

Brown, A. W. A. *Ecology of Pesticides*. New York: Wiley, 1977.

Brown, Martin, ed. *The Social Responsibility of the Scientist*. New York: Free Press, 1971.

Burchett, Wilfred. *The Furtive War*. New York: International Publishers, 1963.

Bush, Vannevar. *Modern Arms and Free Men: A Discussion of the Role of Science in Preserving Democracy*. New York: Simon & Schuster, 1949.

Carson, Rachel. *Silent Spring*. Boston: Houghton Mifflin, 1962.

Cecil, Paul Frederick. *Herbicidal Warfare: The Ranch Hand Project in Vietnam*. New York: Praeger, 1986.

Chomsky, Noam. *American Power and the New Mandarins*. New York: Pantheon Books, 1967.

Chung, Ly Qui, ed. *Between Two Fires: The Unheard Voices of Vietnam*. New York: Praeger, 1970.

Churchill, Ward. *Struggle for the Land: Native North American Resistance to Genocide, Ecocide and Colonization*. San Francisco: City Lights Books, 2002.

Collins, J. L., et al. *Medical Problems of South Vietnam*. Corinth, Vt.: Black Mountain Press, 1967.

Committee of Concerned Asian Scholars. *The Indochina Story*. New York: Pantheon Books, 1970.

Crafts, A. S. *The Chemistry and Mode of Action of Herbicides*. New York: Inter-science, 1961.

Craig, John J. *2,4-D Weed Control: A Guide for the Farmer, Gardener, and Commercial Sprayer for Profitable and Effective Use of Chemicals in the Battle against Noxious Weeds and the Role That the New 2,4-D Herbicide Plays in That Crusade*. Eugene, Ore.: McKenzie Farm Press, 1948.

Crocker, William. *Growth in Plants: Twenty Years' Research at Boyce Thompson Institute*. New York: Reinhold, 1948.

Cross, James Eliot. *Conflict in the Shadows: The Nature and Politics of Guerrilla War*. Garden City, N.Y.: Doubleday, 1963.

Darwin, Charles. *The Power of Movement in Plants*. 2nd ed. New York: D. Appleton, 1897.

Diamond, Jared. *Collapse: How Societies Choose to Fail or Succeed*. New York: Viking, 2005.

Eden, Murray. "Historical Introduction." In *March 4: Scientists, Students, and Society*, edited by Jonathan Allen, viii–xxi. Cambridge, Mass.: MIT Press, 1971.

Ehrlich, Paul R. *The Population Bomb*. New York: Ballantine, 1968.

Eisendrath, Bettie Aldrich. *Military Ecocide: Man's Secret Assault on the Environment*. Washington, D.C.: World Federalist Association, 1992.

Fadiman, Clifton, and Jean White, eds. *Ecocide — and Thoughts toward Survival*. New York: Interbook, 1971.

Falk, Richard A. "Ecocide, Genocide, and the Nuremberg Tradition of Individual Responsibility." In *Philosophy, Morality, and International Affairs: Essays Edited for the Society for Philosophy and Public Affairs*, edited by Virginia Held, 123–37. New York: Oxford University Press, 1974.

Feshbach, Murray, and Alfred Friendly Jr. *Ecocide in the USSR: Health and Nature under Siege*. New York: Basic Books, 1992.

Fitzgerald, Frances. *Fire in the Lake: The Vietnamese and the Americans in Vietnam*. Boston: Little, Brown, 1972.

Ford Foundation. *A Richer Harvest*. New York: Ford Foundation, 1967.

Galston, Arthur. *Green Wisdom*. New York: Basic Books, 1981.

Galston, Arthur, with Jean S. Savage. *Daily Life in People's China*. New York: Thomas Crowell, 1973.

Goldblat, J. *The Problem of Chemical and Biological Warfare*. Vol. 4: *CB Disarmament Negotiations, 1920–1970*. Stockholm International Peace Research Institute. Stockholm: Almqvist & Wiksell, 1971.

Griffiths, Philips Jones. *Agent Orange: Collateral Damage in Vietnam*. London: Trolley Books, 2004.

Grinde, Donald A., and Bruce E. Johansen. *Ecocide of Native America: Environmental Destruction of Indian Lands and Peoples.* Santa Fe: Clear Light, 2000.

Grümmer, Gerhard. *Accusation from the Jungle.* Berlin: Vietnam Commission of the GDR Afro-Asian Solidarity Committee, 1970.

Harvey, Philip. *Vietnam: Documents on Chemical and Bacteriological Warfare.* Holborn, England: Columbia Printers, 1967.

Hayes, Denis, et al. *Earth Day: The Beginning.* New York: Bantam, 1970.

Haynes, W., ed. *American Chemical Industry.* Vol. 6, *The Chemical Companies.* New York: Van Nostrand, 1949.

Henderson, Charles. *Jungle Rules: A True Story of Marine Justice in Vietnam.* New York: Berkeley Caliber, 2006.

Herman, Edward S. *Atrocities in Vietnam: Myths and Realities.* Philadelphia: Pilgrim Press, 1970.

Hersh, Seymour. *My Lai 4: A Report on the Massacre and Its Aftermath.* New York: Random House, 1970.

Hilsman, Roger. *To Move a Nation: The Politics of Foreign Policy in the Administration of John F. Kennedy.* New York: Dell, 1967.

Holmes, Frederic Lawrence. *Meselson, Stahl and the Replication of DNA: A History of "The Most Beautiful Experiment in Biology."* New Haven, Conn.: Yale University Press, 2001.

Horowitz, David, et al. *Eco-Catastrophe.* San Francisco: Harper & Row, 1970.

Institute of Medicine of the National Academies, Committee to Review the Health Effects in Vietnam Veterans of Exposure to Agent Orange. *Veterans and Agent Orange.* Washington, D.C.: National Academies Press, 2004.

Juridical Sciences Institute. *U.S. War Crimes in Viet Nam.* Hanoi: Viet Nam Commission of Social Sciences, 1968.

Kissinger, Henry. *Nuclear Weapons and Foreign Policy.* New York: Harper, 1957.

Knoll, Erwin, and Judith Nies McFadden. *War Crimes and the American Conscience.* New York: Holt, Rinehart, 1970.

Lederer, Edgar. "Report of the Sub-committee on Chemical Warfare in Vietnam." In *Against the Crime of Silence: Proceedings of the Russell International War Crimes Tribunal,* edited by John Duffett, 338–64. London: O'Hare Books, 1968.

Lewallen, John. *The Ecology of Devastation: Indochina.* New York: Penguin, 1971.

Limqueco, Peter, and Peter Weiss, eds. *Prevent the Crime of Silence: Reports from the Sessions of the International War Crimes Tribunal Founded by Bertrand Russell.* London: Allen Press, 1967.

McCuen, Gary. *Ecocide and Genocide in the Vanishing Forest.* Hudson, Wis.: GEM, 1993.

McNew, George L. "The Broader Concepts of Plant Growth Manipulation." In *Plant Growth Regulation,* 3–12. Ames: Iowa State University, 1961.

Meadows, Donella H. *The Limits to Growth: A Report for the Club of Rome's Project on the Predicament of Mankind*. New York: Universe Books, 1972.

Members of Congress for Peace through Law, Military Spending Committee. *Economics of Defense: A Bipartisan Review of Military Spending*. New York: Praeger, 1971.

Merck, George. "Peacetime Implications of Biological Warfare." In George Westinghouse Centennial Forum, *Transportation — A Measurement of Civilization: Light, Life, and Man*, 2:129–46. New York: McGraw-Hill, 1946.

Myrdal, Gunnar. *An American Dilemma: The Negro Problem and Modern Democracy*. New York: Harper, 1944.

National Academy of Sciences. *The Effects of Herbicides in South Vietnam; Part A: Summary and Conclusions and Part B: Working Papers: Beliefs, Attitudes, and Behavior of Lowland Vietnamese*. Washington, D.C.: National Academy of Sciences Press, 1974.

Neilands, J. B., Gordon H. Orians, E. W. Pfeiffer, Alje Vennema, and Arthur H. Westing. *Harvest of Death: Chemical Warfare in Vietnam and Cambodia*. New York: Free Press, 1972.

Nighswonger, William A. *Rural Pacification in Vietnam*. New York: Praeger, 1966.

Nixon, Richard. *RN: The Memoirs of Richard Nixon*. New York: Grosset & Dunlap, 1978.

Osanka, Franklin Mark, ed. *Modern Guerrilla Warfare: Fighting Guerrilla Movements, 1941–1961*. New York: Free Press, 1962.

Pentagon Papers. Gravel ed. Vol. 2. Boston: Beacon Press, 1971. Available at http://www.mtholyoke.edu/acad/intrel/pentagon2/pent11.htm.

Power, Samantha. *A Problem from Hell: America and the Age of Genocide*. New York: Harper Perennial, 2002.

Roberts, Jeremy A., and Richard Hooley. *Plant Growth Regulators*. New York: Chapman & Hall, 1988.

Robbins, William J. "The Expanding Concepts of Plant Growth Regulation." In *Plant Growth Regulation*, 13–24. Ames: Iowa State University Press, 1961.

Rome, Adam. *The Bulldozer in the Countryside: Suburban Sprawl and the Rise of American Environmentalism*. Cambridge: Cambridge University Press, 2001.

Rose, Steven, ed. *CBW: Chemical and Biological Warfare*. Boston: Beacon Press, 1968.

Rothschild, J. H. *Tomorrow's Weapons: Chemical and Biological*. New York: McGraw-Hill, 1964.

Russo, Anthony J. *A Statistical Analysis of the U.S. Crop Destruction Program*. RM-5450-1-ISA/ARPA. Santa Monica, Calif.: RAND, 1967.

Taylor, Maxwell D. *The Uncertain Trumpet*. New York: Harper Brothers, 1959.

Thái, Công Tung. *Natural Environment and Land Use in South Vietnam*. Saigon: Ministry of Agriculture, 1965.

Tukey, Harold B. *Plant Regulators in Agriculture*. New York: Wiley, 1954.

Turner, Ian Michael. *The Ecology of Trees in the Tropical Rain Forest*. Cambridge: Cambridge University Press, 2001.

United Nations. *Chemical and Bacteriological (Biological) Weapons and the Effects of Their Possible Use*. New York: Ballantine Books, 1970.

——. *United Nations Yearbook*. Vol. 22. New York: Office of Public Information, United Nations, 1968.

United Nations Environment Programme. *The Mesopotamian Marshlands: Demise of an Ecosystem*. Early Warning and Assessment Technical Report, UNEP/DEWA/ TR.01–3 Rev. 1. Nairobi: UNEP, 2001.

Verwey, Wil D. *Riot Control Agents and Herbicides in War: Their Humanitarian, Toxicological, Ecological, Military, Polemological, and Legal Aspects*. Leyden: A. W. Sijthoff, 1977.

Viet Nam: Destruction/War Damage. Hanoi: Foreign Languages Publishing House, 1977.

Vogt, William. *Road to Survival*. New York: William Sloane, 1948.

Weed Science Society of America. *Effects of Herbicides in Vietnam and Their Relation to Herbicide Use in the United States*. Report no. 46. Ames: Iowa State University, 1975.

Weissberg, Barry. *Ecocide in Indochina: The Ecology of War*. San Francisco: Harper & Row, 1970.

Went, F. W., and Kenneth V. Thimann. *Phytohormones*. New York: Macmillan, 1947.

Westing, Arthur. *Ecological Consequences of the Second Indochina War*. Stockholm: Almqvist & Wiksell, 1976.

——, ed. *Herbicides in War: The Long-Term Ecological and Human Consequences*. Philadelphia: Taylor & Francis, 1984.

Wilcox, Fred. *Waiting for an Army to Die: The Tragedy of Agent Orange*. Santa Ana, Calif.: Seven Locks Press, 1989.

Wolfle, Dael. *Renewing a Scientific Society: The AAAS from World War II to 1970*. Waldorf, Md.: AAAS Books, 1989.

Young, Alvin L. *The History, Use, Disposition and Environmental Fate of Agent Orange*. New York: Springer, 2009.

Secondary Sources

Adas, Michael. *Dominance by Design: Technological Imperatives and America's Civilizing Mission*. Cambridge, Mass.: Belknap Press of Harvard University Press, 2006.

Barrett, David M. *Uncertain Warriors: Lyndon Johnson and His Vietnam Advisors*. Lawrence: University of Kansas Press, 1993.

Beckett, Ian F. W. *Modern Insurgencies and Counterinsurgencies: Guerrillas and Their Opponents since 1750*. London: Routledge, 2001.

Belknap, Michal R. *The Vietnam War on Trial: The My Lai Massacre and the Court-Martial of Lieutenant Calley*. Lawrence: University Press of Kansas, 2002.

Berman, Larry. *Planning a Tragedy: The Americanization of the War in Vietnam*. New York: Norton, 1982.

Bocking, Stephen. *Ecologists and Environmental Politics: A History of Contemporary Ecology*. New Haven, Conn.: Yale University Press, 1997.

Boffey, Philip. *The Brain Bank of America: An Inquiry into the Politics of Science*. New York: McGraw-Hill, 1975.

Bowie, Robert R., and Richard H. Immerman. *Waging Peace: How Eisenhower Shaped an Enduring Cold War Strategy*. New York: Oxford University Press, 1998.

Boyer, Paul. *By the Bomb's Early Light: American Thought and Culture at the Dawn of the Atomic Age*. Chapel Hill: University of North Carolina Press, 1994.

Boyne, Walter J. *Beyond the Wild Blue: A History of the U.S. Air Force, 1947–1997*. New York: St. Martin's, 1998.

Brigham, Robert K. *Guerrilla Diplomacy: The NLF's Foreign Relations and the Viet Nam War*. Ithaca, N.Y.: Cornell University Press, 1999.

Broadhead, Lee-Anne. *International Environmental Politics: The Limits of Green Diplomacy*. Boulder, Colo.: Lynne Rienner, 2002.

Bundy, William. *A Tangled Web: The Making of Foreign Policy in the Nixon Presidency*. New York: Hill & Wang, 1998.

Busch, Lawrence, and William Lacy. *Science, Agriculture, and the Politics of Research*. Boulder, Colo.: Westview Press, 1983.

Buzzanco, Robert. *Masters of War: Military Dissent and Politics in the Vietnam Era*. New York: Cambridge University Press, 1996.

———. *Vietnam and the Transformation of American Life*. Somerset, N.J.: Wiley Blackwell, 1998.

Cable, Larry E. *Conflict of Myths: The Development of Counterinsurgency Doctrine and the Vietnam War*. New York: New York University Press, 1986.

Califano, Joseph A., Jr. *The Triumph and Tragedy of Lyndon Johnson: The White House Years*. Corpus Christi: Texas A & M Press, 2000.

Chaliand, Gérard. *Guerrilla Strategies: An Historical Anthology from the Long March to Afghanistan*. Berkeley: University of California Press, 1982.

Chomsky, Noam, Laura Nader, Immanuel Wallerstein, and Richard C. Lewontin. *The Cold War and the University: Toward an Intellectual History of the Postwar Years*. New York: New Press, 1997.

Chong, Denise. *The Girl in the Picture: The Story of Kim Phuc, Whose Image Altered the Course of the Vietnam War*. New York: Viking, 2000.

Commoner, Barry. *Science and Survival*. New York: Viking, 1967.

Cotton, Matthew C., and Ronald C. Laura. *Empathetic Education: An Ecological Perspective on Educational Knowledge*. New York: Routledge, 1999.

Craig, Gordon A., and Alexander L. George. *Force and Statecraft: Diplomatic Problems of Our Time*. 3rd ed. New York: Oxford University Press, 1995.

Cronon, William, ed. *Uncommon Ground: Rethinking the Human Place in Nature*. New York: W. W. Norton, 1995.

Curry, Cecil B. *Edward Lansdale: The Unquiet American*. Boston: Houghton-Mifflin, 1989.

Cutler, Lloyd, and Sarah Maza, eds. *A Companion to Western Historical Thought*. Oxford: Blackwell, 2002.

Dallek, Robert. *Franklin D. Roosevelt and American Foreign Policy, 1932–1945*. 2nd ed. New York: Oxford University Press, 1995.

DeBenedetti, Charles, with Charles Chatfield. *An American Ordeal: The Antiwar Movement of the Vietnam Era*. Syracuse, N.Y.: Syracuse University Press, 1990.

Degroot, Gerard J. *Student Protest: The Sixties and After*. London: Longman, 1998.

Dorsey, Kurk. *The Dawn of Conservation Diplomacy: U.S.-Canadian Wildlife Protective Treaties in the Progressive Era*. Seattle: University of Washington Press, 1998.

Dower, John. *War without Mercy: Race and Power in the Pacific War*. New York: Pantheon, 1986.

Duiker, William J. *U.S. Containment Policy and the Conflict in Indochina*. Palo Alto, Calif.: Stanford University Press, 1994.

Dunlap, Thomas. *DDT: Scientists, Citizens, and Public Policy*. Princeton, N.J.: Princeton University Press, 1981.

Egan, Michael. *Barry Commoner and the Science of Survival*. Cambridge, Mass.: MIT Press.

Farber, David, and Beth Bailey. *The Columbia Guide to America in the 1960s*. New York: Columbia University Press, 2003.

Freedman, Lawrence. *Kennedy's Wars: Berlin, Cuba, Laos, and Vietnam*. New York: Oxford University Press, 2000.

Fry, J. Andrew. *Debating Vietnam: Fulbright, Stennis, and the Senate Hearings*. Lanham, Md.: Rowan & Littlefield, 2006.

Gaddis, John Lewis. *Strategies of Containment: A Critical Appraisal of Postwar American National Security Policy*. New York: Oxford University Press, 1982.

Garthoff, Raymond L. *Détente and Confrontation: American-Soviet Relations from Nixon to Reagan*. Washington, D.C.: Brookings Institution, 1984.

Gelb, Leslie H. *The Irony of Vietnam: The System Worked*. Washington, D.C.: Brookings Institution, 1979.

George, Alexander L., and Richard Smoke. *Deterrence in American Foreign Policy: Theory and Practice*. New York: Columbia University Press, 1974.

Gettleman, Marvin, Jane Franklin, Marilyn B. Young, and H. Bruce Franklin, eds.

Vietnam and America: The Most Comprehensive History of the Vietnam War. New York: Grove Press, 1995.

Ghamari-Tabrizi, Sharon. *The Worlds of Herman Kahn: The Intuitive Science of Thermonuclear War.* Cambridge, Mass.: Harvard University Press, 2005.

Gibson, James William. *The Perfect War: Technowar in Vietnam.* Boston: Atlantic Monthly Press, 1986.

Gillespie, Rosemarie. "Ecocide, Industrial Chemical Contamination, and the Corporate Profit Imperative: The Case of Bougainville." In *Environmental Victims: New Risks, New Injustice*, edited by Christopher Williams, 97–113. London: Earthscan, 1998.

Golley, Frank Benjamin. *A History of the Ecosystem Concept in Ecology: More Than the Sum of Its Parts.* New Haven, Conn.: Yale University Press, 1993.

Goodell, Rae. *The Visible Scientists.* New York: Little, Brown, 1975.

Gottlieb, Robert. *Forcing the Spring: The Transformation of the American Environmental Movement.* Washington, D.C.: Island Press, 1994.

Goure, Leon. *Some Impressions of the Effects of Military Operations on Viet Cong Behavior.* Study RM-4517-1ISA. Santa Monica, Calif.: RAND, 1965.

The Great Global Warming Swindle. Produced by Martin Durkin. Originally broadcast on Channel 4 (UK), March 8, 2007. Available at tinyurl.com/26nba9t.

Greene, Lt. Col. T. N. *The Guerrilla and How to Fight Him: Selections from the Marine Corps Gazette.* New York: Praeger, 1962.

Grossman, Karl. *The Poison Conspiracy.* New York: Permanent Press, 1982.

Hagedorn, Hermann. *The Magnate: William Boyce Thompson and His Times.* New York: Reynal & Hitchcock, 1935.

Hargreaves, Hal. *Visions and Discoveries: Reflections on the Nature of Scientific Discovery.* Lanham, Md.: University Press of America, 1990.

Harte, John, and Robert H. Socolow, eds. *Patient Earth.* New York: Rinehart, 1971.

Hays, Samuel P. *Beauty, Health, and Permanence: Environmental Politics in the United States, 1955–1985.* Cambridge: Cambridge University Press, 1989.

Heineman, Kenneth J. *Campus Wars: The Peace Movement at American State Universities in the Vietnam Era.* New York: New York University Press, 1993.

Herring, George C. *America's Longest War: The United States and Vietnam, 1950–1975.* 2nd ed. New York: McGraw-Hill, 1986.

Hixson, Walter. *George F. Kennan: Cold War Iconoclast.* New York: Columbia University Press, 1988.

Hunt, Michael. *Ideology and U.S. Foreign Policy.* New Haven, Conn.: Yale University Press, 2009.

Huntington, Samuel. *The Soldier and the State: The Theory and Politics of Civil-Military Relations.* Cambridge, Mass.: Belknap Press of Harvard University, 2006.

Immerman, Richard H. *The CIA in Guatemala: The Foreign Policy of Intervention*. Austin: University of Texas Press, 1983.

Isenberg, Andrew C. "Historicizing Natural Environments: The Deep Roots of Environmental History." In Cutler and Maza, *Companion to Western Historical Thought*, 372–89.

Jacobs, Seth. *Cold War Mandarin: Ngo Dinh Diem and the Origins of America's War in Vietnam, 1950–1963*. Lanham, Md.: Rowan & Littlefield, 2006.

Jeffreys-Jones, Rhodri. *The CIA and American Democracy*. 2nd ed. New Haven, Conn.: Yale University Press, 1998.

———. *Peace Now! American Society and the Ending of the Vietnam War*. New Haven, Conn.: Yale University Press, 1999.

Jenkins, Virginia Scott. *The Lawn: A History of an American Obsession*. Washington, D.C.: Smithsonian, 1994.

Johnson, Robert David. *Congress and the Cold War*. Cambridge: Cambridge University Press, 2006.

Jones, Howard. *Death of a Generation: How the Assassinations of Diem and JFK Prolonged the Vietnam War*. New York: Oxford University Press, 2003.

Kahn, Herman. *On Thermonuclear War*. Princeton, N.J.: Princeton University Press, 1961.

Kimball, Jeffrey. *The Vietnam War Files: Uncovering the Secret History of Nixon-Era Strategy*. Lawrence: University of Kansas Press, 2004.

Kirby, Celia. *The Hormone Weedkillers: A Short History of Their Discovery and Development*. Croydon, England: BCPC, 1980.

Kleinbaum, David, Lawrence Kupper, and Hal Morgenstern. *Epidemiologic Research: Principles and Quantitative Methods*. Belmont, Calif.: Lifetime Learning, 1982.

Kleinman, Daniel Lee, ed. *Science, Technology, and Democracy*. Binghamton: State University of New York Press, 2000.

Komer, R. W., ed. *The Malayan Emergency in Retrospect: Organization of a Successful Counterinsurgency Effort*. Santa Monica, Calif.: RAND, 1972.

Kuznick, Peter J. *Beyond the Laboratory: Scientists as Political Activists in 1930s America*. Chicago: University of Chicago Press, 1987.

Lauren, Paul Gordon. *Power and Prejudice: The Politics and Diplomacy of Racial Discrimination*. Boulder, Colo.: Westview Press, 1988.

Lear, Linda. *Rachel Carson: Witness for Nature*. New York: Henry Holt, 1997.

LeBlanc, Lawrence J. *The United States and the Genocide Convention*. Durham, N.C.: Duke University Press, 1991.

Lewy, Guenter. *America in Vietnam*. New York: Oxford University Press, 1978.

Littauer, Raphael, and Norman Uphoff, eds. *The Air War in Indochina*. Rev. ed. Boston: Beacon Press, 1971.

Loeb, Benjamin S. "The Limited Test Ban Treaty." In *The Politics of Arms Control Treaty*

Ratification, edited by Michael Krepon and Dan Caldwell, 167–228. New York: Palgrave, 1992.

Logevall, Fredrik. *Choosing War: The Lost Chance for Peace and the Escalation of War in Vietnam*. Berkeley: University of California Press, 1999.

Mao Zedong. *Mao Tse-tung on Guerilla Warfare*. Translated by Samuel B. Griffith. New York: Praeger, 1961.

Marr, David. "The Rise and Fall of 'Counterinsurgency': 1961–1964." In Gettleman et al., *Vietnam and America*, 205–15.

———. "The Technological Imperative in U.S. War Strategy in Vietnam." In *The World Military Order: The Impact of Military Technology on the Third World*, edited by Mary Aldor and Asbjorn Eide, 17–48. Westport, Conn.: Praeger, 1979.

Marshall, Jonathan. *To Have and Have Not: Southeast Asian Raw Materials and the Origins of the Pacific War*. Berkeley: University of California Press, 1995.

McCay, Mary. *Rachel Carson*. New York: Twayne, 1993.

McNamara, Robert S., James G. Blight, and Robert K. Brigham. *Argument without End: In Search of Answers to the Vietnam Tragedy*. New York: Public Affairs Press, 1999.

McNeill, John R. *Something New under the Sun: An Environmental History of the Twentieth-Century World*. New York: W. W. Norton, 2001.

Montague, Peter. "Barry Commoner: The Father of Grass-Roots Environmentalism." In *Barry Commoner's Contribution to the Environmental Movement: Science and Social Action*, edited by David Kriebel, 5–13. Amityville, N.Y.: Baywood, 2002.

Moore, Kelly. *Disrupting Science: Social Movements, American Scientists, and the Politics of the Military, 1945–1975*. Princeton, N.J.: Princeton University Press, 2008.

Myers, Norman. *Ultimate Security: The Environmental Basis of Political Stability*. New York: Norton, 1993.

Nelson, Arvid. *Cold War Ecology: Forests, Farms, and People in the East German Landscape, 1945–1949*. New Haven, Conn.: Yale University Press, 2005.

Neu, Charles E., ed. *After Vietnam: Legacies of a Lost War*. Baltimore: Johns Hopkins University Press, 2000.

Nicosia, Gerald. *Home to War: A History of the Vietnam Veterans' Movement*. New York: Crown, 2001.

Prados, John. *The Blood Trail: The Ho Chi Minh Trail*. New York: HarperCollins, 1999.

Preble, Christopher. *John F. Kennedy and the Missile Gap*. DeKalb: Northern Illinois University Press, 2004.

Primack, Joel, and Frank von Hippel. *Advice and Dissent: Scientists in the Political Arena*. New York: Basic Books, 1974.

Russell, Edmund. *War and Nature: Fighting Humans and Insects with Chemicals from World War I to Silent Spring*. New York: Cambridge University Press, 2001.

Sale, Kirkpatrick. *The Green Revolution: The American Environmental Movement, 1962–1992*. New York: Hill & Wang, 1993.

Schlesinger, Arthur M. *A Thousand Days: John F. Kennedy in the White House*. New York: Mariner, 2002.

Schuck, Peter H. *Agent Orange on Trial: Mass Toxic Disasters in the Courts*. Cambridge, Mass.: Harvard University Press, 1987.

Schulzinger, Robert D. *A Time for Peace: The Legacy of the Vietnam War*. New York: Oxford University Press, 2006.

Schwab, Orrin. *A Clash of Cultures: Civil-Military Relations during the Vietnam War*. New York: Praeger, 2006.

—— . *Defending the Free World: John F. Kennedy, Lyndon Johnson, and the Vietnam War, 1961–1965*. New York: Praeger, 1998.

Seaborg, Glenn T. *Kennedy, Khrushchev, and the Test Ban*. Berkeley: University of California Press, 1981.

Sigal, Leon V. *Fighting to a Finish: The Politics of War Termination in the United States and Japan, 1945*. Ithaca, N.Y.: Cornell University Press, 1988.

Small, Melvin. *Johnson, Nixon, and the Doves*. New Brunswick, N.J.: Rutgers University Press, 1988.

Sterling, Eleanor Jane, Martha Maud Hurley, and Le Duc Minh. *Vietnam: A Natural History*. New Haven, Conn.: Yale University Press, 2006.

Stoll, Steven. *U.S. Environmentalism since 1945: A Brief History with Documents*. New York: Bedford, 2006.

Suri, Jeremi. *Power and Protest: Global Revolution in the Age of Détente*. Cambridge, Mass.: Harvard University Press, 2003.

Thakur, Ramesh. *Peacekeeping in Vietnam: Canada, India, Poland and the International Commission*. Edmonton: University of Alberta Press, 1984.

Tischler, Barbara L., ed. *Sights on the Sixties*. New Brunswick, N.J.: Rutgers University Press, 1992.

Tomes, Robert. *Apocalypse Then: American Intellectuals and the Vietnam War, 1954–1975*. New York: New York University Press, 1998.

Trachtenberg, Marc. *A Constructed Peace: The Making of the European Settlement, 1945–1963*. Princeton, N.J.: Princeton University Press, 1999.

Tucker, Richard P., and Edmund Russell, eds. *Natural Enemy, Natural Ally: Toward an Environmental History of Warfare*. Corvallis: Oregon State University Press, 2004.

Walzer, Michael. *Just and Unjust Wars: A Moral Argument with Historical Illustrations*. New York: Basic Books, 1977.

Webber, Elizabeth, and Mike Feinsilber. *Merriam-Webster's Dictionary of Allusions*. Springfield, Mass.: Merriam Webster, 1999.

Weigley, Russell F. *The American Way of War: A History of the United States Military Strategy and Policy*. Bloomington: Indiana University Press, 1973.

Wells, Tom. *The War Within: America's Battle over Vietnam*. Berkeley: University of California Press, 1994.

Whitehead, Don. *The Dow Story: The History of the Dow Chemical Company*. New York: McGraw Hill, 1968.

Williams, Christopher, ed. *Environmental Victims: New Risks, New Injustice*. London: Earthscan, 1998.

Winston, Mark L. *Nature Wars: People vs. Pests*. Cambridge, Mass.: Harvard University Press, 1997.

Wittner, Lawrence S. *Rebels against War: The American Peace Movement, 1933–1983*. Philadelphia: Temple University Press, 1984.

———. *The Struggle against the Bomb*. Vol. 2, *Resisting the Bomb, 1954–1970*. Palo Alto, Calif.: Stanford University Press, 1993.

Woods, Randall Bennett. *J. William Fulbright, Vietnam, and the Search for a Cold War Foreign Policy*. Cambridge: Cambridge University Press, 1998.

Young, Marylin B., and Robert Buzzanco, eds. *A Companion to the Vietnam War*. London: Blackwell, 2002.

Zubok, Vladislav, and Constantine Pleshakov. *Inside the Kremlin's Cold War: From Stalin to Khrushchev*. Cambridge: Harvard University Press, 1996.

ARTICLES

Primary Sources

"The ABA on Genocide . . ." *New York Times*, February 2, 1970.

"Agent Orange and the Pentagon." *Chemical Weekly*, July 20, 1983, 30–31.

Alland, Alexander, Jr. "War and Disease: An Anthropological Perspective." *Bulletin of the Atomic Scientists* 24 (July 1968): 28–31.

Allman, T. D. "How to Kill the Earth." *Far Eastern Economic Review* 77 (August 19, 1972): 12–14.

Anderson, Jack. "Defoliants May Cause Deformities." *Washington Post*, February 2, 1970.

"Army Scientist Defends Defoliant Use in Vietnam." *Chemical and Engineering News*, January 15, 1968, 17.

Bach, Pham Van. "Law and the Use of Chemical Warfare in Vietnam." *World Federation of Scientific Workers* 15 (1971): 12–14.

Baghat, H. "Vietnam: Where No Birds Sing." *New Internationalist*, 1975, 18–20.

Bailey, Beth. "Earth Day Then and Now." *Reason Magazine*, May 2000. Available at http://www.reason.com/news/show/27702.html.

Baldwin, Hanson W. "Flexibility Aim in Arms Buildup: Kennedy Has Contingency Powers to Meet Different Crises." *New York Times*, July 30, 1961.

Bevan, William. "AAAS Council Meeting 1970." *Science*, February 19, 1971, 711.

Bigart, Homer. "U.S. Spray Strips Foliage Hiding Vietnam Reds." *New York Times*, January 19, 1962.

Blackman, G. E. "A Comparison of Certain Plant-Growth Substances with Other Selective Herbicides." *Nature*, April 28, 1945, 500–501.

"Bright '68 for Ag Chemicals." *Chemical Week*, November 25, 1967, 32.

Bunn, George. "Gas and Germ Warfare: International Legal History and Present Status." *Proceedings of the National Academy of Sciences of the United States of America* 65 (January 1970): 253–60.

Burchett, Wilfred. "War against the Trees." *Novoe Vremia* [New Times], February 1962, 26.

"C-123S Defoliate Jungle Stronghold of Viet Cong." *Aviation Week and Space Technology*, May 8, 1967, 79–83.

Canatsey, J. D. "Bigger Bite for Bulldozers." *Military Engineer* 60 (July–August 1968): 256–60.

Carleton, R. Milton. "New TCP Kills Toughest Weeds." *Better Homes and Gardens*, February 1945, 95.

Celick, Lt. Col. Arnold J. "Humane Warfare for International Peacekeeping." *Air University Review*, September–October 1968, 91–93.

Chamlin, G. R. "Defoliation Saves Lives." *Science*, December 11, 1970, 1153.

Clark, H. M. "The Occurrence of Unusually High-Level Radioactive Fallout in the Area of Troy, N.Y." *Science*, May 7, 1954, 619–22.

Clayton, Anne. "Health in Vietnam." *Nature*, February 10, 1968, 503–4.

Cohn, Victor. "Pentagon Seen Blocking Study of Defoliation." *Washington Post*, September 12, 1970.

Commoner, Barry. "The Fallout Problem." *Science*, May 2, 1958, 1023–26.

———. "Feasibility of Biological Recovery from Nuclear Attack." *Ramparts*, December 1966, 20–26.

———. "Toxicological Time Bomb." *Hospital Practice* 13 (June 1978): 56–57.

Commoner, Barry, et al. "Defoliation Controversy." *BioScience* 18 (December 1968): 1097.

Constable, John D., et al. "Letter: AAAS and NAS Herbicide Reports." *Science*, November 15, 1974, 584–85.

Cullather, Nick. "Miracles of Modernization: The Green Revolution and the Apotheosis of Technology." *Diplomatic History* 28 (April 2004): 227–54.

Cutter, S. L. "Ecocide in Babylonia." *Focus*, Summer 1991, 26–31.

D'Amato, Anthony A., Harvey L. Gould, and Larry D. Woods. "War Crimes and Vietnam: The 'Nuremberg Defense' and the Military Service Register." *California Law Review* 57 (November 1969): 1055–110.

"Defoliants, Deformities: What Risk?" *Medical World News*, February 27, 1970, 15–17.

"Defoliants: Use Still Controversial." *Chemical & Engineering News*, November 25, 1968, 13.

"Defoliating the World." *Milwaukee Journal*, August 23, 1972.

"Defoliation in South Viet Nam: U.S. Partakes of Genocide." *Vietnam Courier*, March 9, 1970, 1.

"Defoliation: Secret Army Study Urges Use in Future Wars." *Science and Government Reporter*, August 18, 1972, 1–4.

"The Desolate Year." *Monsanto Magazine*, October 1962, 4–9.

Dudman, Richard. "Kennedy Would Side-Step Issue over Use of Sprays in Viet Nam." *St. Louis Post-Dispatch*, March 17, 1963.

Dwernychuk, L. Wayne, et al. "Dioxin Hot Spots in Vietnam." *Chemosphere* 60 (2006): 998–99.

———. "Dioxin Reservoirs in Southern Viet Nam: A Legacy of Agent Orange." *Chemosphere* 47 (2002): 117–37.

"The Effects of Modern Weapons on the Human Environment in Indochina." *International Secretariat Commission of Enquiry into U.S. Crimes*, Stockholm, June 2–4, 1972.

Ehrlich, Paul, and John P. Holdren. "Starvation as a Policy: Spraying of Herbicides in Vietnam, Ostensibly a Military Measure, Kills Civilians Wholesale." *Saturday Review*, December 4, 1971, 91–93.

Epstein, Samuel. "A Family Likeness." *Environment* 12 (July–August 1970): 16–25.

"A Fable for Our Times." *Sierra Club Bulletin*. July 1970, 16–18.

Falk, Richard A. "Environmental Warfare and Ecocide: Facts, Appraisals, and Proposals." *Bulletin of Peace Proposals* 4 (1973): 80–84.

———. "United States Policy and the Vietnam War: A Second American Dilemma." *Stanford Journal of International Studies* 3 (1968): 78–98.

Farer, Tom J., et al. "Vietnam and the Nuremberg Principles: A Colloquy on War Crimes." *Rutgers-Camden Law Journal* 5 (1973–74): 1–58.

"FAS Statement on Biological and Chemical Warfare." *Bulletin of the Atomic Scientists* 20 (October 1964): 46–47.

"FAS Statement on Chemical Warfare and U.S. Ratification of the Geneva Protocol of 1925." *FAS Newsletter*, May 23, 1970, 1 and 6.

Ferencz, Benjamin B. "War Crimes Law and the Vietnam War." *American University Law Review* 17 (June 1968): 403–23.

Finney, John W. "Vietnam Defoliation Study Sees Effect of 100 Years." *New York Times*, February 22, 1974.

Flint, Jerry M. "Dow Aides Deny Herbicide Risk." *New York Times*, March 18, 1970.

Ford, Maurice. "The Right to Recruit on College Campuses." *New Republic*, November 11, 1967, 11–13.

Galston, Arthur W. "Changing the Environment: Herbicides in Vietnam, II." *Scientist and Citizen*, August–September 1967, 123–29.

———. "Herbicides: A Mixed Blessing." *BioScience* 29 (February 1979): 85.

———. "Military Uses of Herbicides in Vietnam." *New Scientist*, June 13, 1968, 10.

———. "Plant Biology: Retrospect and Prospect." *Current Science*, January 25, 2001, 143–52.

———. "Plants, People, and Politics." *BioScience* 20 (April 1970): 405–10.

———. "Science and Social Responsibility: A Case History." *Annals of the New York Academy of Sciences* 196 (1972): 223–35.

———. "Vietnamese Journey," *Nature*, November 6, 1975, 2–4.

Galston, Arthur W., et al. "Scientists' Petition to President Johnson against Herbicidal Warfare." *BioScience* 17 (September–January 1967): 10.

Griswold, Deirdre. "The Agent Orange Story: The Toll in Viet Nam Today." *Workers World*, July 6, 1979, 11.

Gruchow, Nancy. "Curbs on 2,4,5-T Imposed." *Science*, April 24, 1970, 453.

Halperin, William E., Patricia A. Honchar, and Marilyn A. Fingerhut. "Dioxin: An Overview." *American Statistician* 36 (August 1982): 285–89.

Hamner, C. L., and H. B. Tukey. "The Herbicidal Action of 2,4-dichlorophenoxyacetic and 2,4,5-trichlororophenoxyacetic Acid on Bindweed." *Science*, August 18, 1944, 154–55.

Harrigan, Anthony. "The Case for Gas Warfare." *Armed Forces Chemical Journal*, June 1963, 12.

Haseltine, William, R. Carter, and Ngô Vinh Long. "Human Suffering in Vietnam." *Science*, July 3, 1970, 6.

Haseltine, William, Robert E. Cook, and Arthur W. Galston. "Deliberate Destruction of the Environment: What Have We Done to Vietnam?" *New Republic*, January 10, 1970, 18–21.

Haseltine, William, and Arthur H. Westing. "The Wasteland: Beating Plowshares into Swords." *New Republic*, October 30, 1971, 13–15.

"Herbicide Controversy May Flare Anew: DoD's Position Remains Unchanged on Issue of Use of Arsenical Herbicides in Vietnam." *Chemical and Engineering News*, September 23, 1968, 27–29.

"Herbicide Hassle: The Army Fires Back." *Chemical Week*, January 13, 1968, 67.

"Herbicides in Vietnam: AAAS Study Finds Widespread Devastation." *Science*, January 8, 1971, 43–47.

"Herbicides: Order on 2,4,5-T Issued at Unusually High Alert." *Science*, November 21, 1969, 978.

Hodgkin, Dorothy Crowfoot. "The Rains of Destruction in Vietnam." *London Times*, December 28, 1970.

Hoffman, Garlyn O. "Economics of Chemical Weed Control." *Down to Earth*, Winter 1961, 3.

Hubbell, John G. "Let's Face the Truth about Gas and Germ Weapons." *Reader's Digest*, August 1960, 77–82.

Human Rights Watch. "The Iraqi Government Assault on the Marsh Arabs." Human

Rights Watch Briefing Paper, Washington, D.C., January 2003. Available at http://
www.hrw.org/legacy/backgrounder/mena/marsharabs1.pdf.

Huntington, Samuel P. "The Bases of Accommodation." *Foreign Affairs*, July 1968,
642–56.

"International: Alphabet of Destruction." *Time*, November 17, 1947. Available at http://
tinyurl.com/yl8bnsx.

"Interview with Matthew Meselson." *BioEssays* 25 (December 2003): 1236–46.

"Ire against Fire." *Time*, November 3, 1967, 57.

Johnson, Julius. "Safety in the Development of Herbicides." *Down to Earth*, Summer
1971, 2.

Johnston, L. Craig. "Ecocide and the Geneva Protocol." *Foreign Affairs*, July 1971,
711–20.

Jones, Franklin D. "Letter to the Editor." *Agricultural and Food Chemistry*, September
16, 1953, 912.

———. "New Chemical Weedkillers." *American Nurseryman*, March 1, 1945, 9–10.

Jordan, Lt. Col. George B. "Objectives and Methods of Communist Guerrilla Warfare."
Military Review, January 1960, 50–59.

Kastenmeier, Robert. "Pentagon Booby-Trap." *Progressive*, December 1959, 28–30.

Kelly, Maj. Joseph Burns. "Gas Warfare in International Law." *Military Review*, March
1961, 42–45.

Kennan, George F. "Rebels without a Program." *New York Times Magazine*, January 21,
1968, 35–46.

———. "To Prevent a World Wasteland: A Proposal." *Foreign Affairs*, April 1970,
401–13.

King, Martin Luther, Jr. "Declaration of Independence from the War in Vietnam."
Ramparts, May 1967, 33–37.

Klare, Michael, et al. *Weapons for Counterinsurgency: Local Research Action Guide.*
Philadelphia: NARMIC, 1970.

Kolko, Gabriel. "The War on Campus: Untangling the Alliances." *Nation*, December 18,
1967, 645–48.

Komer, R. W. Letter to the editor. *Science*, November 6, 1970, 584.

Kraus, E. J. "Remarks by Dr. E. J. Kraus, University of Chicago." In *Proceedings of the
Second Annual Meeting of the North Central States Weed Control Conference*, 78, 80.
St. Paul, 1945.

Kraus, E. J., and John W. Mitchell. "Growth-Regulating Substances as Herbicides."
Botanical Gazette, March 1947, 303.

Lamade, Wanda. "Fact, Not Sensationalism, Needed in Pesticide Evaluation."
Agricultural Chemicals 25 (December 1970): 23.

Langer, Elinor. "Chemical and Biological Warfare (I): The Research Program." *Science*,
January 13, 1967, 174–79.

LeMay, Curtis E. "Counterinsurgency and the Challenge." *Airman*, July 1962, 7.

Leo, John. "Threat of Plague Found in Vietnam." *New York Times*, December 3, 1967.

Lescaze, Lee. "U.S. Study Finds Defoliant Harmless." *Washington Post*, September 21, 1968.

Lewis, Anthony. "Poison Is Good for You." *New York Times*, January 16, 1971.

Marth, Paul C., and John W. Mitchell. "2,4-dichlorophenoxyacetic Acid as a Differential Herbicide." *Botanical Gazette*, December 1944, 224–32.

Mayer, Jean. "Starvation as a Weapon: Herbicides in Vietnam, I." *Scientist and Citizen*, August–September 1967, 116–21.

McArthur, George. "U.S. Reduces Defoliation in South Vietnam." *Los Angeles Times*, March 11, 1970.

McElheny, Victor. "Herbicides in Vietnam: Juggernaut Out of Control." *Technology Review*, March 5, 1971, 12–13.

Meselson, Matthew. "Book Review: *Tomorrow's Weapons*." *Bulletin of the Atomic Scientists* 20 (October 1964): 35–36.

———. "Chemical and Biological Weapons." *Scientific American*, May 1970, 16–25.

Meselson, Matthew, and John D. Constable. "The Ecological Impact of Large Scale Defoliation in Vietnam." *Sierra Club Bulletin*, 1971, 4–9.

Messing, John H. "American Actions in Vietnam: Justifiable in International Law?" *Stanford Law Review* 19 (June 1967): 1307–36.

Mitchell, John W., and William S. Stewart. "Comparison of Growth Responses Induced in Plants by Naphthalene Acetamide and Naphthalene Acetic Acid." *Botanical Gazette* 101 (December 1939): 410–27.

Moore, John Norton. "Ratification of the Geneva Protocol on Gas and Bacteriological Warfare: A Legal and Political Analysis." *Virginia Law Review* 58 (March 1972): 419–509.

Motooka, P. S., et al. "Control of Hawaiian Jungle with Aerially Applied Herbicide." *Down to Earth*, Summer 1967, 18–22.

Nechayuk, Maj. L. "Weapons of 'Civilised Barbarians.'" *Soviet Military Review*, August 1971, 52–54.

Nelson, Bryce. "Studies Find Danger in Defoliation Herbicides: White House Removes One from Use after Tests on Mice Indicate Cancer." *Los Angeles Times*, October 30, 1969.

"New Bag on Campus." *Newsweek*, December 22, 1969, 72.

Newton, Michael, and Logan A. Norris. "Herbicide Usage." *Science*, June 26, 1970, 1606.

Ney, Col. Virgil. "Guerrilla Warfare and Modern Strategy." *Orbis*, Spring 1958, 25.

"The Nixon Administration's Escalations in Chemical Warfare." *Vietnam Courier*, January 18, 1971, 1.

Novick, Sheldon. "The Vietnam Herbicide Experiment." *Scientist and Citizen*, January–February 1968, 20–21.

Nutman, Philip S., H. Gerard Thornton, and John H. Quastel. "Plant Growth Substances as Selective Weed Killers: Inhibition of Plant Growth by 2,4-D and Other Plant Growth Substances." *Nature*, January–June 1945, 498–500.

O'Brien, William V. "Biological-Chemical Warfare and the International Law of War." *Georgetown Law Journal* 51 (Fall 1962): 1–63.

"One Man's Meat." *New Republic*, March 23, 1963, 4–5.

"On the Use of Herbicides in Vietnam." *Science*, July 19, 1968, 253–54.

O'Toole, Thomas. "Pentagon Defends Use of Herbicide on Vietcong Rice Crops." *Washington Post*, August 8, 1968.

Pearce, Jeremy. "Arthur Galston, Agent Orange Researcher, Is Dead at 88." *New York Times*, June 23, 2008.

Pearson, John. "E. W. Pfeiffer: UM's Ultimate Antiwar Activist." *Montana Kaimin*, May 11, 1972, 1.

"Pentagon Denies Charge Defoliation Kills Crops." *Washington Post*, February 24, 1962.

"Pentagon Disputes Defoliation Study." *Facts on File*, January 14–20, 1971, 33.

Petrov, M. "An Important Aspect of Disarmament on Banning Chemical and Biological Weapons." *International Affairs* (Moscow) 2–3 (February–March 1970): 53–56.

Pfeiffer, E. W. "Degreening Vietnam." *Natural History*, November 1990, 11–15.

——. Letter to the editor. "Final Word on Defoliation Effects." *Science*, February 19, 1971, 625–26.

——. "Operation Ranch Hand: The U.S. Herbicide Program." *Bulletin of the Atomic Scientists* 38 (May 1982): 20–25.

——. "Post-War Vietnam." *Environment* 15 (November 1973): 29–33.

——. "Some Effects of Environmental Warfare on Agriculture in Indochina." *Agriculture and Environment* 2 (1975): 271–81.

——. "United States Goals in Vietnam." *Science*, September 11, 1970, 1030.

Pfeiffer, E. W., and Gordon Orians. "Mission to Vietnam." Pts. 1 and 2. *Scientific Research* 4, no. 12:22–23, 27–28, 30; no. 13:26–27, 29–30.

Pokorny, R. "New Compounds." *Journal of the American Chemical Society* 63 (June 1941): 1768.

Race, Jeffrey. Review of *Harvest of Death*. *Annals of the American Academy of Political and Social Science* 403 (September 1972): 177–78.

Raymond, Jack. "Army Seeks Way to Strip Jungles." *New York Times*, June 6, 1961.

——. "Weed Killers Aid War on Viet Cong: They Are Used to Destroy Reds' Shelter and Crops." *New York Times*, March 28, 1965.

Reiss, Louise Zibold. "Strontium-90 Absorption by Deciduous Teeth." *Science*, November 24, 1961, 1669–73.

Robinson, Douglas. "Study Finds Defoliants Change Vietnam Ecology." *New York Times*, September 21, 1968.

Rosebury, Theodor. "Peace or Extinction." *Social Questions Bulletin*, April 1949, 54–56.

Rowley, Peter. "Blood and Fire against the Draft." *Nation*, September 15, 1969, 248–50.

Sachs, Roy M. "Vietnam: AAAS Herbicide Study." *Science*, December 4, 1970, 1034.

Sartre, Jean-Paul. "On Genocide." *Ramparts*, February 1968, 35–42.

Schecter, Arnold, L. C. Dai, O. Päpke, J. Prange, J. D. Constable, M. Matsuda, V. D. Thao, and A. L. Piskac. "Recent Dioxin Contamination from Agent Orange in Residents of a Southern Vietnam City." *Journal of Occupational and Environmental Sciences* 43 (May 2001): 435–43.

Schell, Orville. "Silent Vietnam: How We Invented Ecocide and Killed a Country." *Look Magazine*, March 6, 1971, 57–59.

Schmidt, Dana Adams. "Pentagon Disputes Study of Spraying Devastation." *New York Times*, January 9, 1971.

Schuman, Howard. "Two Sources of Antiwar Sentiment in America." *American Journal of Sociology* 78 (November 1972): 513–36.

"Science and Human Welfare: The AAAS Committee on Science in the Promotion of Human Welfare States the Issues and Calls for Action." *Science*, July 8, 1960, 69.

"Scientists Decry 'Chemical Warfare.'" *Chemical and Engineering News*, January 24, 1966, 26.

"Scientists Protest Crop Destruction." *Science*, January 21, 1966, 309.

Shalett, Sidney. "U.S. Was Prepared to Combat Axis in Poison-Germ Warfare." *New York Times*, January 4, 1946.

Sierra Club. "Conservation Policies: Chemical and Biological Weapons," September 19–20, 1970. Available at http://www.sierraclub.org/policy/conservation/chemwep .aspx.

Skoog, Folke, and Kenneth V. Thimann. "Further Experiments on the Inhibition of the Development of Lateral Buds by Growth Hormone." *Proceedings of the National Academy of Sciences* 20 (1934): 482–83.

Stamper, Earnest B. "Airplane Applications of Herbicides for Johnsongrass Control in Louisiana Sugarcane." *Down to Earth*, Spring 1962, 24–27.

"Statement on the Use of Chemical Agents in the Vietnam War." *Society for Social Responsibility in Science Newsletter*, February 1966, 2.

Stellman, Jeanne M., et al. "The Extent and Patterns of Usage of Agent Orange and Other Herbicides in Vietnam." *Nature*, April 17, 2003, 681–87. Available at http:// tinyurl.com/2bh5fe6.

Stern, Sol. "War Catalog of the University of Pennsylvania." *Ramparts*, August 1966, 32–40.

Stone, Christopher. "Do Trees Have Standing? Toward Legal Rights for Natural Objects." *Southern California Law Review* 45 (1972): 450–501.

Sullivan, E. Thomas. "The Stockholm Conference: A Step toward Global

Environmental Cooperation and Involvement." *Indiana Law Review* 6 (1972–73): 267–82.

Sullivan, Walter. "Zoologist, Back from Vietnam, Notes Defoliants' Value and Toll." *New York Times*, April 4, 1969.

Taylor, Maxwell. "Guerilla Warfare, As the High Command Sees It." *Army*, March 1962, 43–45.

Taylor, Telford, et al. "War Crimes, Just and Unjust Wars, and Comparisons between Nuremberg and Vietnam." *Columbia Journal of Law and Social Problems* 8 (1971–72): 101–34.

Teller, Edward. "Alternatives for Security." *Foreign Affairs*, January 1958, 201–8.

Templeman, W. G. "The Uses of Plant Growth Substances." *Annals of Applied Biology* 42 (1955): 162–73.

Templeman, W. G., and C. J. Marmory. "The Effect upon the Growth of Plants of Watering with Solutions of Plant Growth Substances and of Seed Dressings Containing These Materials." *Annals of Applied Biology* 27 (1940): 453–71.

Troyer, James R. "In the Beginning: The Multiple Discovery of the First Hormone Herbicides." *Weed Science* 49 (March–April 2001): 290–97.

Tschirley, Fred H. "Defoliation in Vietnam: The Ecological Consequences of the Defoliation Program in Vietnam Are Assessed." *Science*, February 21, 1969, 779–86.

———. "Review: Ecological Effects of Extensive or Repeated Use of Herbicides." *Ecology* 49 (November 1968): 1211–12.

"United States Criticizes Vote in UN on Meaning of Chemical Warfare Ban." *New York Times*, December 12, 1969.

"U.S. Added Herbicidal Rape to Its Horrors in Vietnam." *Palo Alto Weekly People*, January 16, 1971, 5.

"Use of CB Weapons in Vietnam Justified, According to Survey." *Industrial Research* 9 (February 1967): 115.

"Vietnam: A Chemical Hiroshima." *Inside Asia Journal* 9 (July–August 1986): 4.

Vinnedge, Harlan H. "Let's Hear It for Pollution (If It's in Asia)." *New Republic*, October 17, 1970, 14–15.

"The War against Weeds." *Time*, February 19, 1945, 67–68.

Westing, Arthur. "America in Vietnam: Democracy for Dead People." *Health PAC Bulletin*, May 1971, 1–9.

———. "Ecological Effects of Military Defoliation on the Forests of South Vietnam." *BioScience* 21 (September 1, 1971): 893–98.

———. "Environmental Warfare: Manipulating the Environment for Hostile Purposes." Paper adapted from a presentation delivered at the Woodrow Wilson Center, May 7, 1996.

———. "Forestry and the War in South Vietnam." *Journal of Forestry*, November 1971, 777–83.

——— . "Leveling the Jungle." *Environment* 13 (November 1971): 6–10.

Westmoreland, William. "Gen. Westmoreland and the Army of the Future." *NACLA Report on the Americas*, November 1969. Available at https://nacla.org/archives.

White, Gilbert F. "Lower Mekong: A Proposal for a Peaceful and Honorable Resolution of the Conflict in South Vietnam." *Bulletin of the Atomic Scientists* 20 (December 1964): 6–10.

Whiteside, Thomas. "A Reporter at Large: Defoliation." *New Yorker*, February 7, 1970, 32–60.

Wisnioski, Matt. "Inside the System: Engineers, Scientists, and the Boundaries of Social Protest in the Long 1960s." *History and Technology* 19 (December 2003): 313–33.

Woodruff, John E. "U.S. Is Expected to End Task of Viet Defoliation." *Baltimore Sun*, August 30, 1969.

"X" [George Kennan]. "The Sources of Soviet Conduct." *Foreign Affairs*, July 1947, 566–82.

Yapa, Lakshman. "What Are Improved Seeds? An Epistemology of the Green Revolution." *Economic Geography* 69 (July 1993): 254–73.

Zimmerman, P. W., and A. E. Hitchcock. "The Aerosol Method of Treating Plants with Growth Substances." *Contributions from the Boyce Thompson Institute* 14 (1944): 313–22.

——— . "Substituted Phenoxy and Benzoic Acid Growth Substances and the Relation of Structure to Physiological Activity." *Contributions from Boyce Thompson Institute* 12 (April–June 1942): 321–43.

Secondary Sources

Aschwanden, Christie. "Through the Forest." *New York Times*, September 18, 2007.

Badash, Lawrence. "American Physicists, Nuclear Weapons in World War II, and Social Responsibility." *Physics in Perspective* 7 (June 2005): 138–49.

Barnes, Bart. "Barry Goldwater, GOP Hero, Dies." *Washington Post*, May 30, 1998.

Barrett, David M. "The Mythology Surrounding Lyndon Johnson, His Advisers, and the 1965 Decision to Escalate the Vietnam War." *Political Science Quarterly* 103 (November 4, 1988): 637–63.

Berenstein, Greg L. "Comment: An Interpretation of the *Feres* Doctrine After *West v. United States* and *In re "Agent Orange" Product Liability Litigation*." *Iowa Law Review* 70 (1984–85): 737–50.

Bernstein, Barton J. "America's Biological Warfare Program in the Second World War." *Journal of Strategic Studies* 11 (1988): 292–313.

Björk, Tord. "The Emergence of Popular Participation in World Politics: The United

Nations Conference on the Human Environment." Paper presented in the Department of Political Science, University of Stockholm, Fall 1996.

Brady, Lisa M. "The Wilderness of War: Nature and Strategy in the Civil War." *Environmental History* 10 (July 2005): 421–47.

Butler, David A. "Connections: The Early History of Scientific and Medical Research on 'Agent Orange.'" *Journal of Law and Policy* 8 (2005): 527–42.

Calamai, Peter. "U.S. Furious at Ecology Attack." *Ottawa Citizen*, June 8, 1972.

Cookman, Claude. "An American Atrocity: The My Lai Massacre Concretized in a Victim's Face." *Journal of American History* 94 (June 2007): 154–62.

Costigliola, Frank. "Unceasing Pressure for Penetration: Gender, Pathology, and Emotion in George Kennan's Formation of the Cold War." *Journal of American History* 83 (March 1997): 1309–39.

Cronon, William. "The Uses of Environmental History." *Environmental History Review* (Fall 1993): 1–22.

Crumpton, Amy, and Albert H. Teich. "The Role of AAAS in U.S. Science Policy: The First 150 Years." *AAAS Science and Technology Yearbook*. Available at www.aaas.org/spp/yearbook/chap26.htm.

Demorlaine, J. "L'importance stratégique des forêts." *Revué des Eaux et Forêts* 57 (1919): 25–30.

Dorsey, Kurk. "Dealing with the Dinosaur (and Its Swamp): Putting the Environment in Diplomatic History." *Diplomatic History* 29 (September 2005): 573–87.

Fischer, Georges. "Environnement: La convention sur l'interdiction d'utiliser des techniques de modification de l'environnefischement a des fins hostiles." *Annuaire Français de Droit International* 23 (1977): 820–36.

Geiger, Roger L. "Science, Universities and National Defense, 1945–1970." *Osiris* 7 (1992): 26–48.

George, Susan. "Financing Ecocide in the Third World." *Nation*, April 30, 1988, 601–6.

Gleick, Peter H. "Environment and Security: The Clear Connections." *Bulletin of the Atomic Scientists* 47 (April 1991): 17–21.

Gough, Michael. "Agent Orange: Exposure and Policy." *American Journal of Public Health* 81 (March 1991): 289–90.

Grotto, Jason, and Tim Jones. "Agent Orange's Lethal Legacy: Defoliants More Dangerous Than They Had to Be." *Chicago Tribune*, December 19, 2009.

Hanes, James H. "Agent Orange Liability of Federal Contractors." *University of Toledo Law Review* 13 (1981–82): 1271–80.

Hudson, Manley O. "The Geneva Protocol." *Foreign Affairs*, 1924–25, 226–35.

Jervis, Robert. "Was the Cold War a Security Dilemma?" *Journal of Cold War Studies* 3 (Winter 2001): 36–60.

Jones, Daniel P. "American Chemists and the Geneva Protocol." *Isis* 17 (September 1980): 426–40.

Joyce, Christopher. "American Government 'Knew about' Dioxin in Herbicides." *New Scientist*, August 18, 1983, 459.

Juda, Lawrence. "Negotiating a Treaty on Environmental Modification Warfare: The Convention on Environmental Warfare and Its Impact on Arms Control Negotiations." *International Organization* 32 (Autumn 1978): 975–91.

Kagan, Robert. "Disestablishment." *New Republic*, August 17, 1998. Available from the Carnegie Foundation at http://tinyurl.com/2d6u9s9.

Kay, David A., and Eugene B. Skolnikoff. "International Institutions and the Environmental Crisis: A Look Ahead." *International Organization* 26 (Spring 1972): 469–78.

Kroll, Gary. "Rachel Carson's *Silent Spring*: A Brief History of Ecology as a Subversive Subject." Available at http://tinyurl.com/25yjdf3.

Lacey, Pamela, and Vincent A. Lacey. "Agent Orange: Government Responsibility for the Military Use of Phenoxy Herbicides." *Journal of Legal Medicine* 3 (1982): 137–78.

Logevall, Fredrik. "The Swedish-American Conflict over Vietnam." *Diplomatic History* 17 (June 1993): 421–45.

Lynn, Frank. "Charles Goodell, Former Senator, Is Dead at 60." *New York Times*, January 22, 1987.

Maechling, Charles. "Camelot, Robert Kennedy, and Counterinsurgency: A Memoir." *Virginia Quarterly Review*, Summer 1999. Available at http://tinyurl.com/2endsse.

Matthews, Kevin. "Hope, Economic Transformation, in Iraqi Marshlands." UCLA International Institute, November 11, 2007. Available at http://www.international.ucla.edu/article.asp?parentid=82857.

McNeill, John. "Woods and Warfare in World History." *Environmental History* 9 (July 2004): 388–410.

Moon, John Ellis van Courtland. "United States Chemical Warfare Policy: A Captive of Coalition Policy?" *Journal of Military History* 60 (July 1996): 495–511.

Palmer, Michael G. "The Legacy of Agent Orange: Empirical Evidence from Central Vietnam." *Social Science and Medicine* 60 (2005): 1061–70.

Peterson, Gale E. "The Discovery and Development of 2,4-D." *Agricultural History* 41 (July 1967): 243–53.

Rasmussen, Nicolas. "Plant Hormones in War and Peace: Science, Industry, and Government in the Development of Herbicides in 1940s America." *Isis* 92 (2001): 291–316.

Ricard, Serge. "Feature Review: Christopher Goscha and Maurice Vaïsse, *La Guerre du Vietnam et l'Europe, 1963–1973*." *Diplomatic History* 29 (November 2005): 879–83.

Rome, Adam. "Give Earth a Chance: The Environmental Movement and the Sixties." *Journal of American History* 90 (September 2003): 525–54.

Schecter, Arnold, and John D. Constable. "Commentary: Agent Orange and Birth

Defects in Vietnam." *International Journal of Epidemiology*, August 16, 2006. Available at http://ije.oxfordjournals.org/cgi/content/abstract/dyl135v1.

Schwabach, Aaron. "Ecocide and Genocide in Iraq: International Law, the Marsh Arabs and Environmental Damage in Non-international Conflicts," August 25, 2003. *Bepress Legal Series*, Working Paper 35.

Sonnenfeld, David A. "Mexico's 'Green Revolution,' 1940–1980: Towards an Environmental History." *Environmental History Review* 16 (Winter 1992): 28–52.

Tierney, John. "Fateful Voice of a Generation Still Drowns Out Real Science." *New York Times*, June 5, 2007.

Tucker, Jonathan B. "A Farewell to Germs: The U.S. Renunciation of Biological and Toxin Warfare, 1969–1970." *International Security* 27 (Summer 2002): 107–48.

Ungeheur, Friedel. "Woodstockholm." *Time*, June 19, 1972, 55.

Warner, Geoffrey. "Review Article: Kennedy and Indochina; The 1961 Decisions." *International Affairs* 70 (1994): 685–700.

Zierler, Aviva E. A. "The Vietnamese Plaintiffs: Searching for a Remedy after Agent Orange." *Temple International & Comparative Law Journal* 21 (Fall 2007): 477–524.

INDEX

AAAS (American Association for the Advancement of Science), 9, 97–98, 104, 116, 148, 153; and government restriction of 2,4,5-T, 124, 125–26; herbicidal warfare viewed by, 99, 140–41, 148; Herbicide Assessment Commission (*see* HAC); and herbicide reviews, 106, 115, 117, 132; inception of, 97; independent investigation into herbicide program called for, 100–101, 105, 106–7, 109 fig. 10, 158; and Pfeiffer, 103, 134; "Resolution on Chemical Defoliants," 147, 198n30; "Settlement of the Vietnam War," 98–99

ABA (American Bar Association), 23

Abrams, Creighton, 132

ACDA (Arms Control and Disarmament Agency), 123, 139, 142, 151, 156

Advanced Research Projects Agency, 70

AFSC (American Friends Service Committee), 122

Agent Blue, 6, 41, 72, 80–81, 116

Agent Green, 71

Agent Orange, 8, 21, 72, 110, 122, 125; accessibility of, 41; components of (*see* 2,4-D; 2,4,5-T); and dioxin, 6, 8, 105; ecological legacy of, 6, 16, 168; government assurances of safety of, 114, 122, 124; and grassy plants, 116; health legacy of, 5–6, 7 fig. 1, 8–9, 26, 91, 121,

132, 135–36, 170n11, 170n14; incinerated on Johnston Atoll, 157; lawsuit against manufacturers of, 10, 12–13, 194n48; literary works on, 11–13; and populated areas, 124, 125; and public policy, 8–9; and racism, 96; scientific campaign against, 3, 4, 140; suppliers of, 93, 105, 110, 194n48; suspension of, 125; teratogenicity of, 16, 121, 122–23, 130, 131; wartime code name, 10. *See also* Operation Ranch Hand

Agent Orange Act of 1991, 8

Agent Orange on Trial (Schuck), 12–13

Agent Pink, 71

Agent Purple, 72, 73, 77

Agent White, 6

agriculture, 1, 2, 35–36, 45, 169nn1–2

American Chemical Paint Company, 37, 46

American Dilemma, An (Myrdal), 24–25

American Relief Administration, 36

anthrax, 150

antiwar activist movement, 19–20, 122, 128, 189n70; and the herbicide controversy, 4, 22, 67, 108; and the Vietnam War, 22, 67, 110

Arendt, Hannah, 19

Army Chemical Warfare Service, 144

ARPA (Advanced Research Projects Agency), 76

arsenic, 116

ARVN (Army of the Republic of Vietnam), 77–78, 139; and Operation Ranch Hand, 27, 69–70, 72, 73, 85, 174–75n55

Aspin, Les, 199n31

Atomic Energy Commission, 90

Australia, 146

baby-tooth survey, 90–91

Bache, Alexander Dallas, 97

Ball, George, 83

Berlin, Germany, 48

Berlin Wall, 53–54

Bernal, J. D., 91–92

Bigart, Homer, "U.S. Spray Strips Foliage," 173n32

Biggest War Criminal of Our Time (Committee to Denounce the War Crimes of the U.S. Imperialists and Their Henchmen in South Vietnam), 173n31

biocide, 21, 95, 173n26

bioethics, 136

Biological Weapons Convention, 157

Bionetics Research Laboratories, 126, 132; cover-up, 122–23, 124, 125, 127; and the teratogenic effects of 2,4,5-T, 122–23, 130

Boffey, Philip, 101

Bohlen, Charles (Chip), 118

Boi, Phung Tuu, 6

Botanical Society of America, 136

Bowie, Robert R., 49

Bowles, Chester, 60

Boysen-Jensen, Peter, 34

BPI (Bureau of Plant Industry), 39

Britain, 20, 63, 92, 152; interwar pamphlet, 145 fig. 16

Brown, James W., 59, 60, 75; and herbicide operations, 70, 72, 73, 74, 76

BTI (Boyce Thompson Institute for Plant Research), 35–36, 37, 41

Buddhists, 78, 79, 81, 128

Bundy, McGeorge, 64, 123, 200n45

Bundy, William P., 54, 62, 70, 96

Bunker, Ellsworth, 117, 126, 127, 128, 132

Burchett, Wilfred, *The Furtive War*, 188n32; "South Vietnam: War against the Trees," 95

Bush, Vannevar, 92

Califano, Joseph, 102; *The Triumph and Tragedy of Lyndon Johnson*, 189n60

Carson, Rachel, 94, 95, 105, 153, 190n76; critique of U.S. politics, science and weaponry, 92–93, 98; and nationalism, 103–4, 161. See also *Silent Spring*

Castro, Fidel, 53

CBW (chemical and biological weapons), 123, 142, 146, 161; and antiwar activism, 110, 122, 189n70; flier protesting, 149 fig. 17; and Nixon, 138, 139–40, 148–49; research on, 97, 108, 139, 148, 190n94; U.S. efforts to ban after World War I, 144, 145 fig. 16

CDTC (U.S./Government of South Vietnam Combat and Development Test Center), 59, 61, 64, 71

Cecil, Paul Fredrick, *Herbicidal Warfare*, 11–12

China, 99, 136, 139, 192n7

Chomsky, Noam, 26, 27

CIA (Central Intelligence Agency), 53, 110

CINCPAC (U.S. Pacific Command), 63, 73

Clary, James, 8

Clausewitz, Karl von, *On War*, 30

climate genocide, 28. *See also* ecological apocalypse

CNI (Committee for Nuclear Information), 90–91

Coghill, Milo B., 76

cold war, 30, 56, 144, 159, 161, 176n72; and the environment, 5, 31, 91, 100; and Kennan, 28; and Kennedy, 49, 66, 159; merged with science, 97–98; and Operation Ranch Hand, 3, 22, 95, 140; relaxation of tensions (*see* détente); and the Vietnam War, 4, 139

Collapse (Diamond), 27

Committee of Concerned Asian Scholars, "Defoliation: The War against the Land and the Unborn," 26

Committee to Denounce the War Crimes of the U.S. Imperialists and Their Henchmen in South Vietnam, *U.S Imperialists' Plan and Methods Regarding the Chemical Warfare in South Vietnam*, 173n31

Commoner, Barry, 89–91, 99, 100, 105, 119, 124; "The Fallout Problem," 90; merger of science with politics denounced by, 92–93, 97–98; and the political repression of scientific collaboration, 90, 100; and the tactical value of Operation Ranch Hand, 116–17, 193n23

communism and communists, 51, 54, 55, 87, 139, 159; and the Kennedy administration, 2, 30, 48–50, 51–53

Congressional Conference on War and National Responsibility, 171n3

Constable, John, 127, 128, 135–36; photograph, 130 fig. 14

containment, 28, 90, 139, 140, 159–60, 185n6; discrediting of, 162; and Eisenhower, 48, 49–50

Convention on the Prevention and Punishment of the Crime of Genocide. *See* Genocide Convention "Convention on the Prohibition of

Military or Any Other Hostile Use of Environmental Modification Techniques," 166–67

Cook, Robert, 122, 128, 130–31

Coolidge, Harold J., 115

counterinsurgency, 48, 53, 56–58, 87, 110, 147; and the shadow metaphor, 57, 58 fig. 3

Crafts, Alden, 45

Cuba, 48, 147; missile crisis, 31, 53

Darwin, Charles, 1, 38, 176n2; *The Power of Movement in Plants*, 33–34

Daschle, Tom, 8

DDT, 9, 10, 18, 39, 93, 177n24

DDT (Dunlap), 9, 11

"Declaration of Independence from the War in Vietnam" (King), 14

"Defoliation: The War against the Land and the Unborn," (Committee of Concerned Asian Scholars), 26

de Gaulle, Charles, 197n6

Delmore, Fred J., 76

Democratic Republic of Vietnam, 21–23, 56

détente, 2, 139, 143, 147, 156

Diamond, Jared, *Collapse*, 27

Diem, Ngo Dinh, 55, 56, 60, 72, 128, 172n20; U.S. support for, 48, 54, 61, 79; coup against, with U.S. support, 81, 185n57; and herbicidal warfare, 21, 59–60, 62–63, 70, 73; and Johnson, 57; portrait, 58 fig. 3; symbolic view of, challenged, 78–79

Dinoxol, 59

dioxin, 6, 13, 135, 170n17; substandard manufacturing, 8, 105, 125, 194n48

disarmament, 139, 140, 141, 148, 153, 155

Doan, Herbert, 111

Lodge, Henry Cabot, Jr., 80
Logevall, Fredrik, 82
Lontz, John, 37, 46

MAAG (Military Assistance and Advisory
  Group), 56, 57, 71–72, 75
MACV (Military Assistance Command,
  Vietnam), 77, 85, 117, 128–29; analysis
  of Operation Ranch Hand, 80, 116,
  192–93n19
mangroves, 16, 76, 112, 113 fig. 11, 135–36
  fig. 15; susceptibility to herbicide, 6, 77,
  119, 127, 132
Mansfield, Mike, 78, 188n35
Mao Zedong, 53
Marr, David G., 58
Marshall, Carl W., 69, 73
Marsh Arabs, 167
McCarthy, Eugene, 28
McGarr, Lionel, 57, 59, 60, 71, 74–75
McNamara, Robert S., 62, 76, 100, 185n59;
  and herbicide operations, 63, 69,
  74–75, 77, 101–2, 104–6
McNeill, John, 31, 79
Mekong Delta, 61, 76, 112
Mendenhall, Joseph, 55
Merck, George W., 39, 42, 44
Meselson, Matthew, 101, 123, 124, 132,
  141–42, 199n30; and the HAC, 17, 22,
  126–27, 128, 131, 135, 141; photograph,
  129 fig. 13; and the SCFR hearings, 141,
  153
Messing, John H., 15
Mikva, Abner, 171n3
Minarik, Charles, 42, 44, 114, 115, 118
Minkowski, Alexandre, 128
Mitchell, John W., 39, 41, 42
Monsanto Corporation, 8, 13, 93, 94, 105,
  199n31
Moore, John Norton, 157–58

MRI (Midwest Research Institute), 104–6,
  114, 117
My Lai massacre, 19–20, 172n19
Myrdal, Gunnar, 24–25

Nader, Ralph, 122
napalm, 76, 111, 141, 152
NARMIC (National Association on
  Research of the Military-Industrial
  Complex), 122
NAS (National Academy of Sciences), 39,
  101, 104, 106, 115, 123; study on herbi-
  cidal warfare, 155, 160, 201n53
National Institute of Environmental
  Health Sciences, 125
National Institutes of Health, 123
NCI (National Cancer Institute), 122–23
Nelson, Bryce, 124
Nelson, Gaylord, 152
New America Foundation, 170n11
New Look policy, 49, 50–51, 52
New Republic, 96, 101, 122, 128
New York Times, 23–24, 133
Nixon, Richard M., 123, 136, 141, 142, 156,
  197n6; and chemical and biological
  weapons, 2–3, 137, 138, 139–40, 148, 156,
  161; and cold war policy, 138–39; and
  détente, 139, 147, 197n2; and disarmament, 142–43, 148, 153; and the end of
  the Vietnam War, 139, 156, 159, 197n2;
  and the Geneva Protocol, 138, 140,
  142–43, 150, 151, 152, 153; and herbicidal
  warfare in Vietnam, 17, 140, 142
Nixon administration, 137, 138, 139, 140,
  143, 156; and the herbicide controversy, 102, 150, 165; interpretation of
  the Geneva Protocol, 142–43; phase
  out of herbicide operations, 147,
  198n30; and U.S. ratification of the
  Geneva Protocol, 148, 150–52, 154, 158

135, 160, 171–72n6; self-perpetuating, 85; soldiers serving in, 11–12; and statistical analysis, 78, 184n43; strategy behind, 5, 58–59, 66, 79, 83, 88; tactical benefits, 5, 67, 128, 161; targets of, 2, 71; three phases of, 71; Tschirley's study of, 117–18; unofficial motto, 71 fig. 5; and U.S. foreign policy, 4, 23; viewed as ecocide, 2, 67, 84, 161; viewed by Galston, 18, 19, 24; volume of herbicides used, 66, 83 fig. 7; as war crime, 19, 20, 25. *See also* Agent Orange; herbicidal warfare

Operation Sherwood Forest, 76

Organic Chemistry Institute, 35

Orians, Gordon, 119, 120

Paal, Arpad, 34

Packard, David, 125

Palme, Olof, 164, 166

Pearl Harbor, 39, 40, 41

Pentagon. *See* U.S. Department of Defense

pentavalent arsenic, 116

Persian Gulf War, 167

Pfeiffer, E. W. (Bert), 17, 103, 108, 116, 117, 128; calls for investigation, 107, 115, 132; criticism of, 121; *Ecocide: A Strategy of War*, 134; field study conducted, 118–19, 120, 193n30; government restriction of 2,4,5-T called for, 125–26; *Harvest of Death*, 134; and nuclear testing, 99; photograph, 120 fig. 12; scientific protest against Operation Ranch Hand launched by, 99–100, 101; "Scientists Committee on Chemical and Biological Warfare," 126; viewed by the AAAS, 134; "Woodstockholm" attended, 165, 166; writings on Operation Ranch Hand, 134

Phuong, Nguyen Tri, 130

"Plant Growth Regulators" (Kraus), 40

plants, 1, 33–35, 36–37; killers of (*see* herbicides)

Pokorny, R., 37

Population Bomb, The (Ehrlich), 23, 153

Power of Movement in Plants, The (Darwin), 33–34

Practice and Theory of Bolshevism (Russell), 20

Price, Don, 100–101, 106

Process of Economic Growth, The (Rostow), 87

Project Agile, 59, 60, 61

Quastel, John H., 38

Race, Jeffrey, 137

racism, 26, 95, 96, 109

RAND Corporation, 30, 147, 184n43, 192–93n19

Raymond, Jack, "Weed Killers Aid War," 173n32

"Resolution Concerning the Study of the Use of Herbicides in Vietnam" (AAAS), 107

"Resolution on Chemical Defoliants" (AAAS), 147, 198n30

riot-control agents. *See* tear gas

Roberts, Walter Orr, 126

Robison, William F., Jr., 73

Rockefeller Foundation, 39

Rogers, William, 132, 152

Rome, Adam, 161

Roosevelt, Franklin, 43, 44, 96

Rosebury, Theodor, 92

Rostow, Walt W., 56, 67, 102; courses of action recommended in Vietnam, 55, 58–59, 60, 61; *The Process of Economic Growth*, 87

Rothschild, J. H., *Tomorrow's Weapons*, 142

rubber plantations, 120, 193n32

rural pacification program, 85, 87

Rusk, Dean, 63, 68, 74–75, 101–2, 173n32, 200n32

Russell, Bertrand, 22, 24; *Practice and Theory of Bolshevism*, 20

Russell, Edmund, *War and Nature: Fighting Humans and Insects with Chemicals from World War I to Silent Spring*, 9, 11

RVN (Republic of Vietnam), 69, 73, 74

Saddam Hussein, 167

Salkowski, E. H., 34

SALT (Strategic Arms Limitations Treaties), 148

Sartre, Jean-Paul, 19, 20

SCFR (U.S. Senate Committee on Foreign Relations), 15, 125, 141, 147, 156, 161; and the Geneva Protocol, 3, 138, 140, 144, 150, 152–55, 156, 157, 158

Schlesinger, Arthur, Jr., 60

Schuck, Peter H., 12–13

Science, 97, 98, 106, 117, 132; Pfeiffer criticized in, 121, 193n37

scientists, 4, 92, 116, 137, 138, 146; and the antiwar movement, 98–99, 160–61; and the chemical and biological weapons debate, 108, 138, 140–42, 143, 190n94; and ecocide, 14, 114, 138, 160; and the environmental movement, 17–19, 103, 160–61, 172n14; and ethics, 98, 100; and the Geneva Protocol, 10, 138, 143–44, 158, 162; herbicidal warfare protested by, 2, 3, 4, 5, 9–10, 12, 14, 15, 17, 20–21, 28, 41, 89, 91, 94–103, 108–9, 114, 116–17, 133, 137, 140,

153, 158, 188n35; herbicidal warfare viewed by, 125, 140–41, 158, 195n60; and international security, 4, 161–62, 168; and politics, 4, 91, 97–98, 161–62, 168; success of, 159–60, 166

"Scientists Committee on Chemical and Biological Warfare" (Pfeiffer), 126

Scientists' Conference on Chemical Warfare in Vietnam, 26

SDS (Students for a Democratic Society), 108, 174n47

Seitz, Frederic, 106

"Settlement of the Vietnam War" (AAAS), 98–99

Sherwin-Williams Chemical Company, 42, 46

Sierra Club, 18, 109; *Bulletin*, 32, 135

Silent Spring (Carson), 9, 10, 31, 32, 92–93, 94; nationalism, 104, 161; technological humility urged by, 153

Skoog, Folke, 35

Soding, H., 34

sodium arsenite, 35, 176n7

South Vietnam: Americanization of war in, 64, 68–69; deployment of ground troops in, 60–61, 64, 82; vegetation in, 76, 112, 113, 192n7; viability of, 81, 185n59. *See also* Vietnam

"South Viet-Nam: War against the Trees" (Burchett), 95

Soviet Union, 28, 31, 99, 138–39, 148, 166; and the Geneva Protocol, 152; and nuclear warfare, 30, 50–51; strategic parity achieved by, 139, 159

SPECTRUM, 147

Spicerack (weapons development program), 110

SSRS (Society for Social Responsibility in Science), 119

Stahl, Franklin, 123
Stimson, Henry L., 39
Stockholm Conference, 163–66, 167,
    199n26
Stockholm Institute for Peace Research
    Studies, 134
Strong, Maurice, 163
strontium 90, 90–91, 99
Stubbs, Marshall, 51
Sweden, 20, 153, 163–64

Tanh, Le Chi, 120 fig. 12
Taylor, Maxwell D., 57, 60, 61; *The*
    Uncertain Trumpet, 50–51
TCDD. *See* dioxin
tear gas, 142, 144, 150, 151, 155
Teller, Edward, 90
Templeman, William Gladstone, 35,
    37–38, 177n21
Tet Offensive of 1968, 83, 116
Thimann, Kenneth, 35
Thompson, Boyce, 35–36
Thompson, Sir Robert, 63
Thornton, H. Gerard, 38
TIBA, 172n13
Tomorrow's Weapons (Rothschild), 142
Train, Russell, 164
Triumph and Tragedy of Lyndon Johnson,
    The (Califano), 189n60
Troyer, James R., 35
Truman, Harry, 44, 144
Tschirley, Fred, 117–18, 121, 126
Tuan, Nguyen Cao, 130–31
2,4-D, 2, 33, 38, 47, 66, 72; discovery
    of herbicidal properties of, 37–38;
    domestic use of, 1, 45, 46, 96; effect
    on plants, 1, 78, 116; production levels,
    46–47; research on, 41–42
2,4,5-T, 33, 37, 47, 66, 126, 152; and Agent

Orange, 2; and Agent Purple, 72;
    and Agents Pink and Green, 71; and
    Dinoxol, 59; and dioxin, 105, 135;
    domestic use of, 1, 44, 96; effectiveness
    on plants, 1, 116; government effort
    to limit human exposure to, 124, 125;
    teratogenicity of, 16, 122–23, 125
"2,4,5-T: Teratogenetic in Mice," 122

UN (United Nations), 19, 92, 107,
    199n25; Conference on the Human
    Environment, 163–66, 167, 199n26;
    "Convention on the Prohibition of
    Military or Any Other Hostile Use
    of Environmental Modification
    Techniques," 166–67; and environ-
    mental issues, 29, 162, 163, 202n5; U.S.
    violation of the Geneva Protocol, 142,
    144–46
Uncertain Trumpet, The (Taylor), 50–51
UNEP (United Nations Environment
    Programme), 5, 162–66, 167, 168
United Nations Conference on the
    Human Environment. *See* Stockholm
    Conference
"United States Policy and the Vietnam
    War" (Falk), 24
USAID (U.S. Agency for International
    Development), 115, 128, 167
U.S. Air Force, 57, 61, 76, 78
U.S. Army, 41, 67, 114
U.S. Army Chemical Corps, 76
U.S. Army Corps of Engineers, 147
U.S. Congress, 3, 138, 142, 148, 159,
    197–98n10; and U.S. ratification of the
    Geneva Protocol, 155, 197–98n10
USDA (U.S. Department of Agriculture),
    39, 43, 47, 117, 124, 194n54; Operation
    Ranch Hand evaluated by, 76, 119

Weinstein, Jack, 13
Went, F. W., 34, 35
Westing, Arthur, 105, 129 fig. 13, 153,
    165, 166; articles on the effects of
    Operation Ranch Hand, 133, 134,
    196n88, 196n90; and the HAC, 126, 128
Westing Associates in Environment,
    Security and Education, 196n90
Westmoreland, William, 79
White, Theodore H., 60
Wilcox, Fred, *Waiting for an Army to Die:
    The Tragedy of Agent Orange*, 12
Wittner, Lawrence, 108

Wolfle, Dael, 115, 118, 126
"Woodstockholm," 165–66
World War I, 11, 16, 26, 27, 43, 143, 144
World War II, 14, 39, 79, 112, 160, 177n24;
    military use of herbicides, 11, 33, 38,
    39, 40, 41, 42–43, 44, 95, 96

Young, Alvin L., 8–9
Young, Stephen, 147

Zacharias, Ellis M., 108
Zimmerman, Percy, 36, 41
Zinn, Howard, *Dow Shalt Not Kill*, 111

CPSIA information can be obtained
at www.ICGtesting.com
Printed in the USA
LVHW031517110523
746742LV00002B/198